AF263658

Other titles by
Eleanor Heartney:

*Critical Condition: American Culture
at the Crossroads*

Movements in Modern Art: Postmodernism

*Defending Complexity: Art, Politics and
the New World Order*

Art and Today

Kenneth Snelson: Forces Made Visible

Roxy Paine

Renee Radell: Webs of Circumstance

Co-authored books:

*After the Revolution: Women who
Transformed Contemporary Art*

*The Reckoning: Women Artists in
the New Millennium*

PRAISE FOR POSTMODERN HERETICS

In this brave and urgently needed study, Eleanor Heartney explains how the work of many of the most controversial artists of recent decades has frequently been due to the "Incarnational consciousness" rooted in their Catholic upbringing. The view that our identity as human beings derives from our bodily condition is inseparable from Catholic doctrine, but its implementation in works of art is often out of phase with the attitudes and beliefs of some members of the religious community, who react to the art as blasphemous and transgressive. Thus the history of postmodernist art has often been a story of bitter conflict. It may be too much to hope that Heartney's compassionate and deeply informed analysis will bring these conflicts to an end, but it has the power to raise the discourse to a new level of healing understanding if read in the spirit in which it is intended. For any reader, however, it is a valuable and indispensible contribution to the appreciation of contemporary art in some of its most extreme and difficult manifestations.

– Arthur Danto, art critic, The Nation

The Catholic imagination is both robust and flexible enough according to Ms. Heartney to influence even those artists whose works many would consider transgressive. Perhaps, she suggests, Catholics could go beyond what they consider to be the bad taste and blasphemy of these works and attend to what they are saying.

– Father Andrew Greeley, author

[Heartney] was the first to identify a Roman Catholic sensibility among diverse artists whose work has demonstrated, often inadvertently, a startling capacity to offend. . . The ultimate and inarguable value of *Postmodern Heretics* lies in demonstrating for those already appreciative of contemporary art the very earnest spiritual passions of the many individuals covered in the book.

– Sue Taylor, Art in America, February 2005

[Postmodern Heretics] is a brave, pioneering work that opens up whole areas of study for future art historians and meanwhile provides fresh insights for anyone interested in the whys and wherefores of recent art.

– Corinne Robins, *American Book Review*, Nov/Dec 2004

Eleanor Heartney's *Postmodern Heretics: The Catholic Imagination in Contemporary Art* is the first book I've read that attempts to bridge the gap (between faith and art) in a comprehensible fashion. She examines some of the most controversial artworks of the past two decades, noting that a majority were created by artists who are, or were brought up as, Catholics. In the process she deftly draws parallels between a kind of physicality that is peculiarly Catholic and these artists' propensity for expressing their ideas through corporeal means.

–Virginia Maksymowicz, *Sojourners*, July 2004

Heartney accomplishes many things with her concisely written, highly accessible study, not the least of which is to offer novel, nuanced readings of familiar works to an art world that, she notes, tends to view ;art that invokes religion in any but a critical way as retrograde and reactionary'.

– Kate Hackman, *Kansas City Star*, May 16, 2004

Cover: Andres Serrano, *Blood Madonna*, 2011

© Andres Serrano, Courtesy of the artist

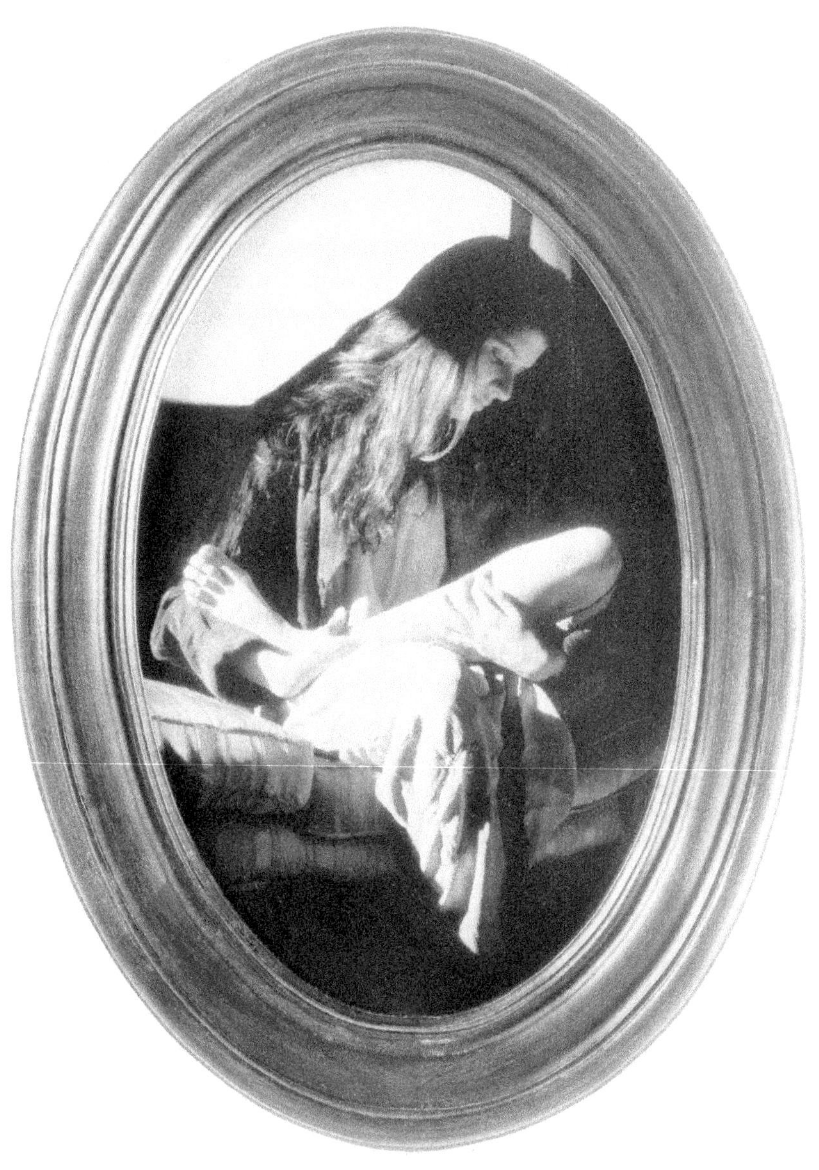

Janine Antoni, *Coddle*, 1999

© Janine Antoni; Courtesy of the artist and Luhring Augustine, New York.

POSTMODERN HERETICS

The Catholic Imagination in Contempory Art

Eleanor Heartney

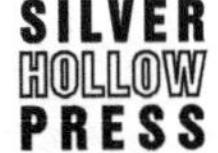

DEDICATION

To Larry, my strongest support and sharpest critic,
who now knows more about Catholicism than
he ever thought possible.

Postmodern Heretics: The Catholic Imagination in Contemporary Art.
Copyright © 2018 by Eleanor Heartney. All Rights Reserved.
For information, contact: silverhollowpress@gmail.com

CONTENTS

INTRODUCTION:

The Age of Trump has revealed a country at war with itself. Savvy political operatives and media figures stoke populist anger toward "elites" while liberals watch in disbelief as social policies that have guided the country since the postwar era are gleefully dismantled. Political, economic and social polarization smothers hopes for a return to civility and bipartisanship. The rise of social media and the splintering, gutting and replacement of mainstream journalism by fringe groups on the Right and Left has exacerbated the siloing of information. The result is a populace cocooned into like-minded groups and disconnected from common cultural touchstones that could be shared across political divides.

Standing astride an acrimonious and often vicious standoff between Left and Right is the President himself. Donald Trump is an outlier whose allegiance to the social goals of the voters who elected him and the conservative establishment that has uneasily pledged fealty to him is tenuous at best. His election has upended conventional pieties about the melting pot, America's role as leader of the free world and the superiority of our democracy. In their place he has fanned a xenophobic nationalism and a culture of resentment that is alarmingly appealing to a large swath of the population. The poles of American society, now defined by red and blue, grow ever further apart.

Bad as things seem, however, we have been here before. In the 1990s the United States was also embroiled in a deeply divisive Culture War. Social conservatives railed against the changes being wrought by feminism, multiculturalism and an assertive gay rights movement. Progressives applauded those developments as landmarks on the road to a more egalitarian society. Politics were contentious and divisive, Right and Left were prone to demonize each other while pundits bemoaned the disappearance of civility's common purpose. Then, as now, the fault lines followed the geographic and demographic divisions opened up by the Civil War, as religious and political conservatives from the rural South led the charge against the permissive mores and amorality of the liberal urban North.

POSTMODERN HERETICS IN THE AGE OF TRUMP

In Culture War One, contemporary art emerged as a focal point for the passions of the day. Artists were low lying fruit, easy targets for right wing politicians eager to use federal funding of the arts to discredit government and shrink all non-military government spending. Conservative activists scanned lists of government grants seeking evidence that tax dollars had been used to support art that was obscene, sacrilegious or otherwise anti-American. Their efforts were particularly aimed at the National Endowment for the Arts, a government agency which, among other responsibilities, provided money to individual artists and to public institutions presenting exhibitions of contemporary art. Small, at times even miniscule amounts of money awarded to artists who had been deemed objectionable by the right's self-appointed arbitrars became fuses for massive controversies. These uproars shut down institutions, brought artists and curators to court and convinced large segments of the population that artists were vile and destructive sociopaths.

I wrote *Postmodern Heretics: The Catholic Imagination in Contemporary Art* in response to the Culture War that engulfed the worlds of art and politics in the late 1980s to the early 1990s. While many books written at this time and later attempted to make sense of the ongoing tumult, *Postmodern Heretics* was unique in its exploration of the role played by religion in these conflicts. I was struck by the fact that virtually all the artists who found themselves in the political crosshairs at that time came from Catholic backgrounds. I searched for an explanation for the incendiary impact of their art. I found it in the peculiarities of Catholic theology, ritual, literature, bodily specific art and the way the culture of Catholicism encourages a potentially transgressive vision of sexuality and carnal experience.

In pursuing the study that was to become *Postmodern Heretics*, I found myself reconnecting with discarded parts of my own history. I was raised Catholic in Iowa in the mid 1960s, during the modernization of the Catholic Church by Pope John XXIII. Though I ceased to actively practice the religion in my twenties, I have come to realize that my own Catholic imagination has profoundly shaped my understanding of art and the world. I wrote *Postmodern Heretics* at a time when art was rife with explorations of identity. Artists and writers were digging deeply into ethnicity, race, gender and sexual orientation as sources of artistic inspiration. This book reflects my conviction that religion is just as potent as a creative force.

Many otherwise confusing aspects of the Culture War become legible when viewed through the lens of religion. *Postmodern Heretics* also challenges the art world's longstanding dismissal of religion as mere superstition. These insights have earned the book a loyal audience among those seeking a less restrictive view of the relationship between art, spirituality and religion. Many readers have told me how they pass around tattered copies of the out of print first edition of *Postmodern Heretics*. The continuing interest in the book, as well as the light it sheds on current events, moved me to bring out this newly designed and re-edited second edition. I wish to thank Silver Hollow Press for its support and encouragement in this endeavor.

Postmodern Heretics was originally published in 2004. However from the perspective of 2017, it is eerily prescient. In revisiting the book for this new edition, I realized that today's abrasive and destructive politics are in fact an extension of the extraordinary cultural and political battles that took place in the late 80s and early 90s. Many of the charges and countercharges hurled between artists and their critics in those days could have been lifted from pro and anti Trump rallies today. The heated rhetoric in the book will have a familiar feel to those following today's debates over "political correctness", reproductive rights, gay marriage and free speech.

Postmodern Heretics exposes the roots of our current conflicts. But the book also points to unlearned lessons that may be helpful in our current crises. One of these is that fundamentalist thinking is dangerous, no matter what position it supports. *Postmodern Heretics* reveals what happened in the 1990s when the righteous defense of patriotism and religion triumphed over reason, tolerance and respect for free expression. The age of Trump is a topsy-turvy world in which the positions staked out in our earlier culture war seem to have reversed. The rhetoric of affirmative action and victimhood has been co-opted by the right on behalf of the beleaguered white working class. Black Lives

Matter is styled a hate group, higher education is seen as a force for evil and the Supreme Court is urged to end preferential treatment for blacks, Latinos, women and other "minorities." Meanwhile on the left, academics, students and artists have been in the forefront of efforts to block college speakers, tear down statues and censor art that offends liberal sensitivities. A new or perhaps newly emboldened absolutism has taken hold on both sides as calls for ideological purity make even the most apparently innocuous actions and language suspect.

In this new version of the Culture War, religion remains a constant flashpoint. Conservatives selectively invoke the first amendment's protection of religion to impose restrictions on abortion, contraception and the expression of sexual preferences. Progressives vociferously defend art that offends religious sensibilities (examples here include Pussy Riot's attack on the Russian Orthodox religion and the Danish and French satirists who incited riots with their mockeries of Mohammed). However, their tolerance does not carry over to art that appears insensitive to race, gender, ethnicity or even animal rights. Social media campaigns shut down exhibitions and call for the destruction of art works perceived as embodiments of white privilege, patriarchal power or animal abuse. There appears to be a double standard in which some offenses are more offensive than others. Attacks on religious belief are not a valid justification for censorship but disrespect for cultural difference evidently is.

Which leads to the second unlearned lesson of *Postmodern Heretics*. Religion is not a monolith, and it is not inherently the enemy of progressive ideals and rational discourse. The heart of the book is an exploration of artistic manifestations of the Catholic imagination in the work of a select group of contemporary artists. Some of them have frequently been immersed in controversy while others explore their Catholic inheritance in less overtly provocative ways. But it is not a matter of separating the "good" Catholics from the "bad" ones. Believers like Chris Ofili and Andres Serrano can unintentionally enrage more orthodox Christians, while the deliberate provocations of artists like Robert Mapplethorpe and Karen Finley are motivated less by an abhorrence of religion than by their disappointment with the gap between its promises and practice.

Such subtleties are generally lost on their critics. It is also often lost on their defenders, who tend to see the past and present Culture

War as simply another salvo in the age-old battle of Reason versus Faith. In this book I argue that contrary to this view, my Postmodern Heretics have a complex relationship to their childhood religion. They embrace the poetry of Catholicism that feeds them as artists even as they roil against its real world shortcomings. The beauty of religious art, music and literature, the slippage in sacramental rituals between the carnal and the spiritual and the compelling metaphors at the heart of Catholicism's religious doctrines provide the raw materials from which they shape their art and lives. But these interests run counter to ingrained assumptions about the natural hostility between artists and religion. As a result, even today the most sincerely spiritual work runs the risk of being received as a mockery of religion.

Thus, in addition to parsing the role played by Catholicism in the 1990s Culture War, *Postmodern Heretics* also suggests an alternative conception of the relationship between art and religion. Since at least the postwar period, religion has variously been derided and dismissed by the cultural intelligentsia as rank superstition; embraced by "anti-modernists" seeking a return to a supposedly more cohesive and fulfilling world; and shamelessly exploited by politicians, pundits and cultural leaders on both sides of the divide. As a result, religion has become divorced in artistic circles from its potential as a force for "world building" and the search for meaning. By examining the myriad ways that religion has worked its way into the creations of artists whom I deeply admire, I hoped in this book to move beyond the either/or relationship that is at the heart of conventional assumptions about contemporary art and religion. I argue that a broader understanding of the poetics of faith can enrich our understanding of both art and religion. Further, I believe that art, as a non-verbal means of communication, is a potential bridge between believers and non-believers in our deeply divided culture.

I was just finishing *Postmodern Heretics* when the destruction of the Twin Towers tore through an already fraught reality. The Culture War receded from public consciousness, to be replaced by the threat of radical Islam, the spread of the surveillance state, the rise of social media and the never-ending Middle East War. However, religion remained contentious. Battle lines were redrawn around the concept of the Clash of Civilizations, with the historical Wars of Religion reformulated as a conflict between the "Christian West" and "Islamofascist" East. In an afterward written in the early days of the G.W. Bush Administration's Iraq War, I was able to reflect on the havoc being unleashed by competing dogmas in an increasingly post-secular world. With apocalyptic fantasies driving the politics of both sides, *Postmodern Heretics'* Postscript constituted a plea for tolerance, an acceptance of imperfection and a recognition of the constructive, communitarian, compassionate side of religion.

Today, those hopes are sadly unfulfilled. Instead of pulling together in the face of external and internal threats, we are more divided than ever. How did we get to the Trump era? Is there any way out of the current impasse between Red and Blue? Or are we doomed forever to replicate the divisions that continually flare up in the United States between North and South, urban and rural, white and non-white, rich and poor, agnostic and believer?

The history recounted in *Postmodern Heretics* reveals that these divisions run deep. However, the book also holds hints of a way forward. One of its themes is the role of art in social change. Back in the 1990s, artists and their supporters may have won some of the lawsuits initiated against them, but they also lost a very strategic battle. Culture Warriors at that time were not able to abolish the NEA, but they did force a reorganization of the agency to eliminate any funding for individual artists, thereby ensuring that "blasphemous," "sacrilegious," "pornographic," and otherwise "offensive" art would not be supported by taxpayer dollars. In the aftermath of this battle, controversial and political art didn't go away, but it lost an important platform. While the post 9/11 years have seen a surge in arrests and convictions of artists in other countries for violation of blasphemy, anti-government or anti-terrorist laws, in the United States dissident artists have generally been muffled by disinterest. Political and cultural agitation have been further sidelined by the emergence of a burgeoning art market underwritten by the same income inequality that exacerbates economic and political divisions in the rest of the society. As the mainstream and art media breathlessly chronicle each new multi-million dollar record in the contemporary art market, it is easy to forget art's potential to challenge the conventions and ideologies that imprison and diminish us.

In the rebooted Culture War, artists are folded into the despised elite who mouth politically correct platitudes while profiting from the globalization that has strip-mined the economies of the Rust Belt.

They are seen to share the values of those who prioritize the needs of immigrants and minorities over those of the "real" Americans who have lost their chance at the American Dream. This time around, instead of godless artists, the foremost "enemy of the people" is the mainstream media that presents lies as truth and promotes a liberal agenda that runs counter to the American virtues of liberty, self determination and independence. The transfer of animus from art to media suggests that in the 1990s artists were simply canaries in the mine, heralding a future defined by growing acceptance of authoritarianism and disdain for the messy business of democracy and free speech.

Thus, *Postmodern Heretics* underscores the importance of establishing a platform from which to challenge the powers that be. A consistent flashpoint of the earlier Culture War was government indifference to the escalating AIDS crisis. Many of the most provocative artworks and the most virulent attacks on art in the early nineties revolved around this issue. Artists attacked the collusion between religious and political conservatives who saw the epidemic as a judgment on the deviant lifestyles of homosexuals. They in turn were attacked as pornographers, enablers of perversion and destroyers of American values. From today's perspective, this battle has been at least partly won. Medical advances have transformed AIDS from a death sentence to a chronic but largely manageable disease. Although condemnation of homosexuality is still a rallying cry in various religious and political circles, by and large society has accepted not only homosexuality, but even, increasingly, expressions of transgender identity. Gay marriage is the law of the land and unlikely to be undone even by zealots in the current Republican regime. This new reality underscores the fact that even in times of great social division and turmoil, change is possible.

In the wake of the Trump election, artists seem newly energized. The Women's March and its aftermath have galvanized the progressive movement; and with it artists who want to work for social change. Political efforts to drag the country back to an imagined halcyon era of white supremacy and patriarchal control have provided a powerful agenda against whom to organize. Here, the examples of artists who chose to resist the reactionary forces of the Reagan and Bush years can be highly instructive. But as the emergence of a new leftist fundamentalism suggests, resistance must be tempered with tolerance, respect for free expression and wariness toward the righteous condemnation of one's adversaries.

The other lesson to be drawn from *Postmodern Heretics* involves the importance of enlisting the support of religious believers and their values in these efforts. One of the peculiarities of the Trump election was the degree of evangelical support for a candidate whose lifestyle, character and prior pronouncements flatly contradict this group's professed beliefs. The fervor of Trump's evangelical base seems to support liberal convictions about the hypocrisy of the faithful and the bankruptcy of religion. But as *Postmodern Heretics* demonstrates, religion is complex. The ascendency of the Trump era has also awakened liberal religious groups to the need for political engagement. In doing so they are reaching back to a rich history of social engagement by religious figures in the abolitionist movement, the battles for social justice, civil rights, the creation of the New Deal and the Great Society.

Unabashed believers like Martin Luther King, Eugene McCarthy, Robert F. Kennedy, Jimmy Carter and Jesse Jackson are evidence that religion can be a force for positive social change. The Left's more recent turn away from religion has separated it from this vital source of inspiration while alienating religious voters who otherwise share its values. Now more than ever it will be important for progressive groups of all stripes to join forces for the good of the country. And in a marked divergence from the early 1990s, the Catholic Church is now headed by a Pontiff whose pronouncements are radically out of sync with those of the Republican Party's conservative Catholic culture warriors. Pope Francis believes climate change is a moral issue and has condemned "the idolatry of money" and the gaping income inequality it has spawned. This tolerant Pope remarked apropos the homosexual community, "Who am I to judge?" Things can change. Allies can appear in unlikely places.

Postmodern Heretics returns at a dark moment in American history. On many fronts we seem to be reaching a tipping point, after which the slide into authoritarianism, endless war and environmental apocalypse will be unavoidable. In this climate the book provides both a warning and a sliver of hope, reviving a period when art was under fire precisely because it mattered. It can matter again, if we dare to take up the challenge.

– Eleanor Heartney, November 2017

PREFACE

When I was a child I briefly dreamed, as do all Catholic girls, of becoming a nun. But it was not really the mysterious women in their voluminous black habits who attracted me. (This was pre-Vatican II, before nuns devolved into ordinary humans with knee length skirts, permed hair and sensible blue suits). Rather I was drawn by the possibility of closer communion with the three pivotal Catholic characters depicted as life-size figures perched around the altar of our local parish Church.

Mary on the right bore an expression of sweet resignation: that faint smile playing across her face mingled feelings of pity and grief. Most of the year she stood above us unadorned by anything but her plain robes and bland beauty. Once a year in May she was festooned with flowers and flowing blue silks. A staircase was built from floor to her lofty perch so that one lucky thirteen year old girl - the May Queen - could don a wedding dress and ascend the stairs to place a crown of roses on Mary's head. Of course I longed to be that girl, but when my year came I had to content myself with being one of the anonymous entourage who processed around the Church grounds before filing into the front row pews for the crowning ceremony.

Her husband Joseph flanked the altar on the left. Stooping slightly he seemed more preoccupied with his carpenter's angle than the faithful gathered below. He was gentle but slightly remote in the way that ideal fathers were supposed to be in the early sixties.

But of course the central focus was Jesus positioned directly above the altar so that he could be seen from all corners of the cruciform church. Jesus was naked but for a slightly fluttering loin cloth. His hands and feet were nailed to a cross. His torso twisted slightly. His legs were bent, resting on a small wooden support at the bottom of the cross. The requisite wound opened in his side. As this was an Irish Catholic Church, nothing about his torture and mutilation was too graphic. Jesus was tastefully carved of the same unpainted blond wood as his Mother and stepfather. The emphasis was on his infinite patience and love, rather than his bloody death. Even to a nine year old the physicality of his perfect male body was unmistakable.

There was one other naked man in my life at that time: a cast of the youngest of Rodin's Burghers of Calais at the Des Moines Art Center where I was taking art classes. This figure too was contorted by pain. Unlike Jesus he grimaced in agony. But they shared an exalted destiny. Both were depicted in the act of sacrificing themselves for the salvation of their fellow humans. And both were endowed with sculpted bodies that rivaled those of the Greek gods.

I used to kneel on the padded kneelers of the empty church for hours staring at the crucified Christ hoping for a vision that would affirm our special relationship. Big questions of evil, sin and complicity were not yet in my focus. In fact, it would be years before I explained my fall from faith to my mother in terms of a complicated analysis of the injustice of a religion which averred that faith was a free gift from God, then punished those to whom the gift was not given. (Needless to say she was not impressed).

Rather, as a somewhat obsessive thirteen year old, I was seeking a means of connection with the supernatural world which seemed so abstract when my teachers tried to describe it. I sought access to God through the representation of the body of Christ on the cross.

In a sense this book began with that experience. The questions I deal with here - the relationship between Catholicism's approach to the body and the physically provocative art work it seems to inspire, the aesthetic and political divide which Catholicism's fleshly orientation has opened up between those raised in different Christian traditions, recent art history's suppression of the extent to which religious concerns have shaped modern and postmodern American art - would all come later. But already at that early moment I sensed the tremendous carnality of the Catholic imagination. Fortunately, I was clearly not alone in this subliminal understanding, as the diverse works of the artists who follow will attest.

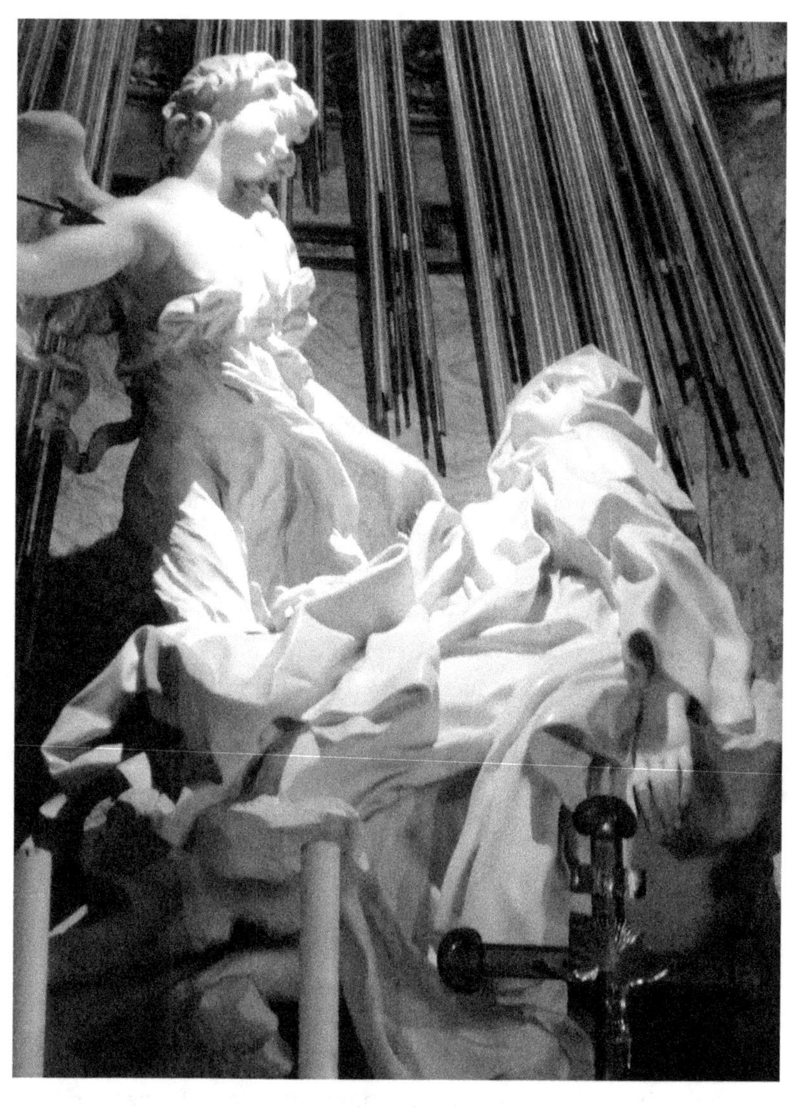

Gianlorenzo Bernini, *The Ecstasy of St. Teresa*, 1652
courtesy of Wikimedia Commons, (CC-BY-SA 3.0) 2005

CHAPTER 1

BODY AND SOUL: THE WORKINGS OF THE INCARNATIONAL CONSCIOUSNESS

Set in a spectacular gilded alcove, flooded with real and sculpted light, Bernini's great sculpture, the *Ecstasy of St. Teresa* depicts the medieval mystic as a beautiful swooning woman. She flings her head back in a transport of emotion, indicating the overwhelming nature of her mystical union with Christ, as the point of an angel's arrow touches her heart. This is one of the world's great devotional sculptures. It is also, as many commentators have pointed out, a remarkably accurate portrayal of a woman in the throes of sexual climax.

For a Catholic viewer, the shock of the scene is compounded by its kinship with the Annunciation, that pivotal event in Christianity, in which the Virgin Mary is visited by an angel who informs her that she is to become pregnant with the child who will be Jesus. Teresa, like Mary, is a Virgin who has been filled with the spirit of God, and it is clear from her written descriptions of her own visionary state that she was aware of the parallels. But while artistic representations of Mary's moment of divine conception downplay the erotic possibilities, presenting her instead as a demure maiden shyly accepting a tremendous assignment, Bernini's Teresa succumbs to her spiritual union with God in a transport of physical excitement.

Even Bernini's contemporaries were struck by the highly sexualized nature of his depiction. One anonymous critic accused him of "dragging that most pure virgin. . . into the dirt, to make a Venus not only prostrate but prostituted."[1] Yet, Bernini was in fact being quite faithful to Teresa's own description of her experience. She writes of being visited by a beautiful angel: "In his hands I saw a golden spear, at its tip, a point of fire. This he plunged into my heart several times so that it penetrated into my entrails. When he pulled it out I felt he took them with it and left me utterly consumed by the great love of God. The pain was so severe that it made me utter several moans. . . This not a physical but a spiritual pain, though the body has some share in it - even a considerable share."[2]

Was it disrespectful for Bernini to borrow from common, carnal experience to give physical form to the experience of religious ecstasy? Or was it a sign of his genius, evidence that he realized that the ineffable can only be effectively expressed in a visual language that draws on familiar and immediately recognizable experiences?

In depicting human union with God as an orgasmic experience, Bernini was pushing the far edge of acceptability. He found himself challenging a church orthodoxy which a century before had ordered the repainting of the exposed genitals of figures in Michelangelo's *Last Judgment* and which, forty years earlier had raised an alarm when Caravaggio used a dead prostitute who had been fished out of the Tiber River as the model for his *The Death of the Virgin*. In sexualizing the spiritual, all three artists flirted with censure. However, they were protected from the most extreme charges of obscenity and sacrilege because they were still operating in an arena in which art was held to be compatible with belief.

Fast forward to present day America. We live in a time when many commentators are convinced that art and religion have reached, in the words of theorist Rosalind Krauss, a point of "absolute rupture." This confirms a seeming tendency within the art world to see art that invokes religion in any but a critical way as retrograde and reactionary. It is further reinforced by the fact that contemporary artists' forays into religious subject matter frequently are met with accusations of blasphemy and sacrilege.

A few cases in point:

In 1988, Donald Wildmon, director of the American Family Association, denounced Martin Scorsese's film *The Last Temptation of Christ*, based on Nikos Kazantzakis' novel of the same name, as sacrilege. Wildmon charged that the movie presented Christ as "a tormented, deranged, human-only sinner."[3] His organization sent out three million letters to Christian lay people condemning the film, sparking threats against theater owners and protests wherever the film was shown. Particularly objectionable to Wildmon's constituency was the depiction of a Christ torn between the seductions of the flesh and the sacrifices required of him as savior of the world. The film includes a fantasy sequence near the end of the film in which Jesus dreams of refusing his mission and leaving the cross to marry Mary Magdalene.

The same year, the rock star Madonna also became the target of a boycott threat by the American Family Association when she released a video *Like a Prayer*. The video tells the tale of a young girl who witnesses a crime and sees a black man wrongfully accused of it. After some hesitation, she is persuaded by a vision in which a black saint transmutes into God, who kisses her, to do the right thing and report her evidence to the police. Charging that in the video "Madonna represented Christ having sex with a priest",[4] Wildmon mobilized his troops and successfully forced Pepsi to cancel a five million dollar ad campaign that featured the singer.

A year later, Andres Serrano, a young photographer of lush art historically derived images became a household name for a work entitled *Piss Christ*. This photograph was one of a series of works in which Serrano photographed religious statuettes through colored light created by various body fluids. Because the work was included in a traveling show partly funded by the National Endowment for the Arts, it became a centerpiece in the political right's efforts to persuade Congress to defund that beleaguered agency.

In 1998, *Corpus Christi*, the production of a play at the Manhattan Theater Club written by award winning playwright Terrance McNally was abruptly canceled during rehearsals under pressure from bomb threats by religious extremists. The play offered a modern day retelling of Christ's passion in which a Christlike character has an off stage sexual relationship with one of his disciples. Conservative religious leaders gleefully praised the cancellation and vowed to "wage war"[5] on any other theater which picked the play up. However, condemnation of the cancellation from the arts community was so powerful that the Manhattan Theater Club reinstated the play to both protestor picket lines and sold out houses.

In 1999, brouhaha ensued over the inclusion of a painting by a young British artist of Nigerian descent in the exhibition *Sensation* at the Brooklyn Museum. Entitled *The Holy Virgin Mary*, it featured an Africanized Virgin Mary embellished with several clumps of rhinestone covered elephant dung. The Mayor of New York, Rudolf Giuliani, courting the Catholic vote for an upcoming Senate race, used this work as a pretext to attack the museum for its anti-Catholic bias, going so far as to attempt, unsuccessfully, to close the city funded museum for daring to exhibit such "sick stuff"[6]. The scenario was repeated a year later when Giuliani renewed the attack on the Brooklyn Museum for including, in a show of Black photography, a photograph by artist Renee Cox which recreated da Vinci's *Last Supper* with a bare breasted Cox standing in for the central Christ figure.

Such incidents, which appear to confirm the adversarial relationship of contemporary art and religion, are elements in what came to be known as the "Culture War", a battle of words and legal wrangles which burst into public consciousness in the late eighties with a campaign to deny public funding to artistic projects deemed pornographic, sacrilegious, amoral or otherwise offensive to the values of the "Christian majority". An effort by political and religious conservatives to purge the nation of what they regard as the relativistic, anti-religious, and anti-family tendencies inculcated by the godless counterculture of the 1960s. The Culture War continues today, exemplified most recently in the effort spearheaded by vice presidential spouse and former NEH chairwoman Lynne Cheney to link the liberal views of various American academics to the attacks of September 11.

In its early days, the Culture War was focused on such goals as outlawing abortion, mandating school prayer and eliminating the National Endowment for the Arts. This latter is a federal agency founded in the 1960s to provide public funding for artists and arts agencies in the form of grants approved by peer panels composed of art professionals.

The campaign against the NEA first became a war in 1989. Combing lists of grant awards to individual artists or institutions, adversaries of public funding discovered a handful that they believed could be classed as pornographic, sacrilegious or otherwise obscene. In order to prevent any further use of taxpayers' dollars to underwrite offensive art, they introduced amendments to eliminate the agency, (which an editorial in the conservative *Washington Times* described as "a kind of federally funded porn palace"[7].) When that proved unrealistic, they persuaded Congress to sharply curtail its funding, and to punish institutions guilty of using NEA money to support offensive art. One of their great triumphs was the institution of the so called decency pledge which required recipients of NEA grants to sign a document promising that the money would not be used to create art which might be construed as obscene or indecent.

The rhetoric surrounding the Culture War has at times suggested a holy crusade. Conservative columnist Pat Buchanan denounced artists like Scorsese and Serrano as paradigms of a secular culture that was "anti-Christian, anti-American, and nihilistic"[8]. In an article for the American Family Association Journal in May 1990, California Representative William Dannemayer went even further. He maintained "My good friends, Christianity is under attack in America." Condemning the moral relativism of these attackers, he averred, ". . . those of us who profess the Judeo-Christian ethic are the primary targets for destruction by the counterculture. In fact, Jesus told us this would happen. He taught his disciples, 'Blessed are ye, when men shall hate you, and when they shall separate you from their company, and shall reproach you, and cast out your name as evil, for the Son of Man's sake (Luke 6:22)"[9]

Such heated rhetoric obscures a crucial element of the Culture War. This is the fact that all of the artists, playwrights, performers and filmmakers discussed above were raised as Catholics. Further, so were other targets of conservative ire whose work was less obviously engaged in religious imagery, among them Robert Mapplethorpe, creator of the infamous "X Portfolio" which contained photographs of explicit sado-masochistic acts, Karen Finley, a performance artist famously described by conservative columnists Evans and Novak as "the chocolate-smeared young woman" and David Wojnarowicz, an artist whose writings and paintings laid the blame for the toll of AIDS at the feet of the political and religious establishment.

These artists' relationship to the religion of their childhood varies considerably - Ofili remains a practicing Catholic, Scorsese describes himself as a devout, though troubled, believer and Serrano, though no a church-goer, lives surrounded by Catholic icons and ecclesiastical furniture. At the other end of the spectrum, Mapplethorpe and Wojnarowicz, who both eventually died of AIDS related ailments, took a more embittered stance toward the religion that negated them as homosexual men, and created works which mingled references to Christ, Satan and tormented sexuality.

But despite the wide variance in their attitudes toward Catholicism, all of these artists have acknowledged its considerable influence over their artistic imaginations. Significantly, the form that influence takes is remarkably consistent. Whether or not they use overtly Christian symbolism, they all create work that focuses in some way on the physical body, its fluids, its processes and its sexual behaviors. And when they run into political trouble, it is almost invariably because the work expresses a carnal vision that is deemed offensive to the American majority.

This brings us to the central questions of this book: Why have artists who were raised as Catholics figured so prominently in the battles of the Culture War? Are there religious roots to their tendency to create work that is perceived as blasphemous, sacrilegious or pornographic by the moral crusaders of the religious right? Why is a carnal vision so potentially inflammatory? Is there something peculiarly American about these conflicts?

We come full circle to Bernini's ecstatic *Saint Teresa*. In this remarkable work, Bernini brings out the carnality implicit in the Catholic vision of man's relationship to God. His sculpture reflects the belief that, as creatures of flesh and blood, men and women require equally physical signs to approach an understanding of Divinity. The central events of the Christian faith - Christ's Incarnation in human form, his physical death and his bodily Resurrection, the Immaculate

Conception and the Transubstantiation of the Eucharist in the Mass also acknowledge this fact. The entire drama of Christian history hinges on the moment when "the Word was made Flesh." When God became man in order to assume mankind's guilt and absolve its sins. St. Bernard presents the standard explanation of the Incarnation: "I think the chief reason why the Invisible God wished to become visible in the flesh... was manifestly this: that he might first win back the affections of fleshly creatures who could not love otherwise than in the flesh."[10]

The preoccupation with flesh and sex in the work of artists who were raised as Catholics reflects an essential aspect of that religion's world view - and, as I will argue throughout this book - may help explain why they so often find themselves the target of attacks in an America whose political and religious establishment is deeply uncomfortable with Catholicism's essential carnality. A recent book by sociologist Andrew Greeley suggests one way to understand this phenomenon. In *The Catholic Imagination* Greeley, himself a Catholic priest, borrows from a book by theologian David Tracy, to posit the existence of a distinctly Catholic consciousness that is immersed in sensuality and sexuality.

According to Greeley, "The Catholic imagination in all its many manifestations . . . tends to emphasize the metaphorical nature of creation . . . Everything in creation, from the exploding cosmos to the whirling, dancing, and utterly mysterious quantum particles, discloses something about God and, in so doing, brings God among us. The love of God for us, in perhaps the boldest of all metaphors (and one with which the Church has been perennially uneasy), is like the passionate love between man and woman. God lurks in aroused human love and reveals Himself to us (the two humans first of all) through it."[11]

Greeley contrasts this with what he calls the "Protestant imagination." "In the Protestant heritage, there is considerable reluctance to go so far as to equate human love with divine," he notes. "Marriage, while good and holy, has never become a sacrament. If one says in this tradition that human sexual union is like the union between God and Her people, there is an immediate need to insist that God's passion is also very different from human passion. Thus, the Protestant imagination... stresses the "unlike" dimension of the metaphor and is in fact very uneasy with the idea of metaphor."[12]

To explain this radically different approach to metaphor, Greeley turns to theologian David Tracy's distinction between the analogical and the dialectical imagination. In *The Analogical Imagination*, a study of the classical theological texts of the Protestant and Catholic traditions, Tracy concludes that "analogically" thinking Catholics assume a God who is present in the world, and thus tend to view the world, and human society, as inherently good and Godlike. "Dialectically" thinking Protestants assume that God is radically absent from the world and discloses himself only on rare occasions. Thus, for them, human society is God-forsaken, unnatural and oppressive. Standing against society, the spiritually inclined human must break away from the world and relate to God as a completely free individual.[13]

An amusing illustration of this thesis can be seen in an interview aired on public television in which Methodist journalist Bill Moyers questions the unlikely media star Sister Wendy Beckett. Sister Wendy, a cloistered Carmelite nun, has gained an enormous following for her populist commentaries on art and art history.[14]

The most interesting part of the interview occurs when Moyers tries to enlist her in America's ongoing war between art and morality. Sister Wendy's responses reveal a remarkably non-judgmental species of Catholicism that flies in the face of Moyer's more Evangelical vision of Christianity.

For instance, Moyers tries to make the point that we owe great art to great sin, to the corrupt, debauched lives of Renaissance and Baroque art patrons. Further, he asks her if she is bothered by the discrepancy between the often immoral character of artists and the great art they produce. Sister Wendy chides him gently about being censorious. She says we must regard the debauched patrons as being "stupid" and "uninstructed" rather than sinful and that we must absolutely distinguish between the art and the artist.

Moyers presses on, asking whether she was offended by *Piss Christ*, a work that, he claims, "denigrates the central figure of your faith." Again, she begs to differ. While advancing her opinion that Serrano is "not a very gifted young man, but he's trying to do his best," Sister Wendy absolutely refuses to see *Piss Christ* as blasphemous. Instead she reads it as an admonitionary work that attempts to say "this is what we are doing to Christ."

Her views on guilt are also illuminating. She declares, "I don't think being truly human has any place for guilt." She elaborates, "Contrition yes. Contrition means you tell God you won't do it again;

you're sorry. Guilt means you go on and on beating your breast . . . You're just sitting in a puddle and splashing."

Finally Moyers raises the question everyone is waiting for. How can it be, he asks, that Sister Wendy feels no shock at the Western canon's immersion in nudity, lust, violence and passion? "It wouldn't ever have occurred to me to be shocked." she replies. "I'm a Catholic".

As for suggestions that artistic depictions of sexuality might be inappropriate viewing matter for a "consecrated virgin", she briskly brushes them aside. "God looked at his creation and saw that it was good, " she maintains serenely. "There is nothing amiss in any part of the human body." She affirms that she and her fellow nuns "are not cramped by the false idea that sexuality is wrong. It's something we have sacrificed." In a final memorable sound bite, she notes, "God wouldn't give you a toy and not let you play with it."

Sister Wendy's unproblematic acceptance of human sexuality needs to be understood in terms of Catholic history and theology. It should come as no surprise that the body has become the battleground in the Culture War. From its earliest days, disagreements about the relationship between body and soul have riven Christianity into opposing camps inaugurating ugly episodes of religious persecution on both sides. Questions about the sanctity of physical experience, the origin of sin and the nature of Christ recur continually throughout the history of Christianity both before and after the great schism of the Reformation.

The theological struggle over the status of the body in Christianity grew out of the doctrine of the Incarnation. Officially instituted in 325 A.D. at the Council of Nicaea, the Incarnation was designed to answer the conundrum that had risen among early Christian theologians about the ontological status of Jesus Christ. Christ, as savior of fallen humanity, had given his life to absolve mankind of the sins of Adam. But how could he be born and die unless he was a man himself? Yet if he was a just a mortal man, how could his sacrifice be sufficient to appease the immortal God?

The Council solved the problem by declaring that Christ was both fully man and fully divine. Only this dual nature made it possible for him to mediate between the realms of heaven and earth. A real sacrifice demanded a real body and a real corpse, while the forgiveness of mankind's sins and the admission of the faithful to heaven required divine intervention.

This official position relegated both those who held the position that Jesus was only a man, and those who declared him only a God, to the status of heretics. In the early years of the Church, dissenters were more likely to deny Christ's divine nature. This was the basis of the Arian heresy promulgated in the fourth century by Arius of Alexandria: that Jesus was simply a very good man who was lifted to the level of divinity by his good works. To counter this heresy, early church doctrine stressed Christ's divinity. In one of his learned sermons, Augustine declared flatly, "This is precisely what constitutes unbelief, that Christ is held to be without any divinity whatsoever".[15]

However, from the second century onwards, there were also those who took issue with the notion of Christ's humanity. The Gnostics, lead by Valentinus, denied that Christ was human, positing instead an unbridgeable gap between Heaven and Earth. According to this rather complex theology, the world that we know is but a perversion of the celestial realm, created not by God but by a jealous pseudo-deity whom unenlightened humans take for the real thing. In this view, the visible world and the flesh are evil, and man's task is to transcend them through gnosis, or special knowledge. Needless to say, the body plays no part in the drama of man's salvation, and is in fact one of his chief impediments. In a pessimistic era, this dark vision took flight, and continued, in various versions, to plague the official Church for centuries.

To counter such threats, Church fathers like Thomas Aquinas and Bonaventure stressed the Incarnation as the central truth of Christianity. From the Incarnation followed a whole host of other doctrines, also based on the human body. For instance, Christ's bodily resurrection from the dead three days after his crucifixion was seen as a foreshadowing of a future event: the resurrection of the bodies of the human dead at the end of time. The faithful would ascend to heaven in their glorified bodies, while the reembodied damned would eternally suffer both physical and spiritual torments in hell.

The Incarnation also dictated the elevation of the Virgin Mary to the status of Queen of Heaven. First promulgated in the 9th century, and adopted as an infallible truth in 1854, the doctrine of the Immaculate Conception maintained that, as mother of the God/Man, Mary herself must have been born free from the curse of Original Sin which had been visited on all the rest of mankind following Adam and

Eve's expulsion from Paradise. She was thus an uncorrupted vessel for the transmission of God into human form.

The Immaculate Conception justified The Assumption, observed as a feast day since the seventh century and officially instated in 1950. According to this doctrine, because of her purity, Mary did not have to wait with the rest of mankind to be reunited with her body. Instead, she was carried bodily to heaven upon her death.

But most important was the doctrine of The Eucharist that solidified the role played by the body in the Mass, the central ritual of the Catholic faith. The Mass is a reenactment of Christ's Last Supper with his Apostles before his Crucifixion (which itself was a celebration of the Jewish Passover). At the pivotal moment of the Mass, the priest, who assumes Christ's role in the ritual, takes bread and wine that symbolize the meal shared with the apostles, and turns them into the actual body and blood of Christ. The bread and wine retain their natural forms, but when consumed by the members of the congregation, replay Christ's sacrifice and seal their commitment to Christ through a physical union with his divine substance. In keeping with the literal nature of the transformation, or Transubstantiation, as the event is officially known, various medieval mystics reported feeling the consecrated bread turn into actual flesh in their mouths.

This theological preoccupation with physical bodies yielded practices and debates that seem bizarre by modern standards. Medieval scholar Carolyn Walker Bynum has reported that belief in the resurrection of the body lead medieval theologians into remarkable speculations, among them: "Will aborted foetuses rise? Will Siamese twins be two people or one in the resurrection? Will we all be the same sex in heaven? The same height and weight? The same age? Will we have to eat? Will we be able to eat? Will deformities and mutilations appear in heaven? Will nail and hair clippings all return to the body to which they originally belonged? Will men have beards in their resurrected bodies? Will we "see" in heaven only when our eyes are open? Will we rise with all our internal organs as well as our external ones?"[16]

The cult of relics is one outcome of such questions. If the bodies of the saints were to be resurrected and glorified at the end of time, the physical pieces that remained behind contained a spiritual power that made them sacred objects to be venerated in the present. Miracles were attributed to bits of bone and hair, vials of blood were said to boil on special days, holy flesh was said to resist decay and exude healing oils. Even scraps of clothing and discarded fingernails could serve as relics.

Meanwhile, living bodies could also be sacralized through the practice of reliving Christ's suffering, an idea popularized by Thomas à Kempis' *The Imitation of Christ*. Pious individuals chose to reenact elements of his passion and death, flagellating themselves, wearing hair shirts, piercing their skin, even walking barefoot on glass, all in an effort to share the physical tortures inflicted on Christ prior to his death. Some of the more fortunate sufferers were miraculously visited by stigmata: bleeding wounds on their feet and hands that mimicked the wounds of Christ sustained when he was nailed to the cross. Others, like Saint Teresa, were overtaken by divine visitations that were equal parts pleasure and pain. As we shall see, this medieval preoccupation with self-inflicted suffering finds a remarkable echo in the activities of a group of late twentieth century artists.

While much about this obsession with the physical body seems alien today, Bynum points out that the medieval belief that the body is an integral part of who we are is crucial as well to the modern idea of selfhood. Medieval theology teaches that, far from being separate and separable entities, body and soul are inextricably linked. The elevation of saints to heaven is not complete until their souls are joined by their bodies, and until then, the bodies they leave behind are imbued with special powers that reflect the exaltation of their souls. Meanwhile, living bodies and their senses can become doorways to the divine through mystical experiences that involve real pleasure and pain.

Such beliefs, she argues, have modern kin in our own preoccupation with the implications of cloning, heart and brain transplants, artificial intelligence and the status of Alzheimer's patients. When we wonder whether the self can continue if the body is significantly altered, and whether mind and memory alone are enough to establish identity, we are confirming our conviction that the body is more than a neutral shell. Instead, we are accepting the belief that identity is a subtle, and still mysterious blend of body and mind, body and soul.

In keeping with this conviction, (and this will have great significance later in our discussion), Catholicism awards the body a dual status. It is not only an enticement for temptation and sin, but also serves as the medium through which we make contact with God.

Medieval art presents striking and often peculiar images of the Last Judgement and General Resurrection, the ordeals of the saints, and the efficacy of holy relics. However, representation of the fuller implications of the Incarnation awaited the Renaissance. As art historian Leo Steinberg has pointed out in his provocative study *The Sexuality of Christ in Renaissance Art and in Modern Oblivion*, it was not until this period that art began to provide a picture of Jesus as a fully human man. Steinberg maintains that "Renaissance Art . . . became the first Christian art in a thousand years to confront the Incarnation entire, the upper and the lower body together, not excluding even the body's sexual component."[17]

Steinberg's thesis, which has been extremely controversial and has even involved him in an extended theoretical quarrel with Bynum, is that Renaissance artists went out of their way to emphasize Christ's sexual organ in order to bolster the theological doctrine of the Incarnation. His book is an exuberant and mind bogglingly comprehensive tour of the varieties of artistic approaches to the subject. He piles up images of the Madonna and Child in which the Virgin seems to be pointing to or even uncovering the baby Jesus' penis. He shows the Magi worshipfully examining the child's genitals. He collects paintings in which Mary touches the holy organ as her Son's adult dead body lays in her lap. He sees displaced phallic emphasis in the furling or bulging drapery which he believes covers or substitutes for an erection in representations of Christ on the Cross or lying on his funeral bier.

The cumulative effect of all these examples is to sustain his conjecture that Renaissance art's phallic focus was completely deliberate. Coming at a moment when art had rediscovered classical models of glorious and strikingly lifelike nudes and when literature and philosophy were celebrating the dignity of man, a focus on Christ the man served a variety of purposes. Art promoted the humanism of the Renaissance while offering a popular line of defense against the heresies that would deny the "humanation" of Christ.

Renaissance art's celebration of Christ's naked body derives from serious theological considerations. As Steinberg says of Michelangelo's *Risen Christ* of 1514 in which the Savior is depicted after his resurrection as magnificently and unabashedly nude as a classical sculpture: "We must, I think, credit Michelangelo with the knowledge that Christian teaching makes bodily shame no part of man's pristine nature, but attributes it to the corruption brought on by sin"[18]. He adds that examples of antique sculpture clearly inspired Michelangelo, "Their unabashed freedom conveyed a possibility which Christian teaching reserved only for Christ and for those who would resurrect in Christ's likeness: the possibility of a human nature without human guilt."[19]

As even Steinberg acknowledges, this moment of freedom was brief, and was quickly shut down with the advent of the Reformation, which among other things, targeted the decadence and idolatry of Catholic religious art. Even the Counter Reformation absorbed some of the prudery of the Protestant assault on nudity. By mid sixteenth century, Michelangelo's conception of glorified human bodies was under attack, and the exposed genitalia of both the saved and the damned in his *Last Judgement* were painted over with modest bits of fluttering cloth. The hysteria of the moment is captured in a 1545 letter to Michelangelo from critic and poet Pietro Aretino, (himself a notorious pornographer apparently hoping to clear his own record). Aretino charged, "Indeed such a fervent display of genital organs . . . would even cause a brothel to blink. Such painting belongs in a voluptuary bathhouse . . . It would be much more appropriate in a theater or a setting for a comedy where something obscene were performed."[20]

The Reformation, which broke Christianity into so many competing factions, turned in part on the perception of Catholicism's decadence, sexual licentiousness and unseemly immersion in things of this world. Efforts to "purify" Christianity took many different forms in the ensuing centuries, often appearing as an emphasis on the gap between body and soul and the incommensurability of the realms of heaven and earth. This vision is particularly evident in English Protestantism, which is, of course, the historical ancestor of many of our American variations. Theologian John Dillenberger describes it thus "...English Christianity was characterized by considerable distrust of the senses. God and God's relation to the world was considered so spiritual in character that the world was not a legitimate mode through which God might be perceived or apprehended. The world and all it symbolizes was the fallen matrix from which, through the resources mind and spirit, humanity must be delivered. God was spirit, the locus of God's relation to humanity was thus essentially and directly spiritual. There was a connection between spirit, breath, sound and words, so that words, not things, became the particular medium appropriate to the mediation of God's presence. Hence, its dominant modality was verbal and auditory."[21]

In America particularly, the lingering effects of this version of Christianity continue to be felt in many ways. It can be seen in the controversies that erupt over public displays of nudity, in the fascinated revulsion with which media and public obsess over the private indiscretions and infidelities of public figures and in the calls to protect people from themselves by banning obscene and objectionable images from the mass media and the internet. (A particularly amusing recent example involves Attorney General John Ashcroft's order that a pair of nude neoclassical sculptures in the Capitol be draped so as not to offend the television viewing public's sensibilities.)

It is clear that in contemporary America, questions of the relationship between body and soul remain vexing. The potentially inflammatory consequences of incarnational thinking are evident in the rage incited by artists embroiled in the Culture War, which so often seems to pit Catholic artists against spokespeople for a "Christian" (read evangelical) America for whom flesh is a condition to be transcended rather than celebrated. However, a schism has also opened up within the American Catholic Church itself about the meaning and practice of sexuality. The official Church stand on homosexuality, abortion and contraception has long been deeply problematic for many American Catholics. More recently, many liberal Catholics see the clerical sexual abuse scandals as the inevitable consequence of the Church's sexual policies regarding priestly celibacy, while conservative Catholics link the problem to the pernicious influence of a licentious secular society. Some commentators have gone so far as to suggest that the current upheavals may be leading toward a second Reformation which could split the contemporary Catholic Church in two.

Thus, in order to make sense of the fury which is frequently visited upon artists imbued with an incarnational consciousness, it is necessary to look beyond distinctions between Catholic and Protestant views on the body to the conflicts opened up by the emergence of a more general stalemate between liberal and conservative manifestations of Christianity in America today. This division, evident within both American Protestantism and American Catholicism, has monumental political implications in a country that, despite its avowal of the principle of separation of Church and State, has always considered itself "a

Christian country". The ease with which crusaders for the cultural right can slip from the charge that contemporary artists are anti-Christian to the assumption that they are thus also anti-American is evidence of how thoroughly our notions of civility and citizenship are tied to religion. Thanks to the superior political organization of the religious right, the definition of religion and morality which has gained most sway in our political life is one which runs counter to the America's deep seated values of tolerance and intellectual freedom.

The Protestant form of religious conservatism goes by the name of Fundamentalism.[22] Fundamentalism is not a denomination itself, but a theological coloration applied to existing sects. As the world has become sadly aware, fundamentalism manifests itself in all the three major monotheistic religions. In its Christian form, It expresses an essential hostility to many aspects of the modern world. Its tenets include the inerrancy of the bible - the doctrine that, since the Holy Spirit inspired the text of the bible, it is "absolutely errorless." Likewise adherence to dispensational Premillennialism, an ideology declaring that after a series of ever darker periods in human history dominated by evil and sin, the earth will descend into complete chaos and catastrophe, after which Christ will reappear for a thousand year reign of peace and justice. This apocalyptic vision, which suggests that the righteous can only wait out the dark times until Christ's Second Coming, received an unexpected boost with the terrorist attack on the World Trade Towers and the subsequent turmoil at home and abroad. This contrasts with the postmillennialist view of liberal Protestants and Catholics that holds that mankind can and should attempt to perfect the world in the period prior to Christ's final return.

In casting the present as an age of darkness and calamity prior to the restoration of the faithful promised by Christ's Second Coming, fundamentalists repudiate the essential principles of the Incarnational consciousness: that the world is a manifestation of God's goodness and that the physical realm offers a mirror of the spiritual one. Meanwhile, the belief in the inerrancy of the bible leads fundamentalists into conflict with many of the teachings of modern science and the society that it has created. Darwinism, socialism, feminism, and popular culture all become manifestations of an anti-Christian secular humanism which tempts the faithful away from the true message of the bible. The note of hysteria which permeates the rhetoric of the religious right when it turns its attention to avant-garde art is a logical consequence of this deeply anti-social and deeply anti-modernist view.

Fundamentalist based political groups like the Christian Coalition, the Moral Majority, and The American Family Association have been remarkably successful in promoting a social gospel based on "family values" which keeps issues like abortion, school prayer, the teaching of creationism on the forefront of the American agenda. These groups target sex education in the schools and government support of condom distribution as insidious attempts to "normalize" the evil of homosexuality. And of course, they were major players in the battle to eliminate the National Endowment for the Arts.

Since the 1980 election campaign, Republican candidates who ignore the agenda of the religious right do so at their peril. And the ever-rightward drift of the Democratic Party is also, in part, an acknowledgement of the political power of religious conservatives. The alliance of conservative politicians and religious leaders has helped skew the country's domestic and international priorities in directions that are often at odds with the views of the nation's populace at large. Its far reaching effects include international health initiatives which can't get funded because they include condoms and family planning; promising avenues of research for the cure of cancer and Alzheimer's abandoned because they involve fetal stem cells, ambassadors, judges and cabinet members whose appointments are held up because of their views on abortion; efforts to censor popular television programs, internet sites, films and pop music whose content includes explicit sex or "anti Christian" messages; and the undermining of the basic premises of "socialist" programs like Welfare, Medicaid and Social Security in favor of "faith based" initiatives. In addition, by cornering the definition of morality in contemporary America, fundamentalist Christians have gained powerful justification for their efforts to condemn "deviant" lifestyles as sinful and to attempt, in some cases to make them unlawful.

In some of these battles, they have been joined by groups that might have been expected to be their natural antagonists. In the drive to eliminate "pornography" in popular culture, fundamentalists have made common cause with a version of radical feminism that equates rape with degrading depictions of women in films, books and on the Internet. Similarly, despite the natural friction between Protestant fundamentalists and Catholics (one of the low points of the 2000 presidential campaign occurred when it was revealed that George W. Bush had appeared at Bob Jones University, a fundamentalist college whose president has proclaimed Catholicism a Satanic cult,) conservative Catholics have been willing to overlook these differences to gain support for their campaigns on issues like abortion, homosexuality and anti-Christian art.

Conservative Catholicism stems from a different source than fundamentalist Protestantism. Its most visible manifestation is the Catholic League for Religious and Civil Rights.[23] Founded in 1973, the League was reinvigorated in 1993 by the appointment of its current media savvy director William Donohue. While fundamentalist organizations like the American Family Association and the Christian Coalition led the battle against godless artists in the 1980s and early 90s, Donohue, through the Catholic League has been the most vocal adversary of irreverence in more recent art controversies.

The League takes as its mandate the defense of "the right of Catholics – lay and clergy alike – to participate in American public life without defamation or discrimination." The League is vigilant, at times to the point of hysteria, in ferreting out instances of anti-Catholicism in American public life. An organization that claims a 350,000 membership throughout the nation, it taps into Catholic fears of the longstanding tradition of American anti-Catholicism. This anti-Catholicism dates from the early years of the country, when Puritan dissenters fled to the colony to escape the "papist" tendencies of Anglican Protestantism in England. This was exacerbated during the American Revolution when loyalists staged rallies against the "Papal Antichrist" represented by Catholic France. However, anti-Catholicism didn't become full blown until the mid nineteenth century when waves of Catholic immigrants poured into the country, bringing different customs and belief systems which threatened to destabilize the comfortable alliance of Protestant religion and politics in this self described Christian country.

Though clearly less visible in contemporary America's diverse cultural landscape, anti-Catholicism has flared up frequently enough in recent years to give credence to the Catholic League's charges. The Catholic League makes forays into politics, taking pro-school voucher, pro-school prayer and anti-abortion stances and supporting various conservative candidates. However, the bulk of its activity is directed toward to anti-Catholic bias in the mass media. Its targets have included CNN, BBC, Showtime, Disney, Salon magazine, and Time Out New York. It also monitors what it perceives as anti-Catholic imagery in corporate advertising campaigns and music videos.

Though it clearly has very different origins, this approach to Catholicism nevertheless shares some aspects of fundamentalism. Both exhibit strongly anti-modernist tendencies that are manifested in a horror of secular culture and a deeply conservative social agenda that makes issues like abortion the litmus test for political support. And both make an argument to higher authority (to the Bible, in the case of the Protestant fundamentalists, to Church doctrine in the case of the Catholic conservatives) that brooks no room for dissent or even discussion.

But from another point of view, conservative Catholicism, at least as embodied by the Catholic League, is a curious mutation of "liberal" focus in recent years on identity politics. Its official website approvingly cites NAACP and Jewish Defense League as models for this crusade to ensure "Catholic civil rights", seeing the Catholic League's battle as yet another effort to gain respect and political power for a beleaguered minority group. The Catholic League has borrowed from the wildly successful tactics of fundamentalist groups like the Christian Coalition and the American Family Association in setting up a network of letter writers and editorialists prepared to flood the media and political leaders with protests when alerted to instances of anti-Catholicism.

However, as a sign of how profoundly contradictory this movement is, its targets in the cultural sphere are with surprising frequency liberal Catholics. In a review of Garry Wills' *Papal Sin,* a book by a noted Catholic scholar that is highly critical of the Vatican's handling of issues like celibacy, contraception, and clerical sexual misconduct, Robert P. Lockwood, the League's Director of Research, begins with a long screed on anti-Catholic Catholics. "Anti-Catholic statements from Catholics, or those with Catholic roots, may seem to be an oxymoron," he writes." But it exists and those Catholics that engage in such inflammatory rhetoric against their own faith rarely see it as bigotry. Influenced by the dominant secular culture, they see anti-Catholicism as a product of enlightened thought, rather than an inherited prejudice. Worse still, by the very nature of their Catholic background, their remarks gain a certain cachet in secular circles that would otherwise ignore them if the source were non-Catholic."[24] It is hard to imagine the NAACP making turncoat African Americans a primary focus, or the JDL turning on "anti-Semitic" Jews.

In the visual arts sphere, the Catholic League has been particularly attentive to this phenomenon of Catholic anti-Catholicism. Many of the controversies that this book addresses surround works by Catholic artists that have been read by the Catholic League and its members as insults to the Catholic faith. In raising the alarm against these apostates, Donohue borrows from the language of liberal identity politics to make a case for censorship and suppression. Often, Donohue's rhetoric reaches a level of hyperbole that seriously undermines his case, reaching for analogies that are patently absurd. Consider, for example, Donohue's query to the curator of an exhibition at the Brooklyn Museum devoted to Black photography. The show featured a photographic recreation of da Vinci's *Last Supper* by Catholic born photographer Renee Cox by which Christ was represented by the bare breasted artist. Donohue asked: "I would love to know whether there is any portrayal of any aspect of history that you might personally find so offensive as to be excluded from an exhibition at the Brooklyn Museum of Art. For starters, would you include a photograph of Jewish slave masters sodomizing their obsequious black slaves?"[25]

Such preposterous analogies would merely be grist for late night comics if Donohue and the Catholic League did not wield real political power. This was most nakedly evident in the close alliance formed by the Catholic New York Major Rudy Giuliani and Donohue in connection with a pair of controversies at the Brooklyn Museum which resulted in a (ultimately unsuccessful) legal battle to close the museum and the subsequent formation of a "decency panel" to monitor "offensive" art in city funded institutions. The irony of this alliance was not lost on commentators, who pointed out that Giuliani was engaged in a highly public extramarital affair during these machinations. In addition, one of the prominent members of the mayor's decency campaign was his own divorce lawyer. (The Catholic Church, of course, officially enjoins against divorce.)

It needs to be stressed that the Catholic League is a minority voice within the larger American Catholic community. It receives no financial support from the Catholic Church, and depends for its funding on individual contributors. The massive press coverage it receives obscures the fact that its positions do not represent the beliefs of the majority of American Catholics. In a study of the relative tolerance for supposedly irreligious art works prepared for the Luce Foundation, Peter Marsden found that as a group Catholics were the most tolerant of the Christian groups.[26] This jibes with Greeley's sociological work, which finds Catholics more inclined than Protestants to take liberal positions with respect to civil disobedience, government intervention in the economy, and redistribution of income.[27]

It is equally important to realize that the Catholic League's campaign against anti-Catholic artists is strictly an American phenomenon. While there are deep divisions within the Catholic Church internationally with regard to the Church's teachings on social issues, the Vatican has taken no interest in these American cultural controversies. An illustration of this is a story told by photographer Andres Serrano, whose *Piss Christ* was exhibit A in the battle against high culture's supposed anti-Catholic bias. Several years after the height of his notoriety, Serrano decided to create a series of photographs of members of the high clergy in France, Spain and Italy. When he took his request to the Vatican, he discovered that Vatican officials were indeed aware of him and the surrounding controversy. However, they were quite sanguine about *Piss Christ* and its larger implications. They expressed more concern about an abstract work in which he had photographed light through a stream of semen, fearing that it violated Church strictures against the unproductive spilling of seed. But none of these concerns were sufficient to prevent Serrano from completing his mission and creating a series of photographic portraits that are quite moving in their sense of reverence and sacred mystery.

This is the context in which right wing efforts to present avant-garde artists as God-hating, anti-American anarchists must be understood. American fundamentalist Protestants, aided at times by conservative Catholics, have managed to impose a definition of morality on the American political landscape that leaves no room for an incarnational theology that celebrates the body and emphasizes the physical and sexual aspects of human experience. The idea that artists who deal forthrightly with human carnality might be expressing a sensibility that comes out of a legitimate Christian consciousness has become almost unthinkable in contemporary American society.

The narrowing of acceptable forms of religious and spiritual creativity has consequences that go far beyond the cultural sphere. In the end, it is not only our understanding of art that suffers. The dismissal of the incarnational imagination has also impoverished our social relationships and our field of political possibilities. By acknowledging the religious dimension of works by artists imbued with an incarnational consciousness we take a first step toward forging a more open definition of public morality which embraces both our spiritual and physical humanity and makes room for the reality of human imperfection.

In the final analysis, the artists in this book are Catholics in conflict. Their conflict stems in part from mixed messages about sexuality and the body within Catholicism itself, many of which originate in a schism between the Catholic Church's official doctrine, and individual Catholic's imaginative sensibilities. Such conflicts are particularly strong in the case of artists whose sexual orientation has been officially condemned by the Catholic Church.

But perhaps even more powerful are the conflicts that arise between these Catholic artists' incarnational orientation and a public morality based on an alien system of thought. The fundamentalist hold on American politics encourages a view of religion that is resistant to metaphor, suspicious of artistic exposure of the body or body processes, and virulently opposed to "deviant" lifestyles and sexual practices. The political battle against "godless" artists denies any validity to their quite different spiritual sensibilities.

I have designated the artists under discussion here as "Postmodern Heretics" because I think the dissonance suggested by this name aptly expresses the contradictions and conflicts which underlie their work and which give it such power. From one perspective, the artistic expressions of these "Postmodern Heretics" are completely in sync with contemporary art theory and production. All of these artists can and, in fact, have been discussed in commentaries on contemporary art without reference to their religion. But "Postmodern" as they are, they are also working through the consequences of an incarnational mode of thinking.

They are "Heretics" meanwhile, because the ways in which they have internalized and reconstituted the elements of the Catholic Imagination are unorthodox and often controversial. But the fact that their work can raise the hackles of more conventional believers does not mean that they are necessarily irreligious. In *The Gnostic Gospels,* her brilliant study of the theology and politics of early Christianity, Elaine Pagels points out that heretical positions are often views that were well within the realm of acceptability until outside threats or external pressures enforced a more narrow definition of orthodoxy.[28] I would like to use the word heretic in this more fluid way, seeing these artists as seekers who may not be intentionally trying to transgress the bounds of established religion.

Defined as a mode of incarnational thinking, the notion of the Catholic imagination presented here allows us to reinject religion into our understanding of contemporary art without limiting artists to the role of propagandists for the Church. It also allows us to include within the category of Catholic, or Catholic influenced artists, not only those who profess an active faith and intentionally express its tenets, but also those who, though they were raised Catholics, may have far more ambivalent feelings about the Church's official teachings. It also makes room for a small subcategory of artists, who, though never officially baptized, have been sufficiently immersed in a Catholic milieu to absorb its incarnational outlook. The work of these Postmodern Heretics provides striking evidence that it is time to move beyond the long standing but erroneous belief that avant-gardism is by definition antithetical to religious sensibility. The study which follows offers a new way to think about the relationship between art and religion which can cast new light, not just on these individual artists, but on the way we define modernism and the way we think about the workings of the creative imagination.

Although there are many possible starting points for this study, I have chosen to begin in the early 1960s, a moment when Catholicism was much in the public mind due to the election of John F. Kennedy to the Presidency of the United States. His instatement was accompanied by fears within the more radical factions of the Republican Party that this first Catholic president would be serving as a 'patsy' for the Pope. Much less recognized at this time was the fact that the most famous progenitor of the movement that came to be known as Pop Art was also a practicing member of the Catholic Church.

* * *

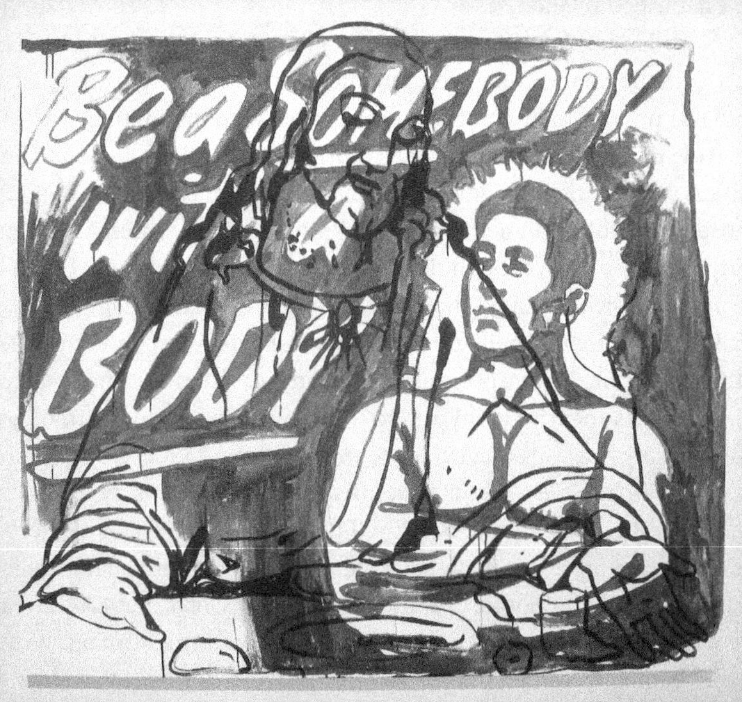

Andy Warhol, *The Last Supper (Be a Somebody with a Body)*, 1985-86

courtesy of Creative Commons (CC BY-SA 2.0) 2007

CHAPTER 2

ANDY WARHOL: SOMEBODY WITH A BODY

Who was Andy Warhol? Common wisdom styles him the great leveler; a fright wigged cynic endlessly recycling the clichés of American popular culture with a postmodernist disregard for value or meaning. "If you want to know all about Andy Warhol," he famously told an interviewer, "just look at the surface of my paintings and films and me, and there I am. There's nothing behind it."[29]

For many reviewers, this statement confirms the apparent emptiness of his work. As Robert Hughes put it in a highly critical essay on the artist, "In general his only subject was detachment: the condition of being a spectator, dealing hands-off with the world through the filter of photography."[30] In this view, Warhol was the human sieve, collecting both the glittering icons of a celebrity besotted culture and the most banal of its consumer products while filtering out anything that could give these images depth and emotional significance. Or, alternately, Warhol was the indifferent mirror that absorbed equally Brillo boxes, the electric chair, movie stars and famous paintings, while reflecting back an image of ourselves constructed out of the blandishments of mass media, advertising and Hollywood. In Warhol's universe, the assassinated president and the anonymous car crash victim, Marilyn Monroe and the FBI's most wanted men, Chairman Mao and the social climbing subject of a commissioned Warhol portrait, the Campbell soup can and the dollar sign all achieve their allotted fifteen minutes of fame in machine-like silk screen paintings which are themselves deliberate negations of traditional ideas of individuality, self expression and personal experience.

If any intentionality was attached to his selection of images, critics writing during his lifetime tended to see it as a form of deliberate sabotage. German critics, in particular, described his work as an effort to destroy the burgeoning system of consumer marketing from within by exposing its essential emptiness.[31] Others regarded him as kitsch's revenge on the high culture represented by the Abstract Expressionists who preceded him. By awarding Mona Lisa and Campbell soup equal status, they believed that he exposed the absurdity of elitist claims for art as a special realm of consciousness.

But in the years since Warhol's death in 1987, commentators have increasingly challenged this picture of Warhol's famed neutrality. Art historian Thomas Crow argued in an article published just four months after Warhol's death that the artist's early work is pervaded with a compassionate empathy for the victims of death and disaster.[32] Curator Trevor Fairbrother has extended that notion to cover a series of skull images from the 1970s, going so far as to assert, "Death was probably the most important underlying theme of Warhol's work after 1960 . . ."[33] Meanwhile, in 2000, a traveling exhibition circulating throughout the United States focused on Andy Warhol as social activist.

Other commentators have borrowed from Susan Sontag's notion of camp as a springboard for a discussion of Warhol's work as an expression of a pre-Stonewall gay consciousness. Art historian Kenneth Silver sees both Warhol's iconography and the flamboyant "swishiness" of his persona as assertions of his homosexuality.[34] Art critic Simon Watney argues that his embrace of camp was a survival strategy in a deeply macho art world.[35]

Meanwhile, even Warhol's greatest critics have acknowledged the presence of some kind of Catholic sensibility in his work. Robert Hughes styles him as a kind of anti-Messiah: "Those whose parents accused them of being out of their tree, who had unfulfilled desires and undesirable ambitions, and who felt guilty about it all, therefore gravitated to Warhol. He offered them absolution, the gaze of the blank mirror that refuses all judgment . . . In this way the Factory resembled a sect, a parody of Catholicism enacted (not accidentally) by people who were or had been Catholic, from Warhol and Gerard Malanga on down".[36]

A more positive spin on Warhol's Catholicism came from art historian John Richardson who revealed the extent of the artist's engagement with religion in his eulogy for Warhol at a memorial service just after the artist's death. "Never forget," he proclaimed, "that Andy was born into a fervently Catholic family and brought up in the fervently Catholic Ruska Dolina, the Ruthenian section of Pittsburgh. As a youth, he was withdrawn and reclusive, devout and celibate; and beneath the disingenuous public mask that is how he at heart remained. Thanks largely to the example of his adored mother, Julia, Andy never lost the habit of going to Mass more often than was obligatory. As fellow parishioners will remember, he made a point of dropping in on his local church, St. Vincent Ferrer, several days a week until shortly before he died.

"Although Andy was perceived, with some justice, as a passive observer who never imposed his beliefs on other people, he could on occasion be an effective proselytizer. To my certain knowledge, he was responsible for at least one conversion. He took considerable pride in financing a nephew's studies for the priesthood. And as you have doubtless read on your Mass cards, he regularly helped out at a shelter serving meals to the homeless and the hungry. Trust Andy to keep these activities very, very dark."[37]

A recent book entitled *The Religious Art of Andy Warhol* by Jane Daggett Dillenberger takes up the challenge offered by this eulogy, and seeks to discover "another Andy Warhol" through an in-depth analysis of the explicitly religious themes that pop up in Warhol's work throughout his career. The book culminates in a detailed analysis of a final series based on Leonardo da Vinci's *Last Supper*. Dillenberger maintains that the Last Supper paintings are Warhol's greatest works and serve as a kind of last will and testament. "In these last paintings the cool and distanced artist abandoned his mask. Warhol finally created paintings in which his secret but deeply religious nature flowed freely into his art," she says.[38]

So the question recurs. Who or what are we dealing with here? There is the saintly Andy of the soup kitchens, the charismatic "holy idiot" who attracts the lost and wounded souls of the amoral affluent society of postwar America, the Marxist Andy whose proletariat origins lead him to a covert battle against capitalism, the affectless dandy who cares only for glamour and celebrity, the demonic voyeur who dispassionately pulls others to their doom, the champion of gay sensibility, the philosopher of mortality, the last purveyor of great religious art. Andy Warhol emerges from all these accounts as a remarkable chameleon whose place in art history is as slippery as the personas attributed to him.

Could the problem be that we are approaching Warhol "dialectically", to use David Tracy's term, rather than "analogically"? The literalism that comes from wanting a single, definitive reading of an artwork eliminates contradictions that may be essential to the work. There is a tendency among contemporary critics to view art as a kind of text to be dissected for its literal meaning. In this view, artists are seen as issuing position papers on politics, society or culture. The task of the critic is to decode the artwork to explain the artist's intention.

This approach ignores the multiple levels on which the best art tends to operate. In Warhol's case, literalism infiltrates the thinking, not only of those who wish to see the work as resolutely neutral, but also of those who hope to invest it with meaning. There is an either/or mentality which plagues even those who acknowledge Catholicism's importance on Warhol's work. It can be seen in Robert Hughes' transformation of the artist into an anti-Christ and in the insistence with which Dillenberger and Richardson maintain Warhol's saintly status. Hughes sees a ruthless, calculating cynic eager to sell his soul for a taste of fame and glamour. Dillenberger and Richardson use the same evidence to construct a thoroughly moral individual who deals seriously with spiritual themes.

Must spiritual art be created by exemplary people? Conversely, is a person associated with a decadent, fast track lifestyle rife with drugs, "deviant" sexuality, and unorthodox behaviors incapable of art that deals profoundly with spiritual issues?

The either/or mentality allows us to see only pieces of the puzzle that is Andy Warhol. Dillenberger is on the right track when she looks for evidence that Warhol's religious upbringing shaped the way he understood and encountered the world. But she falls short of seeing Catholicism's significance for him because she focuses too exclusively on his appropriation of approved Catholic themes. She points out that Warhol periodically based works on well-known religious paintings.

Along with *The Last Supper*, he borrowed from Raphael's *Sistine Madonna*, Leonardo da Vinci's *Annunciation*, Paolo Uccello's *St. George and the Dragon* and Piero della Francesca's *Madonna del Duca Federico*. But it is hard to see how such borrowings can be distinguished from his general interest in brand names and corporate logos. In the larger context of Warhol's work, such religious motifs can be read simply as recognition of their status as a species of designer label for the Catholic Church.

Critics have been lead astray in part, by taking Warhol's own disavowals of depth too literally. Like the paintings themselves, Warhol's statements were careful constructions whose apparent simplicity intentionally obscure a more complex vision. Both words and images display a habit of double play. They offer multiple and even contradictory readings which do not cancel each other out revealing a way of approaching the world which is metaphorical rather than analytical. Warhol uses the most banal references to open up the possibility of a myriad of more profound readings, but without negating or denying the hackneyed nature of the original image.

Dillenberger begins to get at this possibility when she discusses the interpolation of other motifs into some of *The Last Supper* paintings. One such painting is overlaid with the logos of General Electric and Dove soap, complete with abstracted bird image, and a supermarket flyer style price tag for 59 cents. In the context of *The Last Supper* imagery, Dillenberger sees a reference to the Trinity here. The General Electric logo is a metaphor for creation and hence God the father, who like GE, God "brings good things to life." Dove is, of course, the Holy Spirit (and soap the purifying agent, while the Christ figure in Leonardo's painting is the Son and Savior.

However, there is something too pat about this interpretation. The price tag pulls everything back to earth and to the venality of everyday life. One is left to wonder; does this last element signify the conflict between money and religion, the use of kitschified religious imagery to "sell" the church, or the incommensurability of human and divine standards of value? (After all, even in 1986, 59 cents wouldn't buy very much). Or is its effect to downplay the religious implications of the underlying imagery? Is it meant to be read as an interjection that says, "just kidding!" and warns us not to take the spiritual clichés of the work too seriously?

In the face of Warhol's resolute refusal to explain himself - even his closest associates never learned the reason for his obsession with *The Last Supper* - it is possible that the work contains all these meanings at once. And it is precisely this ability to allow ordinary objects to encompass multiple meanings that recurs again and again in the work of artists raised as Catholics.

This way of looking at Warhol gives his rebellion against the aesthetic milieu that preceded him added resonance. Abstract Expressionism, emerging as a radical avant-garde strategy in the mid-1940s, had by the late fifties become the establishment. The group of artists associated with this movement were, significantly for our study, almost exclusively Protestant and Jewish. They espoused an aesthetic of sublimity which critics linked to the transcendentalism of Emerson and Thoreau, the intellectual fashion for Jungian myth and the American landscape tradition. Despite the fact that the most prominent advocate of Abstract Expressionism - the critic Clement Greenberg - disavowed any link between the best art and "literary" influences like history and religion, a number of artists produced works which were understood to have strong spiritual content. Significantly, these were abstract works. Mark Rothko's' Houston chapel, Willem de Kooning's 1984 triptych altarpiece for St. Peter's Lutheran Church in Manhattan and Barnett Newman's *Stations of the Cross* exuded a disembodied spirituality clearly much more akin to the Protestant imagination's focus on transcendence than to Catholicism's carnal obsessions. (It is beyond the scope of this book to consider the Jewish imagination in detail, but for our purposes it will suffice to point out that Judaism's iconoclastic tradition meshes well with this aspect of the Protestant imagination).

Warhol arrived on the New York scene in the early 1950s, spending that decade working as a commercial illustrator, for which he eventually achieved considerable renown. Despite his success, however, he longed to be part of the fine art world and made "serious" paintings throughout the decade. At first these echo the whimsical drawing style which made him such a successful illustrator. However, around 1960, he began making paintings in what was to become known as the Pop Art style. Pop was the antithesis of Abstract Expressionism. Instead of timelessness and sublimity, it celebrated popular culture and the visual language of contemporary advertising. Instead of the expressive gesture and tortured psyche Pop Art honed a machine-like aesthetic presented with cool, knowing irony. Warhol expressed the difference thus: "The Pop artists did images that anybody walking down Broadway could recognize in a split second: comics, picnic tables, men's trousers, celebrities, shower curtains, refrigerators, Coke bottles. All the great modern things that the Abstract Expressionists tried so hard not to notice at all."[39]

Pop's arrival in the early 1960s coincided with major changes in the larger political and social landscape. The election of John F. Kennedy, the first Catholic president and the youngest man to occupy the office, seemed to signal the arrival of a fresh new energy on the political scene. In sharp contrast with the philistinism of the Eisenhower group, the Kennedy administration welcomed artists and intellectuals into its inner circle. Kennedy's beautiful wife became a style setter and the White House the center of art and culture. In this climate, Pop Art seemed a perfect foil for a society that wanted to put World War II behind it and make the most of the new postwar prosperity.

By 1963, Warhol had emerged as one of the most famous of the Pop artists. His canny ability to select subjects that summed up the preoccupations of an American society made him the subject of fascination and outrage in circles far outside the art world proper. With the creation of The Factory in 1964, Warhol stepped even further from Abstract Expressionism, exchanging the existential heroism of the solitary artist for a communal operation that mimicked the processes of industrial production. He announced, "The reason I'm painting this way is that I want to be a machine, and I feel that whatever I do and do machine-like is what I want to do."[40] Everything about his work - the subject matter, the working method, the look of the work and image that he projected - negated everything the Abstract Expressionists represented.

But Warhol's rejection of the orthodoxies of Abstract Expressionism was much more than an Oedipal rebellion against the parental generation. It can also be seen as the expression of a Catholic vision grounded in the concrete reality of the surrounding world. In conformity with the tendencies of the analogical imagination, Warhol was more interested in soup cans as elements of his real environment than in some ineffable notion of the sublime. He said as much in a 1963 interview with art critic Gene Swenson, when he disputed the standard interpretation of his work. Warhol noted, "It confuses me that people expect Pop Art to make a comment or say that its adherents merely accept the environment. I've viewed most of the paintings I've loved - Mondrians, Matisses, Pollocks - as being rather deadpan in that sense. All painting is fact, and that is enough; the paintings are charged with their very presence. The situation, physical ideas, physical presenc: I feel that is the comment."[41]

To locate the spiritual content in Warhol's work, we would do better to look beyond obvious religious motifs and examine instead his obsession with death. During his lifetime, it was still possible to read Warhol's version of Pop Art, particularly throughout the sixties, as a gloss on the optimistic consumerism of that era. Recently, however, scholars have begun to point out the persistence of much darker themes.

At the same time that he was developing his soup cans and his Elvises, Warhol also began a series of Death and Disaster paintings. These were inspired, he later reported, by an article in the New York Daily News. Warhol turned the newspaper article into a painting dominated by the headline *129 Die in Jet*. This was followed by a series of works that focused on other accidents and disasters. *Tuna Fish Disaster*, from 1963 repeated details of a tabloid newspaper account of an incident in which two women were killed from eating tainted tuna fish. As a number of commentators have pointed out, the sinister jars of tuna fish in this work were downbeat cousins to his more famous Campbell soup cans, serving, in Thomas Crow's words, to break "the supermarket promise of safe and abundant packaged food"[42]. He also created works based on news accounts of car crashes, complete with the grainy, grisly news photographs of bodies extruding from mangled cars, of anonymous suicides, of gangster funerals and finally in 1965, the unmistakable mushroom cloud of the atomic bomb.

Between 1963 and 1967, Warhol also produced a series of works based on a photograph of an empty electric chair. The chair, sitting with straps unhooked in an unoccupied execution chamber, has an eerie correspondence to the friendly chairs of our own domestic environments. Warhol produced the electric chair in a variety of formats, sometimes presenting it as a single image, sometimes repeating it in different degrees of clarity in a grid. I recall one *Electric Chair* in particular from his 1989 retrospective at the Museum of Modern Art. The painting presented a single chair, printed in a metallic black on a matte black ground. The image was almost invisible from some vantage points, and depended on glancing light to materialize from the surrounding gloom. The black-on-black format provided an obvious reference to Ad Reinhardt's minimalistic crosses. It also resembled a trace, making me think of the mysterious impressions of the face of Christ or the Virgin miraculously left on sacred relics. Finally, the painting spoke of death, and the absence it engenders, in a remarkably moving and sensitive way. In a flash, a documentary photograph was transformed into a secular crucifixion image drawing, for me at least, a parallel between the condemned men for whom the chair was created and the criminalized Christ executed with equal righteousness by the court of his day.

In Warhol's own mind, the *Death and Disaster* paintings offered a counterpoint for another set of paintings that focused on female celebrities. In each case, Warhol associated the woman with death. He began the famous paintings of Marilyn Monroe just a few months after her death in 1962. *Gold Marilyn*, for instance, surrounds the screen goddess with a flat gold background, transforming her into a modern-day version of the Byzantine icons of his childhood. Marilyn was soon joined by Elizabeth Taylor, or Liz, as she was known in the tabloids. The Liz paintings were begun while the actress was gravely ill following her collapse during the filming of the movie Cleopatra in 1962, and, in Warhol's words, "everyone said she was going to die."[43]

The third member of Warhol's death trio was Jackie Kennedy. She first appeared in a series of paintings that followed the assassination of her husband in November 1963. Warhol juxtaposes "happy Jackie" before the shooting with "sad Jackie" afterwards, using newspaper photos that had become ubiquitous as the nation struggled to come to terms with the senseless death.

In Warhol's mind, the *Death and Disaster* paintings and the tragic celebrities were linked. He said, "My death series was divided into two parts, the first one famous deaths and the second one people nobody ever heard of... It's not that I feel sorry for them, it's just that people go by and it doesn't really matter to them that someone unknown was killed."[44]

Warhol's preoccupation with death had biographical roots. Although these works were completed before his own shooting in 1968 by an outcast member of his entourage, Warhol already had a powerful sense of his own mortality. His father struggled with tuberculosis for four years before succumbing in 1942, Warhol's fourteenth year. He himself was a sickly boy who later reported that he had three nervous breakdowns as a child between the ages of eight and ten. These events marked him with various death phobias reporting that he had trouble going to sleep before dawn because of fears that he would die in the night.

Before the attempt on his life, Warhol had moved on from *Death and Disaster* to less morbid themes, among them his cow wallpaper, flowers paintings, silver pillows, Brillo boxes. He also had announced his intention to abandon painting for filmmaking. Following his recuperation, however, he resumed his production of paintings, and in 1976 embarked on a series of *Skull* paintings based on a photograph of a skull that he had purchased in a French flea market. Again there were many permutations of color and format, but the basic image remained the same: a three quarter view of a human skull from slightly above, shot in such a way that it cast a shadow. Commentators have noted the image resembles the head of a fetus. The skulls appeared at a time when Warhol was also doing a lot of commissioned and celebrity portraits, and may have represented a counterpart to them, just as the anonymous disasters had played off against the tragic celebrities. At the time that Warhol was contemplating beginning this series, his assistant, Ronnie Cutrone remarked to him that painting skulls "would be like doing a portrait of everyone in the world."[45]

Curator Trevor Fairbrother has suggested that the *Skulls* should be seen as a species of 'vanitas,' that genre of Dutch still life painting that presents glittering baubles and over-ripe fruit as harbingers of the death that inevitably awaits their owners. He also links them to the tradition in religious art that sounds a similar warning by depicting skulls as attributes of saintly hermits. The theme recurs in other late works by Warhol, among them a set of paintings of shadows cast by a candle, a self portrait in which Warhol holds a skull next to his head, and a late portrait of Warhol patron Philip Niarchos which used a CAT scan to represent the subject's head. [46]

From a Catholic perspective, Warhol's preoccupation with death flows from the Incarnational consciousness that is such an important part of the Catholic imagination. While other Pop artists - Lichtenstein, Wesselmann and Rosenquist, for instance, - created works that seemed to freeze snippets of pop culture in states of unapproachable perfection, Warhol returned again and again to the idea of fragility, temporality and loss. His people and things, for all the glamour of their presentation, were also subject to the cycle of life and death. Even the images, which resemble photographic reproductions which have been copied so many times that contrasts and details have begun to fade, seem themselves on the road to oblivion. For Warhol, death was an inescapable reality hovering just out of reach, and no amount of campy posing could obscure that ultimate fact.

But we are still missing a crucial piece of the story. As a Catholic artist, we would expect Warhol to create work imbued with physicality. However, the literature on Warhol is permeated with references to his asexuality. Art critic Carter Ratcliff, writing in 1983, notes "Warhol, our leading connoisseur of glamour, has little use for physicality. "Fantasy love is much better than reality love," Warhol has said. "The most exciting attractions are between two opposites that never meet."[47]

In searching for the "other Andy Warhol", Dillenberger also deaccentuates the physical, noting an exchange reported by one of Warhol's biographers:

S.C. You're still a virgin?

A.W. Yeah, I'm still a virgin.

S.C. With all these beautiful people hanging around, don't you ever get turned on?

A.W. Well, I think only kids who are very young should have sex, and people who aren't young should never get excited. After twenty-five you should look, but never touch. [48]

If we are to make a convincing case for Warhol's Catholic Imagination, it seems we will also need to look for 'another Andy Warhol', quite different from the one Dillenberger is seeking. Revisionist accounts have recently begun to refute reports of Warhol's asexuality. In fact a whole literature has sprung out of looking at Warhol from the point of view of Queer Theory. This theory maintains that mainstream criticism has deliberately "dehomosexualized" Warhol in order to make him acceptable to mainstream taste. Queer Theorists like Simon Watney and Jennifer Doyle have pointed out the persistence of homosexual couplings and provocations in his films, the crowd of drag queens and transvestites who hung around the Factory and starred in his movies, the existence of early drawings of beautiful nude boys and penises with bows and kiss marks and the later silkscreen paintings of nude male torsos [49]. There is even a series of silkscreen paintings entitled *Sex Parts* that offer close-up views of male sexual organs with explicit homosexual acts. These were done in 1978, the same year that Robert Mapplethorpe was creating the photographs for his *X Portfolio*, and they bear a rather remarkable resemblance to those more notorious works.

Also countering his avowed lack of interest in sex are published statements by Warhol about his love of pornography. In *POPism*, he writes, "Personally, I loved porno and I bought lots of it all the time - the real dirty, exciting stuff. All you had to do was figure out what turned you on, and then just buy the dirty magazines and movie prints that are right for you, the way you'd go for the right pills or the right cans of food. (I was so avid for porno that on my first time out of the house after the shooting I went straight to 42nd street and checked out the peep shows with Vera Cruise and restocked on dirty magazines.) " [50]

All this provides compelling evidence of the essentially carnal nature of Warhol's imagination. His body obsession plays out in short films that document, usually to the point of boredom, ordinary body functions like sleeping, eating, and showering, as well as more explicitly sexual activities. One short film, *Blow Job* is a thirty-minute depiction of the face of a man as he is being fellatiated. In Warhol's films, which gained an underground and often largely homosexual audience, there are male strip teases, wrestling scenes, strip poker games and soft-core sex acts.

As the Queer Theorists maintain, Warhol's "public work" does seem carefully denuded of much of this sensibility. There are oblique references to homosexuality in works for general consumption - many commentators have pointed out double meanings suggested by *13 Most Wanted Men,* a 1964 installation of FBI mug shots for the Worlds Fair. In general, though, Warhol was shrewdly playing to an audience that would embrace the camp side of the gay sensibility far more readily than its explicit sexuality.

But there was a further reason for Warhol's reticence. As a practicing Catholic, he went to church several times a week, but never went to confession or took communion. Dillenberger reports that the parish priest preached regularly against homosexuality, and this condemnation no doubt explains Warhol's unwillingness to participate fully in Church rituals.

Yet, if the Church establishment censured Warhol's sexuality, Catholicism also provided him with unofficial images of homoeroticism and male desire. Though countered by the official abhorrence of homosexuality, the undercurrents of homoeroticism in Catholic art and literature create conflicts that emerge in an outlaw sensibility and sensuality. This is, after all, a religion whose central image is a near naked man on a cross and whose prayers and teachings are filled with often startlingly erotic exhortations to love that man. The historical link between homosexuality and Catholicism will be explored more fully in a later chapter, when we consider why the conflicted gay Catholic artist is such a familiar figure in contemporary art.

For now, it will suffice to look at a Warhol's 1985 painting *Be Somebody with a Body.* The slogan, taken from a bodybuilding ad, is laid over an image of a smiling, bare chested body builder whose face, Dillenberger suggests, resembles a photograph of the young Andy Warhol. The body builder's head is surrounded by a halo-like aura. The other half of this diptych is a line drawing of Christ from the Last Supper. Cropping out the apostles, Warhol focuses on Christ's outstretched hand at the moment when he is saying, "This is my body", thereby transforming the bread of the meal into his mystical flesh.

Taken together, this pair of images might be an advertisement for our Incarnational consciousness. The slogan "Be somebody with a body" suggests a Pop restatement of Steinberg's thesis. If applied to the body builder, it can be seen as a celebration of the physical experiences so often denied Warhol by his critics. If applied to the Christ figure, it could be taken as a confirmation of Christ's human status.

But the most intriguing possibility is that it serves as a link between the two figures, suggesting both identification and sexual attraction. The aura around the body builder's head suggests that he has been transformed through an encounter that, the slogan suggests, has physical as well as spiritual aspects. The notion of Christ as lover is, as we suggested in our discussion of Bernini's *St. Teresa,* a time honored Catholic theme. Applying it to a same sex context is more unorthodox, though not unheard of in the writings of male and female mystics. We will see this theme reappear in the work of other twentieth century artists from Catholic backgrounds.

The importance of Warhol's Catholicism can't be overestimated. It is not simply a matter of religious iconography and it is not negated by the "amoral" or "immoral" aspects of his life. Catholicism permeated Warhol's thinking, encompassing his obsessions with physical death and physical love, his transformation of ordinary objects into icons with multiple resonances, his interest in the body and its processes and most of all, the conflict manifested in his work between the Church's official teachings and Catholicism's subliminal messages. Neither saint nor Satan, our Catholic Warhol can be seen as a conflicted human being whose flawed spirituality found its expression in works which express all the contradictions of his situation. As a result, his complexities set the stage for a deeper investigation of the rich and multifaceted workings of the Catholic Imagination in contemporary art.

* * *

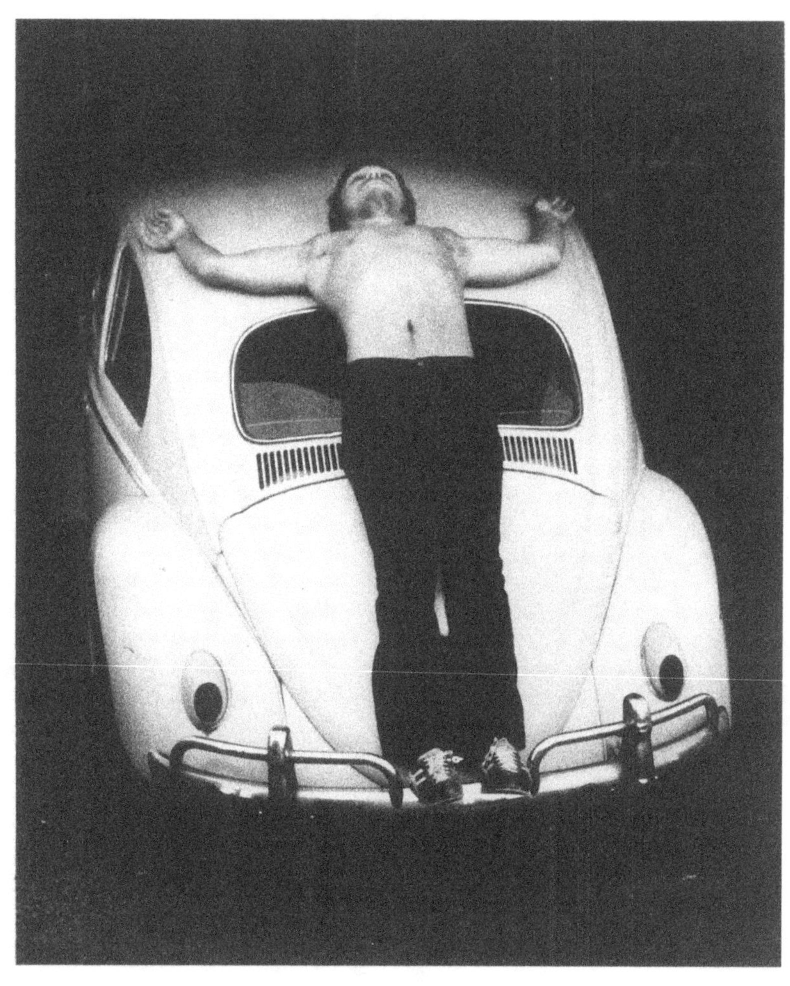

Chris Burden, *Trans-fixed*, 1974

© 2017 Chris Burden / licensed by The Chris Burden Estate
and Artists Rights Society (ARS), New York

CHAPTER 3

THE TRIALS OF THE BODY ARTISTS: BLOOD RITUALS AND ENDURANCE ART

Inside a small garage in Speedway Avenue, I stood on the rear bumper of a Volkswagen. I lay on my back over the rear section of the car, stretching my arms onto the roof. Nails were driven through my palms into the roof of the car. The garage door was opening and the car pushed halfway out into Speedway. Screaming for me, the engine was run at full speed for two minutes. After 2 minutes, the engine was turned off and the car pushed back into the garage. The door was closed.

– Chris Burden, description of *Trans-fixed*, 1974

Though in flagrant rebellion against the transcendental rhetoric and the self-important seriousness of his predecessors, Warhol still felt compelled to keep his more explicitly homoerotic images under wraps. But as the sixties melted into the seventies, the body suddenly emerged as a focal point for contemporary art. Whether drenched with buckets of blood, shot, burned, mutilated or stabbed, engaged in public acts of masturbation or sexual intercourse, or turned into art works by an artist's signature, bodies were everywhere doing things that had never been considered art before. The phenomenon was international extending from France, Austria, Italy and the United States to Japan and Brazil.

There seemed to be multiple reasons for the emergence of what came to be known as "body art." Some art critics argued it was an extension of the gestural emphasis of Abstract Expressionism. That the next logical step after what Harold Rosenberg had titled "Action Painting" was art as Action, pure and simple. But if there was a theoretical continuity with the works of artists like Jackson Pollock or Willem de Kooning, the new ethos also represented a dramatic rejection of the arts-for-arts sake mentality of the older generation.

Other commentators meanwhile, linked body art to Minimalism, described by critic Barbara Rose as "an art whose blank, neutral, mechanical impersonality contrasts so violently with the romantic, biographical abstract expressionist style which preceded it that spectators are chilled by its apparent lack of feeling or content."[52] Critic Michael Fried declared that the essence of minimal sculpture was its "theatricality" by which he meant that, by reducing work to its most literal essence, for instance a slab of steel or a pile of bricks, the artist displaced the viewer's attention from the object itself onto the work's relationship with the surrounding world.[53] While Fried viewed this as a breach of the modernist faith, body artists took it as a permission to move from things to actions. Suddenly it became possible to think of the body as an art object and art as an extension of the body.

But beyond these aesthetic progenitors, body art seemed to spring from the complex and deeply troubled political and social atmosphere of the 1960s. In the United States, it could hardly be separated from the turmoil engendered by the Vietnam War and the daily television images of body bags and reports of casualty counts. Vito Acconci, one of the most prominent progenitors of body art, reflected years later that he would never "have thought of this kind of life stuff without the context of that time, without the context of demonstrations against American involvement in the Vietnam War."[54]

Intersecting with these political protests were the upheavals created by the social revolutions of the time: the sexual revolution, the emergence of the feminist and gay rights movements, the mutation of civil rights activism into more radical movements like Black Power, and the birth of political terrorist groups like the Weatherman and the Symbionese Liberation Army, the latter famous for its kidnapping and indoctrination of heiress Patricia Hearst. Outside the United States, anger at the Vietnam War was simply one element in a larger crisis of authority that led to riots in 1968 on the streets of Paris.

In a world in which Buddhist monks were setting themselves on fire as a protest against the Vietnam War, it did not seem so perverse for artists to nail themselves to Volkswagens or walk barefoot across broken glass. Nevertheless their motivations were multiple and complex, rooted in a variety of personal, political, social and philosophic considerations. Some of the more benign versions of body art appeared in France in the early 1960s. In France, Yves Klein conceived of the "Living Brush", covering a nude model with blue paint and pressing her body against a canvas to create a physical imprint of her body. In Italy Piero Manzoni, inspired by Klein, created living sculptures by signing the backs or arms of his models. But he is best known for his production of ninety cans of artist's "shit" to be sold at the same price per gram as gold.

In Vienna, body art took a darker turn in the works of the Viennese Actionists whose works were said to be responses to Viennese socio-religious repression and the legacy of Nazism. Actionism manifested itself in blood rituals that made reference to both Dionysian and Christian rites. Arnulf Rainer made paintings by smearing paint on canvas with his hands, often working them until they bled. Hermann Nitsch disemboweled slaughtered animals and covered himself and participants in their blood. Gunter Brus enacted performances involving self-mutilation and degradation, and Rudolf Schwarzkogler staged apparent self-mutilations for the camera. His death in 1969 gave rise to the unfounded rumor that he had committed suicide during a performance by slowly cutting off his penis piece by piece.

American style body art varied widely. On one side were celebratory works like Carolee Schneemann's 1964 *Meat Joy*, in which she and a group of male and female performers rolled semi-naked on the floor, embracing each other amid mountains of paper, red meat, fish and dead chickens, and pseudo scientific works like Dennis Oppenheim's *Reading Position for Second Degree Burn* (1970) in which he allowed himself to be "painted by the sun" by lying bare-chested in the sun for five hours. On the other were more overtly disturbing and potentially dangerous works like Burden's *Trans-fixed,* in which he nailed himself to a Volkswagen and Acconci's *Trademarks,* from 1970 in which he bit himself all over his body and made ink impressions of the bite marks.

These latter actions which involved feats of endurance and voluntarily self inflicted pain, found parallels outside the United States in the works of figures like Yugoslavian artist Marina Abramovic and French artist Gina Pane. In 1974, Abramovic undertook a seven-hour performance during which audience members were invited to do anything they wished with her body using seventy-two objects that included scissors, razors and a loaded gun. The performance came to an abrupt end when other audience members took this last item from a participant who was holding it to Abramovic's head. Gina Pane staged elaborate scenarios involving self inflicted wounds, cutting her face with a razor blade, walking over broken glass and putting out fires with her bare hands and feet.

An international phenomenon, body art was not confined to any single ethnic or national group, nor did all the artists come from the same religious backgrounds. But what interests us here is why so many of the artists involved in the more confrontational and masochistic approaches to body art were raised in Catholic countries or come from Catholic backgrounds, and why they so often undertake actions which seem to echo Catholic ritual and tales of the tortures of Christ and the saints.

Commentators on so called "masochistic" body art have often pursued a psychoanalytic interpretation, seeing the works as an expression of a masochistic impulse rooted in the libidinal need to reconstitute the self as a objectified whole. Accompanying this interpretation is a tendency to reference psychoanalyst Theodor Reik, who in the 1940s made a study of the relationship between masochism and Christianity[55]. Reik saw the Christian martyr as the embodiment of the social masochist whose desire for suffering is fed by the adulation of his peers. Reik suggested that the "collective phantasy" of Christ's suffering and death promulgated by the Church drove the martyrs to embrace ever more grisly fates in Christ's name. Noting that "whoever humiliates himself so deeply wants to be exalted", Reik maintained that exhibitionism and a striving for "publicity" lay behind the early Christians' longing to emulate Christ's Passion.[56]

Applying this analysis to the activities of twentieth century endurance artists proved irresistible to many commentators. Writing of Burden's *Trans-fixed*, critic Donald Kuspit invokes Burden's own statements about the piece, noting "The car 'had to be a Volkswagen', the people's car, rather than for example, 'a falcon' a car symbolic of predatory individuality, as if Burden, like Christ, could redeem all the people, not just himself, with his crucifixion. I can't help thinking of psychoanalyst Theodor Reik's conception of Christ as the ultimate masochist, who expects to win the world through his sacrifice of himself."[57]

In a related mode, art historian Amelia Jones suggests that figures like the French artist Orlan, who has subjected herself to a series of publicly broadcast plastic surgery operations designed to recreate the idealized features to be found in various Renaissance paintings, and the American artist Bob Flanagan, who turned to sadomasochistic sexual practices to counteract the painful progress of cystic fibrosis, have "ritualized (their) pain through performances that borrow from and transgress the flamboyant fetishization of suffering and martyrdom in the Catholic tradition."[58]

And indeed, these artists' voluntary acceptance of violence or abuse to their bodies does seem to contain parallels with the Catholic preoccupation with the Imitation of Christ. This form of devotional practice which became increasingly widespread with the doctrinal insistence on Christ's humanity during the second century, encouraged the faithful to assume such a passionate identification with Christ's bodily suffering that they willingly undertook physically painful trials or courted agonizing deaths. In a typical expression of such religious devotion, Ignatius, Bishop of Antioch, joyfully proclaimed as he waited to be killed by wild beasts in the Roman amphitheater: "Let there come upon me fire, and the cross, and the struggle with wild beasts, cutting and tearing apart, racking of bones, mangling of limbs, crushing of my whole body . . . May I but attain to Jesus Christ!"[59] Chris Burden's catalogue of terrors was not quite so final, but there does seem to be a strange echo in his efforts to risk death or mutilation by electrocution, shooting, stabbing, drowning, burning and crucifixion.

But one person's pathology may be another's religious practice. Looking beyond the psychoanalytic interpretation of so called "endurance art" as a form of social masochism, it is possible to give another interpretation to the parallels between Catholic ritual and belief and the work of Burden and other body artists. Art historian Kathy O'Dell invokes Reik's analysis of the components of masochistic acts to elaborate her own theory about "masochistic" body art as a form of contractual agreement. From her perspective, the endurance artist's apparently perverse actions can be seen as serving a rational function - they create an imaginative bond between spectator and actor which allows for heightened sympathy and understanding. O'Dell notes that "Such performances reminded viewers of their own roles as witnesses and of their own capacity to occupy the position of either perpetrator (subject) or victim (object) of violence."[60]

Further, she notes the importance of the photographic record in "masochistic" body art. Because such actions are viewed by only a small number of people, the photographic documentation ultimately becomes the piece. And because these photographs focus on the artist's body they allow for a level of identification which goes beyond ordinary recording. "Encountering the shared ontology of the body makes the viewer mindful of his or her own physical presence as witness to the pictured event (even if it is well after the fact). One's involvement in the event - the choice to become a "contracted partner" - is thus made tangible."[61]

The recurring representations in Renaissance and Baroque art of Christ being whipped, beaten, pressed with a crown of thorns and nailed to the cross and of saints undergoing unspeakable physical torments and agonizing deaths in his honor would seem to fulfill a similar function. They demand an imaginative identification with the physical experience of bodily suffering in order to, in a sense, ratify the "contract" by which the faithful bind themselves to their religious beliefs.

I do not mean to argue here that contemporary twentieth century endurance artists are deliberately mimicking the trials of the saints that, of course, were undertaken for quite different purposes. The point is that Catholicism provided an imaginative structure which artists from Catholic backgrounds have been able to exploit for their own ends. And, in keeping with the atmosphere of social experimentation that permeated the 1960s and 70s, these ends involved a radical breakdown of the distance between audience and artist through self inflicted pain or body based ritualistic activity that simulates the Catholic believer's submission to Christ or to the Christian community.

The degree to which this exploitation of Catholic models was explicit varied widely. The Viennese Actionists blended Christian and pre Christian blood rituals in a way that emphasized communal activity while bringing out the "pagan" underpinnings of the Catholic mass. The Actionists' attitude toward their Catholicism was ambiguous. One of the leading practitioners, Hermann Nitsch announced that the blood rituals that he devised were orchestrated to liberate the performers from the "sado-masochistic neurosis" of Christianity. But he also picked up on the positive body emphasis embedded in the Catholic imagination, noting, "Body and flesh, though part of the divine plan denied by some ascetic religious communities, in no way represent a factor of sin or suffering, but become festivity.[62]"

Viennese Actionists were most active during the 1960s, during which time their performances attracted the attention of the art public, the media and the police. After a performance in 19[63] in which, according to his own description "I lie down on a bed, entrails, mangled cow's udders, hair, hot water being stuffed and poured under the feather bed. I hit, kick, slap in the face, stone, whip, bite wet the body. I sacrifice my body to public libation", Nitsch was sent to jail for fourteen days for "causing a public nuisance.[63]"

Undeterred, Nitsch has continued to organize his performances under the auspices of his Orgy Mystery Theater (OMT) which he founded following his first action in 1958, he continues to organize day and week long rituals in which participants are invited to share in precisely choreographed rituals in which animals are slaughtered, nude men and women are taped to crosses and spattered with animal blood or led in processions through the fields around the artist's castle in Prinzendorf Austria.

Other Actionists have long ceased their activities, for a variety of reasons. Otto Muhl, known for acts of coprophilia in the 1960s, was imprisoned for seven years in the 1970s for child molestation in connection with practices he engaged in at a commune based on his increasingly messianic beliefs. Schwarzkogler has, as mentioned above, passed into art world legend based on erroneous report that he died while enacting a self-mutilation (In fact he did die after falling from a window in 1969, presumably a suicide).

Gunter Brus eventually moved from physical actions involving the manipulation of body fluids, self mutilation, and public masturbation to painting, but not before being sentenced to six months in jail for degrading state symbols during a performance in which he undressed, cut his thigh and chest with razor blade, urinated in a glass, defecated on the floor, drank the urine, rubbed feces over his body, lay down and masturbated while singing the Austrian national anthem.

Arnulf Rainer was arrested for a performance in which he painted dried blood in streaks down his face to attack the complacency of bourgeois society. Eventually, he also turned back to painting, creating works in which he smeared paint on canvas with his hands and feet, and literally attacked photographic self-portraits, violently marring them or over painting them to the point of invisibility.

While there was a good deal of variation in the operations performed by individual Actionists, the underlying premise they shared was the desire to liberate modern man from the constrictions of civilization by tapping back into primitive fertility rites and blood rituals. The Actionists were adamant about the connections between early Christianity and pagan nature worship, taking literally the notion of the Catholic Mass as a reenactment of human sacrifice.

By contrast, American body artists in the 1960s and 70s tended to be less interested in public ritual than in individual acts which posed ethical and psychological challenges for their viewers. Distinguishing himself from the Viennese Actionists, Chris Burden suggests that their work is an extension of the emotional excess of abstract expressionism, while his was derived from the much cooler ethos surrounding minimalism.

Though he has not performed for over twenty-five years, Burden is still notorious in certain circles for a series of actions that he undertook between 1971 and 1975. Designed like a set of endurance tests (though it was never entirely clear whether the artist or the viewer was the true test subject), many involved potentially dangerous or actually harmful situations. Significantly, the forms of the actions and the names that Burden affixed to them often had religious connotations.

Trans-fixed, described at the beginning of this chapter, involved a literal crucifixion in which his hands were nailed to the hood of a Volkswagen. Afterwards, Burden described the marks left by the nails on his hands as "stigmata", a reference to the bleeding holes that mysteriously appeared on the hands and feet of saints in sympathetic emulation of the bleeding wounds of the crucified Christ.

The same year, Burden undertook a number of performances with equally religious overtones. For *The Confession*, performed at the Contemporary Art Center in Cincinnati, he invited a small group of people who he had just met to sit in circle around a video monitor showing the artist confessing the most intimate details of his personal life.

Visitation at Hamilton College in New York, conjured the specter of a divine apparition. For this performance Burden sat in a niche in the gallery basement facing glowing coals and across from an empty chair. Audience members, who had been given no information what to expect, were brought down to the basement one by one, where they were left to discover his presence and accept the invitation implied by the empty chair.

O Dracula at the Utah Museum of Art transformed Burden into a work of religious art. Here he wrapped his body in a "chrysalis" of fabric that was then mounted on the wall of a gallery devoted to Renaissance religious painting. Lighted candles were placed below his head and feet and the hanging object, which was in place for a single day, was labeled as an artwork.

The religious references in these and other works were not accidental. Though not a baptized Catholic, Burden spent his childhood in Italy and France where, he recalls, all of his friends were Catholic. He accompanied them to Sunday Mass and Thursday catechism classes and absorbed a great deal about Catholic culture. He notes, "Catholicism was just part of the landscape I grew up in."[64]

While works like those above have a more poetic quality, the performances that garnered the most attention were those which, like *Trans-fixed*, involved real or potential bodily harm. *Shoot*, from 1971 may be his most famous work. Captured on video, it shows Burden being shot in the arm by a friend. In fact, he admits today, he never intended to be seriously injured, expecting instead that the bullet would just graze his arm producing a few drops of blood. A photograph taken just after the event reveals the artist with a dazed expression, still in a state of shock.

Other works involved equally calculated risks. *Doorway to Heaven*, (1973) involved the threat of electrocution. As several onlookers watched, Burden pushed two live electric wires into his chest. The wires crossed and exploded, burning his flesh but preventing electrocution. *Doomed*, performed in 1975 at the MCA in Chicago, was in fact designed as a test of the spectators. Burden lay without moving behind a piece of glass in the gallery. What the museum staff had not been told was that the performance would only end when someone intervened. This finally happened forty-five hours and ten minutes later when an employee, concerned about Burden's health, furtively slipped him a glass of water.

Doomed, in particular, raised questions about whether thrill seeking audiences would in fact be willing to fulfill their part of the contract implied by these works and intervene when Burden put his fate in their hands. Not long after, Burden stopped doing performances and started making objects, which he continues to do to this day.

Reflecting on his performance career, Burden disputes interpretations that lay these works to clinical masochism, insanity or a hunger for publicity at any cost. Rather, he points out, they were carefully planned situations whose risks often appeared far greater than they were. And he notes, "while the performances were art experiences, they were also other worldly experiences, where my senses were heightened. For a long time people thought I was unbalanced, but when I did those performances, I felt that I was at my most lucid and clear, more in control. It was like being in an altered state."[65]

So, from one perspective, Burden's performances were a way to use his body to attain a higher state of consciousness in a manner strikingly reminiscent of the mystical visions that allowed religious figures like Saint Teresa to make contact with the divine realm through the sensations of their physical bodies.

But an equally vital aspect of these works is their ethical dimension: the contractual element that required spectator's imaginative involvement with the artist. "It was important that these works asked the viewer to put themselves in my place," Burden says. "When I locked myself in the locker for five days or lay hidden on a platform just under the gallery ceiling, it was about what you imagine is inside. It is a reminder that the imagination is stronger than visual evidence."[66]

Though Vito Acconci also performed actions which involved a degree of physical pain, in *Trademarks* (1970) he bit himself all over his body. In *Conversions*, from that same year, he burned the hair around one of his nipples, then tried to pull it out in a vain attempt to create a woman's breast. He points out that the discomfort was mild and that he never drew blood. However, he does admit that the focus of his early body work was on "tests, trials and training."[67] And, he adds these tests were, like Burden's, undertaken in the service of forging a relationship with the spectator, who was forced to become an active participant in the performance.

His most notorious body work was *Seedbed* from 1972, in which he hid himself beneath a ramp on one end of his gallery and masturbated while he audibly fantasized about the gallery goers walking overhead. In an untitled work from 1971, he invited people to meet him in a dark shed on the Hudson River from 1 to 2 am, where he divulged embarrassing secrets about himself. Other works were more assaultive. *Claim* (1971) staged a threatening encounter with a viewer. Acconci positioned himself in the basement of a building, blindfolded and guarding the entrance with lead pipes and a crowbar. A video monitor upstairs conveyed the artist's activity and his ravings ("I am alone here in the basement . . . I want to stay alone here in the basement") to anyone foolish enough to consider entry. His last body work was "Command Performance" in 1974. A video installation, it consisted of a pair of monitors. One faced a stool and played a tape of Acconci enjoining the viewer to sit on the stool and become the performer ("Come on, baby, move . . . Move into the spotlight . . . That stool's all yours") and to engage in a strip tease act. The other monitor focused on the stool, allowing other viewers to watch the spectator who had agreed to go on show.

Acconci's performances lack the overt religious references found in Burden's work. He suggests that this may stem in part from the reaction he was feeling against seventeen years of Catholic schooling. And he notes that at the time, he was more consciously reacting to the social upheavals of the early 60s instigated by the war in Vietnam, the emergence of the feminist movement and the general crises of authority. However, in retrospect, Acconci acknowledges that he was probably influenced on a more subterranean level by his Catholic upbringing. "In a lot of the early pieces, I put myself in kind of an isolation chamber," he recalls. "Could that have happened without the confessional booth? I just don't know"[68].

But even more striking was, to return to O'Dell's formulation, the contractual aspects of these works. Viewers who entered a gallery filled with the sounds of Acconci masturbating and fantasizing about them, or who confronted a live video of a crowbar-wielding artist, could hardly remain neutral. Some commentators have read a sadistic element into such works, or seen them as promoting the idea of artist as creatures of superior power. Feminist critics like Amelia Jones also see a gendered quality to his works, which both reinforced and undermined masculine assumptions of control.[69]

While admitting that there may have been unintended assertions of male domination in such works, Acconci argues that his intentions were very different. "Vulnerability is the basis of my early work," he says. "My idea was, if I present myself to you, I have to make myself vulnerable, and strip away the conventional social armor. That way there is more chance that you will be able to coincide with me." This, he admits, is not dissimilar to Catholicism, where, he points out, "God as Christ becomes vulnerable to temptations and pain."[70]

He adds, "In Catholicism, rhetoric is always connected to the body in some way. The Saints are very tangible; they have been assigned a body with attributes. You go to a priest to confess; you pray face to face with a statue; you are always in front of a person." Similarly, he notes, "I always thought my work was about rhetoric and persuasion, about having a tangible presence in the world."[71]

More overtly Catholic is the performance work of Linda Montano. A former novitiate who spent two years with the Maryknoll Sisters before turning to art, Montano's career has involved a concerted effort to turn her life into art. She has melded her early Catholic training with more recent study of yoga, tantric philosophy and eastern religion. Among her best-known works was *One Year Performance*, a yearlong action in 1983, in which she spent an entire year tied by a rope to Taiwanese performance artist Tehching Hseih. For this performance, she deliberately chose a partner with whom she was not intimate and laid out the ground rule that the two must never come into physical contact during their year together. In the same vein was *Seven Years of Living Art*, which took place at the New Museum in New York over a seven-year period. She took up residence once a week in the window of the museum, and invited spectators to join her for discussion and fortune telling. During this performance, she assigned herself a different color for each year, based on the seven energy centers of the body described in the teachings of the yoga chakras. During the year she wore clothing and decorated her home exclusively in the color for that year.

While such performances did not involve the possibility of bodily harm or physical pain inherent in many of Acconci and Burden's actions, their duration and strict rules certainly turned them into tests of endurance. From one perspective, this approach to art/life is in keeping with the asceticism and discipline which are parts of yoga training. But it also reflects Montano's interest in Catholicism and her early experience as a novitiate in a convent. And in fact, her earlier work, in the 1960s and 70s, often had explicitly Catholic references. She assumed the persona of the Chicken Woman who would lie in a cruciform chicken bed or walk in a cruciform pattern during a "trance dance." At times the Chicken Woman embraced such diverse roles as nun, saint, martyr, plaster statue, angel, totem and twin. In keeping with the experimental atmosphere of the time, Montano also broke down the barrier between art and life by undertaking 'performances' in which she become a bell ringer for the Salvation Army, declared her house a museum, and took odd jobs which she viewed as art works. In 1975, she assumed the role of the Screaming Nun, in which she dressed as a nun, screamed and heard confessions at Embarcadero Plaza in San Francisco.

Reflecting on the religious roots of her preoccupations, Montano has written, "During my childhood I was deeply influenced by the Catholic church and its rituals. I attended church for years, it was my theater, my sanctuary, and my teacher. There I encountered mystery, terror and awe . . . Terror that I would drop communion out of my mouth, or accidentally chew it, terror that my breath would smell during confession, terror that I would sin and break the sixth commandment. But along with these frightening experiences, there was also the comfort that came from being engulfed in ancient rituals. I'm convinced now that I was rehearsing my subsequent performance role as I knelt in church for hours praying, asking plaster statues to talk to me or forgive me. I'm also convinced that the images that I internalized then are those which appear, reappear and shape my work even today."[72]

Body art that focused on blood rituals or endurance trials slipped from view during the late 70s and early 80s and many practitioners moved on to more permanent and less risky artistic expressions. In the latter half of the eighties, however, action based art, now more commonly known as performance art, returned to center stage, as a new group of practitioners came to the fore. However, things were subtly different. Instead of the Vietnam War and the civil rights struggle, the social backdrop against which they worked was dominated by the AIDS crises and the militancy of the religious right. And the issues dominating the art world had changed as well. Artists were no longer obsessed with subverting the institutional system, escaping the gallery or erasing the boundary between art and life.

As a result, while performance art of the 1980s and 90s owed much to its predecessors (Acconci and Burden in particular emerged as important influences on the younger generation), it was also strikingly different. Even when exploring "masochistic" or endurance activities, artists tended to take more overtly political stands, using these as a metaphor for the condition of the marginalized and victimized members of society. And they also tended to pursue a more theatrical format, acting on stage before real audiences, rather than setting up actions to be observed only by a few friends, or by a still or video camera.

The difference is particularly striking in the work of Karen Finley who gained notoriety in 1990 when her performance *We Keep Our Victims Ready* became the focus of a renewed effort by opponents of the NEA to convince Congress to abolish the agency. A Catholic girl turned avant-garde activist, Finley developed an eclectic, confrontational performance style that centered on her own body as exemplar of woman's secondary status in a patriarchal society. The masochistic acts in her performances serve as an indictment of the callousness of the powerful. Her targets have been many and her approach unvarnished. She has compared the Christian fundamentalists who have vilified her with the Nazis, cited rape and incest as symptoms of sickness of a woman hating society, indicted the Catholic Church for its stand on homosexuality and AIDS, and pointed out the perverse psycho-sexual underpinnings of supposedly innocent childhood entertainments.

While there is lots to offend the right wing in Finley's work, including nudity, profanity, explicit descriptions of "perverse" sexual acts, and broadsides against the politics of the religious and conservative right, what propelled her into the public eye was a description of her performance in a May 1990 column in the Washington Post written by conservative columnists Rowland Evans and Robert Novak. Alerting the public to a new round of grants for art taken by the right to be "obscene," the columnists singled out "the performance of a nude, chocolate-smeared young woman in what the NEA memorandum calls 'a solo theater piece'"[73] and what the artist herself, Karen Finley, describes as a performance "triggering emotional and taboo events."[74]

Despite the fact that the work in question dealt with a variety of issues, including the oppression of women, people with AIDS and various minorities, Finley instantly became "the chocolate-smeared young woman" just as Serrano had become the originator of "the crucifix dipped in urine" and Ofili would become the creator of "the Madonna splattered with dung". Again, the offense was connection to the public exposure of body excretions (in Finley's case a reference to excrement by way of chocolate.) What seemed most objectionable to these conservative critics was the foregrounding of the physicality of the human body and its excretory functions.

As Finley explains the piece, *We Keep our Victims Ready* used faux body substances to make a political point. "I smeared my body with chocolate, because I said in the piece, I'm a woman, and women are usually treated like shit. Then I covered myself with red candy hearts because, after a woman is treated like shit, she becomes more lovable. After the hearts, I covered myself with bean sprouts, which smelled like semen and looked like semen because, after a woman is treated like shit, and loved for it, she is jacked off on. Then I spread tinsel all over my body, like a Cher dress because, no matter how badly a woman has been treated, she'll still get it together to dress for dinner."[75]

The Evans and Novak column that thrust Finley into the public eye was part of a campaign by opponents of the NEA to uncover grounds for the agency's elimination. The subsequent press brouhaha persuaded the agency's beleaguered chairman John Frohnmayer to overrule the decision of the peer panel to award grants to Finley and three other artists, Holly Hughes, John Fleck and Tim Miller, whose work also dealt with sexual themes. Frohnmayer hoped that this act of self-censorship would shield his agency from outside interference. This proved to be a serious miscalculation. In 1990, the US Congress, under pressure from political and religious conservatives, passed legislation forcing the NEA to consider "standards of decency" when awarding grants.

Several months later Finley, Fleck, Hughes and Miller, now dubbed the "NEA four" by the media, filed suit against the NEA for violation of their first amendment rights. An eight-year legal battle ensued. In 1992 a federal judge ruled in favor of the plaintiffs and declared the "standards of decency" clause in the 1990 legislation to be unconstitutional. The artists settled part of the lawsuit against the NEA in exchange for a reinstatement of the denied grants and privacy damages. But the question of the constitutionality of the so called "decency pledge" dragged on. In 1994, the U.S. Government appealed the verdict and lost. Then in 1998 the Clinton Administration took the appeal to the Supreme Court, which, by a narrow majority, ruled that it was constitutional for the NEA to consider "general standards of decency and respect for the diverse beliefs of the American public" when awarding grants.[76] But by this time, the point was essentially moot. In order to defend itself against the continuing conservative onslaught, the agency has already undergone a radical reorganization that eliminated the troublesome grants to individual artists altogether.

Like her close friend David Wojnarowicz, whom we shall examine in a subsequent chapter, Finley's work is shaped by her rage against a religious and social culture that negates the humanity of those who refuse to abide by its dictates. Often she takes explicit aim at religious and political figures like Jesse Helms, one of the primary architects of the case against the NEA, Donald Wildmon, director of the conservative American Family Association and Pope John Paul II and the late Cardinal John O'Connor, representatives of a Catholic Church whose positions on abortion and AIDS were, in her view, deeply homophobic and patriarchal.

But, at the same time, her work is deeply influenced, in both form and content, by the visual and literary traditions of Catholicism. Finley's use of her own body as foil for the degradations visited on society's discards draws on the Catholic tradition of self-flagellation. Along with chocolate, she has smeared her body with raw eggs, yams and gelatin, transforming food, the symbol of female nurturance, into a symbol of victimization. Meanwhile, religious imagery pervades both her performances and her written work. She has enlisted the Virgin Mary in the pro-choice cause and called for the installation of a female Pope. In *A Certain Level of Desire* a performance piece that Finley wrote at the height of battle with the religious right, she creates an imaginary dialogue between a depressed housewife and her male psychiatrist. It opens by tracing her problems to a repressive religious system that denies female sexuality:

MAN - Why don't you start with the beginning?
WOMAN - You mean Adam and Eve?

MAN - You said it, not me -

WOMAN - You asked me to start at the beginning - Adam and Eve.
Let's get it right. The snake was his dick, the apple his balls. So don't
blame Eve.

MAN - What about God?

WOMAN - You should know better than me, because God is in your
image. God is in your image. The image of man.[77]

Finley's work is full of anger and anguish at organized religion,
but in the end what she is really expressing is anger at the Catholic
Church's failure to live up to its message of love and forgiveness. In the
same performance she details a litany of wrongs against women and the
poor that ends with the cry: "JESUS CHRIST, where are you now?"
This echoes another work from 1990 entitled "The Black Sheep" which
she describes as her version of the psalm "The Lord is my Shepherd".
A homage to the disenfranchised and outcasts of the world, it contains
the refrain:

"We are sheep with no shepherd

We are sheep with no straight and narrow

We are sheep with no meadow

We are sheep who take the dangerous pathway through the mountain range
To get to the other side of our soul."[78]

As the contretemps over Finley's *We Keep Our Victims Ready*
demonstrates, a surprising number of the controversies which have
erupted as part of the Culture War center around the artist's use of
body fluids. Urine, excrement (as itself, or referred to by analogy with
chocolate), blood, and semen have all been central elements in art works
which have raised the hackles of the religious right. A discomfort with
these overt evidences of bodily processes is, in part, a lingering legacy
of American Puritanism. It also conforms to the Cartesian tendency to
see the body as a mere machine that is animated by the injection of the
mind or spirit. (Curiously, this same distinction has been reinforced
by the electronic era's distinction between hardware and software.) In
such a schema, the workings of the body, though necessary, are of a
lower order of importance than those of the mind. Or, to take another
contemporary analogy, fluids are waste products of a system that must
be controlled and regulated, but certainly not celebrated. Meanwhile the
AIDS crisis has placed a political spin on body fluids like semen and
blood, which become potential carriers of disease.

Taken together such tendencies have produced a culture in which a focus on body fluids and processes is seen as embarrassing, perverse, infantile or dangerous. Needless to say, this is in fundamental contrast with the Incarnational consciousness that sees body and soul as one. Far from stifling our awareness of the body's physical processes, the Catholic tradition has long fetishized body excretions. Among the many examples of this, we might point to the bloody sweat of Christ eternally imprinted on Veronica's veil; the invocation of the Virgin Mary's breast milk as metaphor for God's mercy; reports of miraculous secretions as, for instance, when the Baroque statue of San Gennaro in Naples bleeds once a year. This emphasis also appears in reports of the cheerful consumption of leper's pus or vomit by mystics like Catherine of Sienna and Veronica Giuliani as part of their spiritual trials. Even Saint Augustine, that austere church father, includes a humorous discussion of farts in his seminal theological tract, *The City of God*, while reporting dourly, "We are born between feces and urine."

Thus artists who revel in body fluids are, consciously or not, partaking of a long Catholic tradition. The clash between the incarnational and anti-carnal consciousnesses becomes acute in cases of performance art where the real substances are produced on stage. One such controversy involved the performance artist Ron Athey who falls into our subcategory of artists from other religious backgrounds who nevertheless manifest an Incarnational consciousness.

Athey was raised by his grandmother and aunt to be a minister in what he describes as an "underground Pentecostal church" which featured such charismatic activity as faith healing, speaking in tongues, stigmata and dances in the spirit. Pentecostals take issues with the fundamentalist fixation on the written Word of the Bible. Instead, they wish to reclaim the mystical aspects of early Christianity, and instead of approaching God through their minds, claim to literally experience the effects of faith in their bodies. In this, they share a kinship with the incarnational focus of Roman Catholicism.

Now an HIV positive gay man covered with tribal tattoos, Athey draws on this unusual background, combining it with ritualistic symbolism drawn from Catholic tales of Christ's Passion and the trials of the saints. He uses these in performance works that deal with his internal conflicts and with the psychological and social toll of AIDS. Athey is active in the S&M subculture, and elements of those activities appear in his art.

His performances have titles like *Martyrs and Saints* and *Deliverance* and include onstage piercings, mummification, flagellation and bloodletting. He notes a special fondness for Saint Sebastian, who was ordered executed by bows and arrows as a result of his use of his position as officer in the Roman army to shelter persecuted Christians. Saint Sebastian has emerged, thanks in large part to his sinuously erotic portrayal by artists like Mantegna, Botticelli and Bernini, as a gay icon, and Athey has paid homage to him by including a sequence in some performances in which he pierces himself with an arrow. Athey also references Christ's agonies by donning a literal crown of thorns.

Athey was thrust into the public eye, as were many of the artists discussed in this book, through a controversy generated by the opponents of the NEA. In 1994 he presented a performance at a Minneapolis nightclub that had been sponsored by the Walker Art Center in conjunction with an annual Lesbian, Gay, Bisexual and Transgender Film Festival. In one portion of the show, Athey cut a ritual design on the back of another man, blotted the blood with paper towels and strung the towels on a clothesline above the audience. When a local critic questioned whether the blood on the towels was HIV infected and hence a risk to public health (in fact it was not), the performance came to the attention of Senator Jesse Helms. Helms used the incident as further evidence of the depredation of the NEA. In fact, it was eventually revealed that the total of NEA funds allocated for Athey's performance was $150, but this did not stop Congress from using it as justification for an 8.5 million dollar cut in the agency's budget.[79]

While the free flow of blood in Athey's performances plays on the public's fear of gay men in the age of AIDS, the artist argues that the works ultimately serve as an exorcism of the self hatred which he acquired in his early Pentecostal years. He finds masochistic play transformative and cathartic, and his performances are designed to reenact the positive aspects of his early experiences.

Athey says, "It took a decade for me to find that life could be worth living without a God. Maybe that's at the bottom of it, I didn't have God, and after my glorious spiritual upbringing, it left a huge hole in me. I was furious, I hated my family for lying to me. I hated them even more because in their truth they didn't lie to me, they took their belief system with them to the grave.

"Of course this doesn't explain everything, but I see in a way, that I'm doing the same thing with my performances that my family did with their whole lives, I make an alternative reality that's one-half based in creating utopia, the other half facing unspeakable horrors. Luckily, I try to leave this world on stage, and let my hostages go free after the show."[80]

For Athey, masochism becomes an act of healing which, despite his professions of atheism, adopts the visual and theological symbols of the Imitation of Christ. This tactic is also a crucial element in the work of performance artist Bob Flanagan. While Acconci and Burden have disavowed any intentional masochism in their work, and Finley uses it to direct attention to society's victims, Flanagan, like Athey, was an active member of the S&M subculture. In fact, he came to performance art through the photographs which his partner Sheree Rose took of their mutual practice of bondage, piercing and consensual torture.

Flanagan, who died in 1996, was a lifelong sufferer from cystic fibrosis, a genetically inherited disease involving the over production of mucus, when eventually fills the lungs and makes the sufferer susceptible to viruses, bacteria and other infections. Most cystic fibrosis patients die very young, and Flanagan attributed his relatively long life in part to the focus provided by his S&M activities.

In a series of remarkably forthright interviews published in 1993, Flanagan traced his initial interest in masochism to his long stays in the hospital during which he was tied to the bed so he wouldn't thrash about when he was injected with needles to extract the fluid from his lungs. But despite the pain, there was a positive side. "While horrible things were happening to me, I was getting extra love and attention, so the two contradictory feelings probably fused together...the horrible things happening to me were made into something better; a sweetness was overlaid."[81]

Sadomasochism (SM) provided Flanagan with a sexual release that recalled this commingling of pain and pleasure. In addition, the physical pain involved in activities like nailing his scrotum to a board (an act which eventually became a staple element in his public performances) and hanging from his wrists, as well as the more subtle psychological tortures inflicted by his partner and SM mistress Rose (he was once ordered to eat nothing but oatmeal for the forty days of Lent), became a way to redirect and sublimate the physical pain inflicted by his illness. He remarked, "SM makes fun of what I have to do. This is why I never lose my sense of humor about SM. In some ways its dark and serious, but in other ways its the goofiest kind of activity, like any kind of sex that humans do. There's no way to make fun of an illness that can make children die at an early age, that's serious, but SM mocks it all."[82]

In the beginning, Flanagan's SM activities were private, pursued furtively as he immersed himself in the Los Angeles poetry and music scene. Eventually he began to haunt SM clubs, but found sessions with professional dominatrixes psychologically unfulfilling. Meeting Sheree Rose changed his life, and together the two forged a lifelong partnership which was on one level surprisingly conventional. They lived together in a suburban house raising her two children by a previous marriage while also involved in SM role playing in which Flanagan was enslaved to Sheree.

Thanks to Flanagan's ties to the Los Angeles art scene and Rose's interest in photography their inventive SM activities are copiously documented. The couple eventually began to present versions of their endeavors on the avant-garde performance and college circuit. They finally attained a more or less mainstream audience in 1992 with the presentation of *Visiting Hours*, an installation/performance exhibited first at the Santa Monica Museum of Art, then at the New Museum in New York.[83]

Visiting Hours was organized around the conceit of the hospital room, complete with a hospital bed outfitted with a device to lift Flanagan up so that he could hang nude suspended by his feet, a candy colored reception area in which covers of the children's magazine Highlights were inserted with SM magazines and a wall of children's blocks confined to the letters CF (for his disease) and SM (for his release). There were also a bed of nails, a cage and videos of Flanagan being force fed, pierced, carved and slapped interspersed with clips of Jesus on the cross. However, the centerpiece of the installation was Flanagan himself, a disarmingly friendly man who sat on the bed and chatted with visitors about his life, philosophy and sexuality.

In reviewing his influences, Flanagan cited an eclectic array of pop culture sources including cartoons of Porky Pig being tortured, the lashing scenes from *Mutiny on the Bounty* and *Jesus Christ Superstar*, Tony Curtis's *Boston Strangler*, flagellation as depicted in the film version of *The Pit and the Pendulum* and Jerry Lewis serving as humiliated slave to his sisters and stepmother in *Cinderfella*. Interestingly, hard core

SM magazines were less significant, perhaps because they didn't allow enough room for the imagination.

But equally important, Flanagan made clear, was his Catholic upbringing. "I was intrigued by (and perhaps identified with) the idea of being a martyr, especially since I was sick a lot. Saints always had something they were burdened with, and I remember thinking, 'I'm suffering. Maybe I'm a potential saint!' Suffering, sacrifice, and pain are themes of the Catholic religion: I remember going to church and kneeling for hours, enduring the horrible torture of just having to be there. It seemed like it was always hot, about 200 degrees, so that was endurance too."[84]

While Flanagan eventually lost his faith in God, he remained deeply affected by the Catholic imagination. He saw his preoccupation with SM not as a rejection of his background but as an extension of it. Speaking of himself and his fellow SM practitioners, whom he noted, tended to come from Catholic or Jewish backgrounds, Flanagan pointed out, "In Catholicism, torture was considered something beautiful and spiritual; something to rise above and change your life. And as kids those influences stuck with us . . . We never shirked from torture or pain because of the church. So it's not a reaction against, it's a reaction to. The Catholics teach Stations of the Cross, where whipping and scourges end up in crucifixion: death by torture. Jesus always has this great smile on his face and this expression of release when it's all over."[85]

In the end, Flanagan saw his artistic mission as the teaching of tolerance. He emphasized the consensual nature of SM practices, remarking, "We also aren't trying to proselytize; we don't say 'SM is the greatest thing in the world and you should do it.' We say, 'Don't put people down.' We try to dispel the whole idea of making judgements against people, when you don't even understand what they're doing."[86]

Body art as practiced by the artists described above is motivated by the belief that one can gain knowledge through the body. In this it differs from performance based work like that of non-Catholics like Bruce Nauman or the German artist Rebecca Horn which attempts to reduce the body to a kind of machine or inanimate object. It also stands in marked contrast to the more Zen-like approach to art found in the works of artists like Robert Irwin and James Turrell which seem designed to produce a release from embodiment into the realm of pure spirit. Instead of attempting to either reduce or transcend the body, the artists here employ it as the medium for their explorations. Like St. Augustine, who believed that the soul rises to God through the things of this world, they seek greater understanding of themselves and others through the exploitation of the senses, through the cultivation of pain and through the literal or metaphorical immersion in blood, body fluids and viscera.

The knowledge they attain is rooted in the concreteness of flesh. When Burden notes that the effect of his experiments was to make him feel more deeply in control, when Flanagan explains that the voluntary embrace of bondage allowed him to accept the unbidden physical pain of his illness, when Acconci invokes the vulnerability which comes from physical and psychological self-exposure, they are all acknowledging a kind of understanding which is inseparable from physical experience. And by framing their actions as performances, they invite audiences to participate in this experience.

Hence, it is not surprising that physical pain and sympathetic suffering are recurring themes in body art. As Elaine Scarry notes in her seminal book *The Body in Pain*, " . . . for to be oneself in pain is to be more acutely aware of having a body, as so also to see from the outside the wound in another person is to become more intensely aware of human embodiments."[87] Pain, perhaps more than any other sensation, affirms our shared corporeality. For contemporary body artists, pain, endurance and the frank acknowledgement of our status as creatures of flesh and blood become ways to reinforce the ethical, imaginative and empathetic bonds that underlie the social contract. In this these artists echo the Christian contract whereby Christ's Incarnation and embrace of physical suffering ensures the possibility of man's salvation.

In this chapter we have seen how the AIDS crises and the religious right's campaign against homosexuality helped shape performance art in the 1990s. We turn now to the effects of those developments on artists who worked in more apparently conventional art forms as well.

* * *

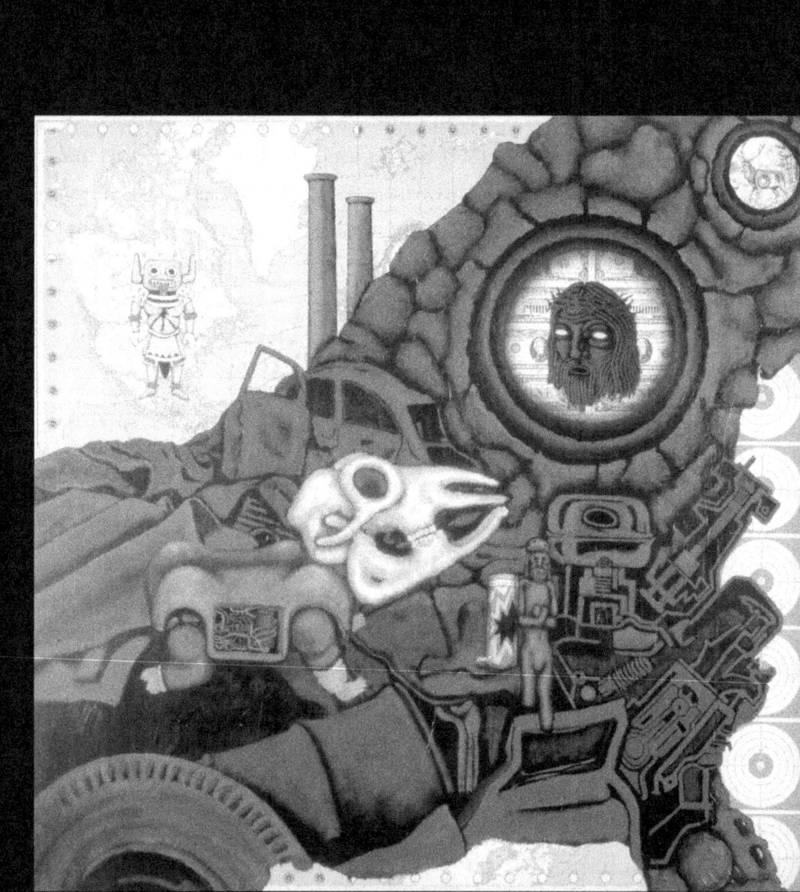

CHAPTER 4

OUTLAWS/OUTCASTS: CATHOLIC GAY ARTISTS

The first man I was ever in love with was Jesus. He was sweet. He was strong. He didn't play football or scream at me and he wore great clothes. This feeling I had for him from a very early age is part of my love for other men. I imagine him as a generous and sensitive lover, ready to give and receive pleasure. I see him there for the other person. Rubbing tired muscles with all those sweet smelling balms and ointments that they keep talking about in the New Testament. My relationship to Jesus is in a direct heartbeat to my gay identity.

–Tim Miller[88]

Is homosexuality a sin? Or is the official denunciation of homosexuality - one of the points of convergence between official Catholic doctrine and fundamentalist Christianity - the real transgression? How does the Christian doctrine of love and acceptance square with the rabidly anti-gay statements issued by Catholic conservatives and fundamentalist Protestant church leaders and politicians at the height of the AIDS epidemic? Do believers who are homosexual have a place within the Catholic Church or are they, in the words of Patrick Buchanan "lost souls, fighting a war against the Author of human nature, a war that no man can win?"[89]

We have already seen one effect of the official condemnation of homosexuality in Warhol's self-imposed exile to the back of the Church. Other artists have met the message of exclusion with sorrow, rage or reciprocal rejection. As we shall see, Robert Mapplethorpe chose to invert the cosmic order of Christianity, identifying himself with Lucifer, the fallen angel. David Wojnarowicz took a more explicitly political view. He laid blame for the cataclysmic death toll from AIDS on Christian leaders who applauded the disease as a just punishment for an immoral lifestyle. Yet others, like performance artist Tim Miller and playwright Terrence McNally have attempted to reimagine a Christianity whose spirit of unconditional love embraces a homosexual lifestyle.

One reason the official interdiction against homosexuality sits so heavily on such artists is that simple rejection of Christianity as a homophobic institution is not really an option. Christianity's, especially Catholicism's, relationship to homosexuality is not as simple as official proclamations against "unnatural sex acts" might suggest.

There is first of all, the tradition of ideal brotherhood, represented by the intense relationships between Jesus and his disciples, who were advised to leave all, including wife, parents and children, to join the Master. This spills over into Christianity's aesthetic tradition of homoeroticism, which can be discerned in some of the most venerated masterpieces of religious art.

For example Michelangelo's idealization of the male body, an idealization that extends even to his masculinized representation of women, was in part a reflection of his sexual interests. Leonardo da Vinci too was known in his own time to have a weakness for young boys, and in fact, when he was twenty four, he spent two months in a Florentine jail for having sex with a seventeen year old youth. Homoeroticism permeates his representations of androgynous angels, beautiful male saints and a sweetly feminine *John the Baptist*. It extends as well to his archetypal representation of the *Last Supper* that eliminates all female characters and emphasizes the bond between Christ and John "the apostle whom Jesus loved." As well Caravaggio, the preeminent exemplar of Counter Reformation art, was also given to homoerotic mythological and genre scenes of musicians, biblical figures and classical gods.

There is also in the contemporary Catholic Church the officially embarrassing issue of gay priests. (This is an issue that should not, but frequently is confused with the recent explosion of cases against pedophile priests). Garry Wills points out that the insistence on priestly celibacy has discouraged heterosexuals from accepting vocations, resulting in a tilt toward homosexuals. He notes, "Gays themselves register the change. In a survey of 101 gay priests, those ordained before 1960 remember their seminary as having been 51 percent gay. Those ordained after 1981 say their seminaries were 70 percent gay."[90]

Thus, while official Catholic policy sternly condemns homosexuality, the incarnational consciousness creates a climate very receptive to homoeroticism and homosexuality. Literary critic Eve Kosofsky Sedgwick speaks only partially tongue-in-cheek when she insists, "Catholicism in particular is famous for giving countless gay and proto-gay children the shock of the possibility of adults who don't marry, of men in dresses, of passionate theatre, of introspective investment, of lives filled with what could, ideally without diminution, be called the work of the fetish." She continues, "And presiding over all are the images of Jesus. These have indeed, a unique position in modern culture as images of the unclothed or unclothable male body, often in extremis and/or in ecstasy, prescriptively meant to be gazed at and adored."[91]

Gay religious scholar Mark D. Jordon notes the pervasiveness of what he calls "the paradox of the 'Beloved Disciple' which sends the mixed message: "Come recline beside me and put you head on my chest, but don't dare conceive of what we do as erotic." He adds, "Perhaps it is even more clearly seen in the paradox of the Catholic Jesus, the paradox created by an officially homophobic religion in which an all-male clergy sacrifices male flesh before images of God as an almost naked man."[92]

The mixed messages that Catholicism conveys about homosexuality create a situation in which gay artists are forced to question either their sexual orientation or their religious beliefs. These conflicts are exacerbated by a political climate in which large numbers of political and religious leaders have equated homosexuality with immorality, anti-Americanism, and enmity to religion. The AIDS crisis which erupted in the 1980s only confirmed the homophobia of those dedicated to the promotion of 'family values', as gay promiscuity was linked in the public mind with the growing incidence of the disease. Representative William Dannemayer expressed the political right's sentiments when he wrote in an anti gay screed "... we must reinstate traditional prohibitions against homosexuality in order to establish a sense of order and decency in our society, to reconnect us with our normative past."[93]

The Right's discomfort with homosexuality was a key factor in the Culture War that erupted at the end of the 1980s. We have already discussed Karen Finley's role as the most visible protagonist in the legal battles which swirled around attempts by the so called 'NEA Four' to reinstate their canceled grants and to challenge the constitutionality of the NEA 'decency pledge.' Interestingly, though Finley (who is heterosexual) emerged as the figure in this group with the greatest public name recognition. She was only added to the list of canceled grant recipients at the last minute, when her name appeared in an anti-NEA column written by conservative columnists Evans and Novak. A study of the proceedings reveals that the other three performance artists were denied grants on the basis of their homosexuality.[94]

Each was identified with performances that dealt in some way with their sexual orientation. John Fleck is a performer who works in TV, film and theatre. His solo performance works, for which he applied to the NEA, included works like *Blessed are All the Little Fishes* (1989), a performance where he turns an on-stage toilet into an altar. He urinates, mimes vomiting into it, and hauls out a live goldfish, while talking about his family's alcoholic background, sexual orientation, fears of AIDS, ageing and his career. Another work is *I Got the He Be, She Be's*, in which he addresses androgyny by tucking his genitals between legs to appear to be a woman and simulates making love to himself.

Holly Hughes is a performance artist whose main theme is women's sexuality from a lesbian's perspective. At the time of her grant cancellation, she was known for works like *The Lady Dick, World Without End* and *Dress Suits for Hire.* In this last, she depicts a lesbian relationship in which sexual expression is not fixed. Instead each of the two-character shift between polarities of butch and femme by which lesbians are frequently defined.

Tim Miller was more blatantly political in his anger over AIDS and the conservative attack on civil liberties. His works mixed autobiographical vignettes with, as he put it "growing up queer," explicit commentaries on gay sex and defiant politics. The publicity still from his 1989 performance *Stretch Marks*, for instance, shows the artist mounted as if crucified on a backboard cut into the shape of a bomber plane.

While none of these three performers is Catholic, each has had a complicated relationship to Christianity. Fleck frequently employs religious imagery. Hughes reports that she went through a "born again" phase in high school.[95] Meanwhile Miller, a self described "good ole protestant"[96] has a Roman Catholic partner and has gone on the road with a series of performance art sermons with Priest Malcolm Boyd designed to employ Christian liturgy to raise consciousness of the need for social justice in America.

Miller, in particular, is immersed in the paradoxical position of the gay believer who attempts to find a place for himself in a religious culture that is hostile to an essential element of his identity. Miller resolves this by returning to the original Christian commandment of love. He says, "I approach Jesus as a friend and helper. He is someone I meet at an ACT UP action. He is there in the circle with us in my performance art workshop. He is part of the fellowship of my gay friends. I know his lips. He is around to help me find my way through the biggest challenges of understanding my own heart, the pain in my world, the Gospel as a social document and the love commandment as an ultimate moral yardstick. We must love one another."[97]

In this, Miller echoes the approach of another homosexual artist whose work was engulfed in controversy ten years later. Catholic Playwright Terrence McNally's reenactment of the Passion of Christ became a cause célèbre for conservative Catholics when news leaked out that the Manhattan Theater Club would produce it in the fall of 1998. *Corpus Christi* is a reworking of Christ's life and passion in the form of a contemporary tale about a boy from Corpus Christi, Texas. The action careens between recreations of traditional biblical scenes and contemporary references. The hero, renamed Joshua, is born in a motel room during football weekend; James Dean makes a brief appearance during his adolescence; on Prom night Joshua is drawn into a sexual relationship with Judas. Eventually he gathers a motley group of disciples who include a gay hustler, a tax lawyer, a high school teacher and a masseur. In this company, he performs miracles and preaches unconditional love. Following the biblical script, Joshua is betrayed by Judas to the high priests and Romans, is crucified and dies.

The point of McNally's retelling becomes clear in scenes that deal with the question of Joshua's sexual orientation. In his interrogation by Pontius Pilate, it appears that Joshua's crime is not, as in the New Testament telling, blasphemy. Rather it is his homosexuality. Pilate asks him, not "are you the Son of God," but "Are you queer?" To which Joshua offers the traditional response "Thou sayist I am."[98]

This builds on a pivotal moment earlier in the play in which the apostles James and Bartholomew ask Joshua to bless their gay union. The dialogue stresses Joshua's message of unconditional love:

JAMES: Bartholomew and I had wanted our union blessed for a long time - some acknowledgement of what we are to each other.
BARTHOLOMEW: We asked, Josh. They said it was against the law and the priests said it is forbidden by scripture.
JAMES: "If a man lies with a man as with a woman, both of them have committed an abomination: they shall be put to death, their blood is upon them."
JOSHUA: Why would you memorize such a terrible passage? "And God saw everything that He had made, and behold it was very good." I can quote scripture as well as the next man. God loves us most when we love each other. We accept you and bless you. Who's got the ring?[99]

While overly didactic, the play is clearly reverential. In its plea for tolerance, it comprises an appeal to the original spirit of Christianity as a religion of love and acceptance. However, it was precisely this idea that Christianity might include an embrace of homosexuality that drew the ire of its conservative Catholic critics. Alerted to the imminent opening of the play, Catholic League President William Donohue issued a strongly worded protest against the play in the New York press and in the organization's internal newsletter.[100] Mobilized by this supposed threat to their faith, members signed petitions, flooded letters to the editor columns and organized protest rallies. Following a bomb threat, the theater announced it would cancel the play.

However, the Catholic League's victory was short lived. Following a firestorm of protest from arts groups and civil rights organizations, the play was reinstated. A circus like atmosphere surrounded the short sold out run of the play, as protesters clashed with supporters and ticketholders, who had to run the gauntlet of metal detectors. Despite the buildup, reviews were lackluster, leaving some conservative commentators to wonder whether their cause might have been better served by ignoring the whole situation.

Although descriptions by Donohue were inflammatory and inaccurate (in one missive he describes it as a play about Jesus having sex with the twelve apostles), the League's larger objections throw light on the internal fault lines exposed by the question of homosexuality and contemporary Catholicism. In keeping with the particular attention paid by the Catholic League to 'anti Catholic' Catholics, here again it is heretical believers, rather than atheists or agnostics, who pose the greatest threat to its established beliefs.

In a long unsigned article in the November 1998 issue of *Catalyst*, the Catholic League's on line magazine, a writer (presumably Donohue) opines, "It needs to be asked why McNally found it necessary to write this play. Above all, I believe it has to do with his need to justify his lifestyle. And this is certainly something that many other gays can relate to, especially if they were brought up Catholic, as McNally was.

... Instead of rejecting God, they are driven by a passion to seek His approval for their behavior. To be blunt, sodomy is not a sin that these gay men can accept. Unlike other gay men, they find it impossible to simply dismiss the Bible as fiction. No, they want to believe in God, but they don't want to believe in God as we know Him. To do that would be to admit to their sin, and their sin is their lifestyle. Better to rework Him than to reject Him. But God cannot be rehabilitated, and they know it. This is what drives them crazy."[101]

This screed tellingly articulates the bind that constricts homosexual Catholic believers. It also helps explain why homosexual artists feature so prominently in our litany of Postmodern Heretics. The irreconcilable conflicts posed by the combination of an outlawed sexual identity and a persistent Catholic imagination leads to artistic expressions which are powerful, provocative, and frequently deeply transgressive.

The artist who has become identified most indelibly in the public mind with homosexuality is, of course, Robert Mapplethorpe. It was Mapplethorpe's 1988 traveling retrospective *The Perfect Moment* that sparked the most contentious and long playing controversy of the Culture War. Ironically Mapplethorpe, who had a voracious appetite for publicity, and who consciously played with pornographic themes as a means to that end, never knew about the imbroglio which made his name synonymous with degeneracy among the broad American public. He died of AIDS related complications three months before the director of the Corcoran Museum of Art canceled his show and set off the Congressional battle to eliminate the NEA for contributing $30,000 to the exhibition. Before it was over thousands had stood in lines to see the exhibition at its seven venues and Dennis Barrie, director of the Cincinnati Art Center where the show made one of its stops had been indicted and tried for pandering obscenity.

At the heart of the controversy were a series of photographs known as the *X Portfolio* that contained explicit images of sadomasochistic homosexual acts. Among these were photographs of one man's fist disappearing up another man's anus, a man clad in leather S&M gear urinating in the mouth of another man, a close-up of a finger being inserted into the tip of an erect penis and a close cropped crotch shot of a black man's extraordinarily large penis dangling out the open zipper of his cheap polyester pants. Exhibited in a room set apart from the rest of the exhibition, these were accompanied in the retrospective by other examples of the artist's more socially acceptable subjects: floral still lifes, celebrity portraits, male (and occasionally female) nude studies which lovingly focused on the near perfection of the subject's bodies.

There were also two photographs that featured children. *Jesse McBride* is a photograph of a nude fourteen-year-old boy staring with self-possession at the camera as he perches on a stuffed chair in a pose that reveals his childish penis. In *Honey*, a three year old girl sits unselfconsciously on a park bench with her dress was pulled up to partially expose her vagina. In the Cincinnati trial these two latter works were cited as examples of child pornography, despite affidavits from the children's parents that they had attended and approved the sessions.

The thread connecting these works was Mapplethorpe's aesthetic sensibility. Each subject, be it still life, society matron or erect penis, was placed against a neutral background and bathed in a dramatic, raking light. Despite the sharply captured details, the objects or figures were subjected to an abstracting effect, presented as arrangements of swelling, modulated forms. Commentators noted that flowers photographed in this way became as erotic as the sensuously posed nudes. And in fact, Mapplethorpe claimed not to distinguish between the two, telling an interviewer, "I don't think there's that much difference between a photograph of a fist up someone's ass and a photograph of carnations in a bowl."[102]

During the controversy, and especially during the trial in Cincinnati, some supporters defended the more salacious works against charges of obscenity on the grounds that their style, compositional sophistication and attention to the conventions of beauty raised them from pornography into the realm of high art. Though this argument ultimately convinced the Cincinnati jury, who deferred to the "experts" to acquit Dennis Barrie, it was not a very satisfactory answer to the question of the works' relationship to pornography. Nor would it likely have pleased Mapplethorpe, who declared: "I think it (my art) could be pornography and still have redeeming social value. It can be both, which is my whole point in doing it: to have all the elements of pornography and yet have a structure of lighting that makes it go beyond what it is."[103]

Rather, as critic Arthur Danto has argued, any real understanding of Mapplethorpe's photographs must acknowledge that their transgressive content is absolutely integral to their meaning. In a review of a Mapplethorpe show mounted at the Whitney Museum in 1988, he remarked, "It would have to be a pretty cool cat for whom the triptych *Jim and Tom, Sausalito* of 1978 which shows, in each of its panels, what looks like Jim pissing into Tom's eager mouth, recommends itself as a particularly good example of what gelatin silver prints look like."[104]

How did a good Catholic boy from Floral Park, Queens become the most famous artistic interpreter of homosexual S&M practices? Even during his lifetime many commentators sensed the presence of a Catholic sensibility in Mapplethorpe's work. Janet Kardon, who organized his controversy plagued retrospective, located it in his still lifes: She declared, "Yet, of all Mapplethorpe's objects, the flowers offer the greatest evidence of his Catholic background . . . Because flowers are presented in a state of absolute perfection, they suggest a realm more sacred than profane. The blossoms seem to emerge from a rarified atmosphere in which Nature, like Heaven, is in array."

In this she echoes Mapplethorpe himself, who acknowledged the influence of Catholicism on his sense of composition; "... being Catholic is manifest in a certain symmetry and approach. I like the form of a cross. I like its proportions. I arrange things in a Catholic way. But I think it's more subconscious at this point."[106]

Viewed from a strictly formal perspective, Mapplethorpe photographs reveal other debts to traditional religious art, among them his love of dramatic lighting, his icon-like placement of subjects in the center of the picture, his frequent use of the triptych format, even, on occasion, his employment of poses directly drawn from sacred art.

However, there is something rather unsatisfactory about limiting Catholicism's influence on Mapplethorpe to strictly formal concerns. After all, this is an artist who once told an interviewer that the two most profound influences on his art were Coney Island and the Catholic Church, who exhorted his sexual partners to "do it for Satan" and whose walls were covered with crucifixes and religious icons. We must delve deeper to discover the real significance of Mapplethorpe's religious upbringing upon his work.

A more comprehensive view of Mapplethorpe's Catholicism emerges from Patricia Morrisroe's *Mapplethorpe,* a biography that draws on a series of interviews that the author conducted with the artist during the last months of his life.[107] Her book offers a fascinating portrait of a man torn between his unconventional desires and his powerful sense of sin and guilt. She draws a picture of his early life as an awkward, slightly effeminate boy born into a working class family in Queens, drawn equally to the Catholic Church and Coney Island. She traces his early efforts to assert his masculinity to a disapproving father and his enrollment at Pratt Institute where he evolved from ROTC cadet to drugged-out hippie. Following graduation he moved to New York with his soul mate, the rock poet Patti Smith, with whom he maintained a close, lifelong friendship. Smith and Mapplethorpe haunted the downtown art scene, longing for acceptance by the luminaries who held court at the avant-garde club Max's Kansas City. Eventually Mapplethorpe, whose efforts to settle down into a heterosexual relationship with Smith were clearly futile, gravitated toward the gay S&M scene which would provide the subject matter for his most controversial work. Mapplethorpe, who had been experimenting with the themes of religion and homosexuality in intentionally bizarre works that mixed photography and objects, found a mentor and lover in the wealthy photography collector Sam Wagstaff. With the help of Wagstaff's financial support and social connections, Mapplethorpe finally gained the acceptance he craved.

The biography offers a sympathetic, but unflinching look at Mapplethorpe's radical lifestyle, raw ambition, and the toll taken on his psyche and body by AIDS at the height of his fame. Summing up his internal conflicts, Morrisroe notes, "Mapplethorpe had fashioned a life for himself that precluded love, yet he, too, worried that he would end up alone. "Just because I was out at the bars all the time didn't mean I wasn't looking for someone to love," he said. "I wanted that as much as anyone else... Only it was hard for me." Morrisroe adds, "It was nearly impossible, in fact, for the same dramatic tension that pervades his work - the push-pull of black and white, good and evil, Catholicism and homosexuality - was emotionally tearing him apart."[108]

In order to fully understand the nature of Mapplethorpe's incarnational imagination, it is necessary to acknowledge the degree to which the conflict between his physical desires and his spiritual aspirations defined his life. From one perspective, many of the more transgressive elements of both his lifestyle and his photographs are simply exaggerations of orthodox Catholic beliefs. For instance, the fascination with bondage and sadomasochistic rites, as Allen Ellenzweig points out, "call upon an iconography of sin, guilt, punishment and martyrdom."[109] His friend Kelly Edey recalled to Morrisroe that Mapplethorpe and his circle were obsessed with the search for the perfect body, which they agreed, was a "manifestation of the divine."[110]

However, it is also undeniable that Mapplethorpe self-consciously challenged the taboos set up by the Catholic Church. He photographed himself with devil's horns and merged the iconography of religious art and gay porn. Perhaps the most illuminating clue to his inner state came when he responded in an interview to the question: "What is sacred to you?" Mapplethorpe replied: "Sex."[111] While this could be taken as flip response to an intrusive question, in fact it also suggests the degree to which Mapplethorpe allowed the carnal to usurp the place normally occupied by the divine in conventional Catholic thinking. Instead of embracing physical desire and ecstasy as a metaphor for union with God, in the manner of St. Teresa, Mapplethorpe used the tropes associated with spirituality to explore the all encompassing role sex played in his life.

The notion of sex as sacred magic has a place in numerous non-Christian religions, but for Mapplethorpe it was translated into the theological structures of Catholicism. Arthur Danto, who argues that the notorious triptych *Jim and Tom, Sausalito* can be read in relation to a traditional religious theme, explores one striking example of this. The work depicts a man in full bondage regalia urinating into the mouth of his kneeling partner. The lighting is deeply dramatic. Bars of light from an unseen window fall over graffitied walls while the two protagonists, angled in such a way that they illuminate the standing man's penis and the kneeling man's open mouth, leaves the former's face in shadow.

Danto connects this to the story of Roman Charity, in which a daughter presents her milk-laden breasts to her starving father who has been imprisoned by the Romans for his Christian beliefs. He argues "Undoubtedly, the Roman Charity paintings subserved prurient interests inasmuch as they allowed, under the guise of filial devotion, the artist to show and the viewer to admire a pretty breast; there was a moral overlay on a piece of lubricity, which is the inverse of our experience with *Jim and Tom Sausalito*. Still it was a depiction of a generous act, an act of devotion, whatever else complicates the viewers experience, and in some way Jim here confers a benefit on Tom, though most people might have a hard time appreciating that fully or not being disgusted by it."[112]

Other works in the sadomasochistic vein can also be read in this way. *Dominick and Elliot* (1979) depicts the submissive partner in an S&M relationship hanging upside down in a pose that suggests an inverted crucifix, recalling the martyrdom of Saint Peter, who declared that he was not worthy to be crucified in the same manner as Christ. *Joe* (1978) depicts a man fully encased in a rubber suit. He is presented on his hands and knees, wearing a dog collar with a rubber tube coming from his mouth. He is a picture of complete and total submission, willingly abjuring any trace of will or individuality in a manner that echoes Saint Ignatius' calls for the perfect submission of the soul to God.

Meanwhile *Dennis Speight with Calla Lilies* (1983) is a clear reference to the theme of the Risen Christ, who reappears on earth after his resurrection in a luminous and transfigured state. In traditional representations, he carries a lily as a symbol of his triumph over death and his body is so purified and perfected that he must warn Mary Magdalene at the tomb, "Noli me tangere" ("Do not touch me"). Mapplethorpe presents a naked black man holding a lily in the pose of Christ. His body is perfectly modeled and the picture is cropped so that we have a glimpse of his large penis. Thus the work takes the idea of physical beauty as a manifestation of divinity into the sexual realm, once again intermingling the sacred and the profane.

However, the most personal statements of Mapplethorpe's complicated relationship to his Catholicism are his self-portraits. These suggest a changing self-image. In his first published book of portraits, the dust cover front and back display a pair of self-portraits. In one Mapplethorpe appears as the tough, leather clad macho artist. The other is his alter ego. Rouged and painted with mascara and lipstick, he presents his feminine side. The spirit of play continues in later self-portraits. One of the most notorious is his photograph of himself, taken from behind, with a bull whip coming like a tail out of his anus. He is dressed in chaps and hip boots while peering back at us sardonically. The bullwhip tail suggests a transformation of the artist into the devil, a metamorphosis that is even more explicit in a 1985 self-portrait in which he sports goat like horns. The reference in both of these is to Satan, or perhaps more explicitly to the figure of Lucifer, who was the most beautiful and beloved of all the angels until his prideful challenge to God's authority caused him to be cast from Heaven. Like Lucifer, Mapplethorpe saw himself as the outcast, dedicated to recreating in inverted detail the kingdom from which he had been exiled.

By 1988, Mapplethorpe's struggle with AIDS had begun to tell on his face and ravaged body. In one of his most powerful self-portraits he stares unsmilingly out at the viewer clutching a cane carved with a skull. He is dressed in his signature black and his face is gaunt. With this work he is obviously acknowledging the way that illness is wearing away his once beautiful features, leading them toward the inevitable state suggested by the death's head in his hand. In this work, he becomes a figure in a medieval morality play, the reminder that even in the plenitude of life, death waits for us all. A final, very late work completes the sequence. Here he has simply photographed a real skull on a shelf.

The raking sidelight emphasizes the deep hollows in the eyeholes and toothy mouth, making it a photographic version of the medieval 'memento mori'.

Mapplethorpe's trajectory from altar boy to cultural symbol of sexual excess brings to mind Susan Sontag's analysis of the sources of the "pornographic imagination." She suggests that in Western culture, pornography blooms when the religious imagination becomes impoverished. She traces this to "the traumatic failure of modern capitalist society to provide authentic outlets for the perennial human flair for high temperature visionary obsessions, to satisfy the appetite for exalted, self-transcending modes of concentration and seriousness." She continues, "The need of human beings to transcend "the personal" is no less profound than the need to be a person, an individual. But this society serves that need poorly. It provides mainly demonic vocabularies in which to situate that need and from which to initiate action and construct rites of behavior. One is offered a choice among vocabularies of thought and action which are not merely self-transcending but self-destructive."[113]

While Mapplethorpe's work can be seen in terms of a personal struggle between his sexual identity and his Catholic imagination, it also must be placed in a larger cultural context. Many commentators have linked his work to the homoerotic, anti-rationalist and deliberately backward looking fantasies of the so-called Decadents, a group of late nineteenth century writers and artists in France and England. On the continent, the Decadents were grouped around writers like Charles Baudelaire, Paul Verlaine and J. K. Huysmans, while in Britain the most visible figures included the artist Aubrey Beardsley, the poet Oscar Wilde and critic Walter Pater.

The Decadents were at war with the materialism and emptiness of bourgeois society and they, like Mapplethorpe, often turned to Catholic themes to bolster their case. Much of the power of their work derived from the contradictory elements within Catholicism itself. They played in the borders between the Church's subliminal homoeroticism and its condemnations of homosexuality, between its spirituality and its sensuality, between the rich visual excess and voluptuous worldliness of Catholic rituals and architecture and the official exhortations to simplicity, renunciation and repentance.[114]

Artists Gustav Moreau and Aubrey Beardsley and writers Oscar Wilde and J.K. Huysmans exploited the titillating eroticism of biblical stories like the tale of Salome whose lascivious dance won her the head of John the Baptist. Gustav Flaubert's *Temptation of Saint Anthony*, which lovingly evokes the tortured dreams of lust, death, evil and redemption plaguing the imprisoned hermit saint, became a touchstone for writers on both sides of the English Channel. Other masterworks of the decadent movement dealt with a specifically homoerotic spirituality. In *De Profundis*, Wilde identifies with Christ as a sexually ambiguous aesthete. The forbidden love between a priest and his beloved acolyte appears as the subject of works by writers like John Francis Bloxam, Samuel Butler and Frederick William Rolfe. Richard Wagner's Christ-like *Parsifal* serves as a model for idealized love in a sonnet by poet Paul Verlaine.

By the early 20th century, decadence was largely played out in Europe, but its traces remained in the United States. These converged with the growing popularity of the new medium of photography which offered new possibilities for artists who wanted to recreate an idealized past. One artist who gained particular notoriety in this area was the photographer and publisher F. Holland Day.[115] Among his other projects, Day published an American edition of Wilde's Salome with illustrations by Beardsley. Day's own photographs, which have recently come back in vogue, include numerous depictions of nude young men with classical accoutrements. They also include a series of staged religious tableaux, including a depiction of Christ's Crucifixion with himself in the lead role.

The ostensible purpose of these works was to promote the artistic acceptance of the fledgling art of photography by using it to represent the great subjects of the Western art tradition. To prepare for his impersonation of the crucified Christ, Day sequestered himself for months in order to grow his hair and beard and starve himself into a suitable emaciation. His representation follows the standard lines for this subject, with the gaunt and near naked Day gazing down from a wooden cross upon a group of actors made up to represent the two Marys, Joseph of Arimethea and Saint John.

Though Day took pains to adhere to time honored pictorial conventions in his religious scenes, an inevitable gloss of homoeroticism creeps in. This is especially evident in Day's photographic version of the martyrdom of Saint Sebastian. Reportedly based on a painting by the 17th century painter Guido Reni, the work draws on Reni's twisting, arrow ridden original. However, Day's version exaggerates the figure's languorous eroticism to the point that his Saint Sebastian almost feels like a model for a Calvin Klein underwear advertisement.

While Day himself never married, it is not known whether he had an active homosexual life. Nor did his work achieve public notice for its homoerotic qualities during his lifetime. In those more closeted times, the nude or near nude male body could be depicted without comment if placed in a narrative that seemed to justify its appearance. And in fact, controversy swirled around Day, not for any erotic irregularities in his depictions but for having the temerity to deem the lowly art of photography a suitable medium for sacred subjects.

The soft focus treatment of male bodies in culturally defensible genres remained the norm well into the twentieth century. Gay photographers like George Platt Lynnes and Minor White developed a set of cultural codes that could be read by insiders one way and by outsiders another. This all changed after the Stonewall Rebellion of 1969. This event is generally regarded as the turning point for gay consciousness in the United States. Stonewall is a gay bar in Manhattan's Greenwich Village. One evening in 1969, when police entered the bar to pursue what had become a well-established pattern of harassing the gay patrons, the clientele rebelled and began to fight back. The ensuing melee, which resulted in the arrests of a number of patrons and bystanders, came to be seen as the opening salvo in a gay liberation movement that shared its philosophy with the concurrent black power and feminist movements.

Post-Stonewall, many gay men and women became militant about their homosexuality to the point that they tended to see the efforts of others to hold back as a betrayal of their shared identity. The result was a conflict within the gay community about the degree to which homosexuals should be open about their lifestyles and the degree of risk they were able to accept in their encounters with a homophobic society. One can detect the clash of pre and post Stonewall sensibilities in the very different ways in which Mapplethorpe and Warhol presented themselves to the public and in the way they regarded each other.

While Warhol was the first openly gay artist to achieve widespread popular success in 20th century America, he tended to underplay the sexual aspects of his persona. He succeeded to the extent, as we have seen, many commentators were convinced he had no sex life at all. When Warhol did create sexually explicit imagery, it was for a more underground audience. By contrast, Mapplethorpe made his sexual adventures part of his public persona. His public work was a mix of more conventional genres with hard core sexual imagery. Interestingly, in his first years in New York, Mapplethorpe had longed to be part of Warhol's circle. However, though they were acquainted, Warhol rebuffed him, complaining to a confidant: "He's so dirty. His feet smell. He has no money. And that horrible Patti Smith..."[116] For his part, his biographer reports, the mature Mapplethorpe remained wary of Warhol and kept his distance.

But if the gap between them represented the distance between pre and post Stonewall consciousness, by the late 1980s another schism was beginning to appear in the gay world as the AIDS epidemic exploded to crises proportions. While Mapplethorpe was one of the virus' most prominent fatalities, his work never made explicit reference to the disease or to the political controversies surrounding it. That was left for the younger generation, for whom AIDS became the impetus for an avalanche of works expressing rage, grief, black humor and anguish.

Among these, one of the most passionate was David Wojnarowicz. Wojnarowicz, a painter and writer identified with the East Village art scene, became the centerpiece of yet another clash in the ongoing Culture War in November 1989. The occasion for his notoriety was an exhibition organized by guest curator Nan Goldin for Artist Space, a well-respected alternative space in downtown Manhattan. Goldin is herself a photographer who has chronicled the devastating effect of AIDS on her own circle of artistic friends. For *Witnesses: Against Our Vanishing* she invited a variety of artists to reflect on the impact of the disease. As one of the invited artists, Wojnarowicz submitted several paintings and provided one of his texts for the catalogue.

The exhibition was scheduled to open at a politically precarious moment, the summer before had seen the cancellation of Mapplethorpe Corcoran exhibition. In the preceding months, the congressional debate over indecent art had lead to the passage of a modified version of the so called Helms amendment. Meanwhile, a new director, John Frohnmeyer, had just been appointed to head the NEA, and he was clearly being pressured to weed out any potentially inflammatory awards.

Artist Space director, Susan Wyatt, knowing that the NEA had pledged to cover $10,000 of the $30,000 cost of the show, decided it would be politic to provide Frohnmeyer advance warning about the content of the show and its catalogue. Of particular concern was Wojnarowicz's catalogue essay. Himself an HIV positive man who had buried his longtime lover the year before, Wojnarowicz unleashed his fury in a highly charged, hallucinatory text. In this essay, entitled *Postcards from America: X-rays from Hell,* he laid the blame for the prolongation of the AIDS crises on government officials who refused to allocate money for AIDS research and treatment and on a Catholic Church whose representatives forbade the distribution of condoms and condemned homosexuality as a sin.

Particularly inflammatory in the highly charged political atmosphere of that moment was the way that Wojnarowicz named names. Laying the blame for "thousands and thousands" of unnecessary deaths at the feet of the Church's outspokenly anti-gay representative Cardinal John O'Connor, he raged, "This fat cannibal from that house of walking swastikas up on Fifth Avenue should lose his church tax-exempt status and pay retroactive taxes from the last couple of centuries." Nor were the representatives of the government spared. """At least in my ungoverned imagination I can fuck somebody without a rubber or I can, in the privacy of my own skull, douse Helms with a bucket of gasoline and set his putrid ass on fire or throw Rep. William Dannemeyer off the Empire State Building." [117]

Initially, Wyatt's strategy appeared to have backfired. Upon receiving the catalogue, Frohnmeyer announced that the show was political rather than artistic, and that he was suspending the grant. This announcement took place a week before the exhibition was scheduled to open. An all too predictable media circus followed. The *New York Post* denounced the show as an "obscene mockery at public expense" while composer Leonard Bernstein announced he was declining a National Medal of Arts in protest. [118] Artist Space refused to return the portion of the money it had already received, Frohnmeyer met with Wyatt and altered his position, and in the end, the part of the funding designated for the exhibition was returned. However, Frohnmeyer refused to provide the promised funding for the catalogue, which, of course had already been printed. In the end, the newly formed Mapplethorpe Foundation made up the shortfall.

The response to Frohnmeyer's turnabout in this matter underscored how impossible the job of NEA director had become. The art world was not mollified by his partial reinstatement of the grant, while the congressional opponents of the NEA were outraged at what they decried as Frohnmeyer's failure to uphold the public trust. Having now been alerted to Wojnarowicz existence, they waited for a further opportunity to use him as an example of the misuse of public funds.

They didn't have to wait long. In January of 1990 an exhibition of Wojnarowicz's work partially underwritten by a $15,000 grant from the NEA opened at Illinois State University in Normal, Illinois. Accompanied by a catalogue containing an extensive selection of Wojnarowicz's writings, the exhibition engendered only minor controversy locally. However, the catalogue became grist for new attacks in Congress on "federally subsidized porn." Representative Dana Rohrabacher sent members of Congress a letter that described Wojnarowicz's work as "sickeningly violent, sexually explicit, homoerotic, anti religious and nihilistic."[119] He accompanied it with a detail from a painting that depicted Jesus with a syringe in his arm. The American Family Association's Donald Wildmon, working in tandem, sent a similar letter to Congress accompanied by a pamphlet containing images that purported to prove the objectionable nature of Wojnarowicz's work. In fact, Wildmon had extracted fourteen images of sex acts that had appeared as small details in a number of Wojnarowicz's large paintings and presented them as autonomous works of art.

As it turns out, the New York Artists and Authorship Rights Act makes it a crime to mutilate or willfully misrepresent a work of art. Wojnarowicz was able to make this infraction the basis of a five million dollar lawsuit against the American Family Association. After a faceoff in court, a judge ordered Wildmon to cease distribution of the pamphlet and awarded Wojnarowicz a symbolic $1 in damages.

Wojnarowicz's notoriety in the last few years of his life, he died from AIDS complications in 1992, was exacerbated by his untempered expressions of anger at a society which seemed intent on obliterating all he held dear. However, it would shortchange the complexity of his extraordinary writings and art works to see them purely in political terms. Along with his desire to expose the hypocrisy of social and religious attitudes toward AIDS and homosexuality, he was also engaged in a search for an authentic spirituality which was inspired by the almost Dostoyevskian difficulties of his life.

Wojnarowicz's biography has the improbable quality of fiction. Born in 1954 in Red Bank, New Jersey, Wojnarowicz had an abusive, alcoholic father who, he later recounted, killed his pets, shot guns in the living room and beat his wife and son with two by fours and dog chains. He was sent to Catholic school where he was further abused by the nuns who made him kneel on bags of marbles and told him he was "in the devil's wings and would go to hell."[120] In his adolescent years, he ran away to Times Square where he lived on the street and supported himself as a gay hustler. For a time he led a drifter's existence which took him to Canada, Mexico, San Francisco and for a brief period, Paris and Normandy. He eventually settled in the East Village of downtown Manhattan just as the area was becoming home to a gritty underground art scene. He joined a band named after a news headline, *3 TEENS KILL 4: No Motive*, which used tape recordings of street sounds as percussion. With fellow band member Julie Hair he undertook a series of rebellious 'action installations' including the depositing of one hundred pounds of bloody cow bones on the staircase of the Castelli art gallery in Soho. He also stenciled images of burning buildings, bomber planes, and recoiling figures on gallery doors, creating the beginnings of an artistic vocabulary of images that he would continue to draw on throughout his career.

An important turning point came in 1980 when Wojnarowicz met the photographer Peter Hujar who became his lover and mentor. Older and more established, Hujar provided Wojnarowicz with a new stability. In the next few years, Wojnarowicz began to gain recognition as a prominent member of the newly emerging East Village art scene. He worked in many media, among them writing, photography, painting, video and performance, and exhibited his work extensively both within the East village, in numerous national and international galleries and museum shows.

Following Hujar's death from AIDS in 1988 and his own discovery that he was infected with the AIDS virus, Wojnarowicz's work grew increasingly dark and political, leading to the last phase of his life where he spoke out frequently about the conservative backlash against gay men in the wake of the spread of AIDS.

In both his visual art and his writings, Wojnarowicz explored the meaning of a life lived on the edge of respectable society. In both formats he evolved a complex, layered style that drew on surrealist juxtaposition, Beat rebellion, Emersonian notions of transcendence and the visionary hallucinations of Symbolist poetry. The written texts effortlessly merge sharply rendered social observations and vignettes about life on the street with dreamlike fantasies of escape, destruction and sexual ecstasy. The paintings are similarly constructed from concatenations of apparently disparate images. A single painting may bring together torn bits of real maps or money, painted images from a repertoire which included cowboys, crumbling cities, prehistoric beasts, industrial gears and rotting skulls, and tiny photographic vignettes of trains, gay porn and microscopic cells.

In both texts and paintings, Wojnarowicz's focus is on the duality of the world, which he divides into the "World" of authentic feeling and experience versus the "Other World." This latter, which he frequently refers to in his writings as the "pre-invented world", is the progeny of industrial civilization and coercive social structures into which we are born. This pre-invented world is dominated by technology, science, language, law and official history. The authentic world, by contrast, is the domain of nature, which provided Wojnarowicz a much-needed refuge during his horrific childhood, and serves in his paintings as the symbol of an imagined preindustrial life. The split between the two reflect the split in the modern world between culture and nature, and between the material and spiritual world.

Interestingly, sex and physical desire belong to the latter realm, bringing with them the indescribable sweetness that arises from the momentary submission to nothingness. In Wojnarowicz's writings, it is striking how harsh descriptions of the struggle for survival on the street suddenly melt into moments of lyrical beauty experienced in the midst of an anonymous sexual encounter. In the paintings, flashes of beauty similarly break through images of the bleak devastation wrought by human action. From one perspective both the paintings and the writings are chronicles of attempted escape in which death looms, less as a fearsome extinction than as a passage to a realm of spiritual and imaginative freedom. As Wojnarowicz wrote in a meditation on the death of a close friend from AIDS, "Hell is a place on earth. Heaven is a place in your head."[121]

Despite his rage at official Church pronouncements about homosexuality and AIDS, Wojnarowicz' work suggests an identification with the suffering Jesus, who makes frequent appearances in his paintings. One of the most controversial, a painting entitled *Untitled (Genet)* which was reproduced in the catalogue for Wojnarowicz's retrospective at Illinois State University, brought a number of hate letters and was later used by Representative Rohrabacher as evidence of Wojnarowicz's enmity toward religion. The work places a number of found and collaged images within the architectural framework of a gothic Church. The images include Renaissance angels, modern soldiers, a haloed portrait of Genet and, in the right corner, a holy card image of the crucified Christ with a hypodermic needle sticking from his arm.

Taken as a whole, the work appears to be a meditation on suffering, evil and salvation, but Wojnarowicz's critics fixated on the idea that he had defiled the image of Christ by portraying him as a drug addict. As Wojnarowicz explained to his lawyer David Cole, this image was actually inspired by an incident in which he witnessed the diabetic grandfather of the family with whom he briefly lived in France administering his own insulin. He told Cole, "I was thinking about medicine in terms of how it's used as a benevolent treatment of an illness, or else it's used by sensitive people in order to nullify their sense of life or what their lives feel like living in this societal structure.

"So I thought about my upbringing. I thought about what I had been taught about Jesus Christ when I was young, and how he took on the suffering of all the people in the world and I wanted to create a modern image of that, if he were alive physically before me in the streets of the lower East side, I wanted to make a symbol that would show that he would take on the suffering of the vast amounts of addiction that I saw on the street. And I did this because I saw very little treatment available for people who had this illness."[122]

The Christ head reappears in numerous other works. In these, again, it seems to rebuke the modern world for deserting true Christian values. *Spirituality (For Paul Thek)* (1988), centers on a black and white photograph of a rather grisly crucifix in which Christ's painted face is covered with ants. This is set off against a group of smaller photographic images which draw on Wojnarowicz's personal iconography of spiritual and material death; among them a clock, a pile of bills and coins, and an AIDS victim on the verge of death blowing smoke from a cigarette which circles his wasted head like a departing spirit.

In *Excavating the Temples of the New Gods* (1986), the Christ head turns sinister with glowing eyes. This work contains many of Wojnarowicz's symbols for the false idols of the pre-invented world, among them a set of factory chimneys, a field of five dollar bills, a map delineating the world's arbitrary borders and a giant animal skull like form created of machine parts, old tires, abandoned cars and other detritus of industrial society.

Other religious symbols appear as well, often with lighter connotations. A humorous red devil pops up occasionally almost as a form of comic relief from the surrounding devastation. There are occasional angels as well, dotting the darkness as symbols of hope. These play off more earthbound images of cowboys, ants, urban rubble and rotting skulls.

Reflecting on his recourse to cartoonish and mythic imagery, Wojnarowicz explained to an interviewer, "Spirituality has become a dirty word in this society because of the destructive nature of organized religion and the controls exerted by its human structure. Myths get played out only in pop culture, in the forms of toys and cartoons, animals, monsters and fantastic creatures."[123]

Especially in his later years, Wojnarowicz's life and work became a referendum on the hypocrisy of American society and the Catholic Church. But, like Mapplethorpe, beneath the anger and the rebellion, it is clear that a Catholic imagination was at work. For both artists, the search for redemption led through the body. For Mapplethorpe, sexual desire and ecstasy provided momentary transcendence from his personal hell. For Wojnarowicz, they were manifestations of nature, havens of authentic feeling in a world that had become a mechanistic nightmare.

Like the Decadents and the Romantics who were their spiritual ancestors, both Mapplethorpe and Wojnarowicz exhibited a fascination with death. Such a focus remained, as it had for Wilde, Huysmans and other anti-modernists, one way to rebel against a society fixated on rationalism and soulless progress. But for artists in the age of AIDS, death was also an urgent and ever present reality. The artist Felix Gonzalez-Torres, in a much quieter way, also took on the mayhem.

On the surface, Gonzalez-Torres' work could not seem farther from the in your face sexuality of Mapplethorpe or the high decibel rage of Wojnarowicz. But this Cuban born gay activist artist who died of AIDS complications in 1996 shared many of their concerns. In his work the politics of AIDS and the seductions of homoerotic desire were transmuted into an aesthetic of absence and disappearance.

At first glance Gonzalez-Torres' works seem remorselessly spare and abstract, reflecting his allegiance to the reductive aesthetics of conceptualism and minimalism. But Gonzalez-Torres embeds worlds of emotion within deceptively simple formats. Consider some of his signature works: Two bare light bulbs glow together, their cords entwined like the bodies of lovers. A pair of battery operated clocks on the wall tick away in comfortable companionship until they slowly fall out of sync and one gradually winds down, a harbinger of death and loss. A billboard appearing simultaneously in twenty-four sites throughout New York City contains nothing more than the black and white photographic image of an empty double bed with two rumpled pillows bearing the imprint of recently vacated heads. Again, the emptiness is poignant and suggestive. A stack of paper sheets imprinted with the image of a tiny bird flying across a vast sky literally disappears as visitors peel pages off and take them home. A pile of glittering cellophane wrapped candies proves similarly ephemeral, as it diminishes piece by piece with each acquisitive visitor.

Such works are understated meditations on Gonzalez-Torres' recurring focus on love and loss (works like the pair of clocks and the empty beds make reference to his devotion to his lover Ross Laycock who succumbed to AIDS after a long battle in 1991). A constant undercurrent is the political world in which these personal experiences take place, which for Gonzalez-Torres encompassed the divisive and cold hearted politics of the Reagan era and the history and struggles of the gay liberation movement.

These, of course, were concerns he shared with Wojnarowicz. However, in place of Wojnarowicz's inflamed polemics, Gonzalez-Torres exploited a more subtle strategy to convey his messages. Everyday objects, displaced from their ordinary contexts, were transformed into vessels of poetry and politics. Often, an interactive element was built into the work. Take, for instance, the candies. Different piles employ different mixes of sweets. A pile, or "spill" as Gonzalez-Torres preferred to call them, of 700 black licorice pieces from 1991 was labeled "*Untitled (Public Opinion)*". Its sickly sweet odor and excremental color suggested the muddy nature of public discourse in late 20th century America.

Untitled (USA Today) was more spritely, composed of candies in shiny red, white and blue wrappings to reflect the reflexive patriotism favored by that paper's constituency. More poignant were the silver candies of *Untitled (Placebo)*. First exhibited in 1991, just after Ross's death, the title suggests the futility of his long medical treatment. Meanwhile the combined weight of the pile, which was to shrink as visitors carried pieces away and then be replenished throughout the course of the show, was equal to the combined weight of the two lovers.

Reflecting on his obsession with the ephemeral, Gonzalez-Torres remarked, "In a way, this letting go of the work, this refusal to make a static form, a monolithic sculpture, in favor of disappearing, changing, unstable and fragile form was an attempt on my part to rehearse my fears of having Ross disappear day to day right in front of my eyes."[124]

The spills were characteristic of his approach to art. Tottering on the verge of non- art (after all anyone could create a similar pile of candy, and Gonzalez-Torres expressed surprise to one of his curators that people didn't just do that instead of purchasing a "signature" piece) they threw an oblique challenge to the whole idea of art as a precious, expensive, one of a kind commodity. At the same time, the invitation to viewers to take away a piece of candy was a deliberate violation of the museum's 'do not touch' rule. In each spill, the choice of scale and color was deeply significant and meant to suggest a host of personal and social meanings. But for the uninitiated viewer, such theoretical niceties were secondary to the simple visual and sensual pleasures that the candy promised.

In his own description of the operations of the spills, we can see Gonzalez-Torres' Catholic imagination at work. He described their operations to curator Nancy Spector in terms that evoke both erotic desire and Holy Communion. "It's a metaphor," he remarked. "I'm giving you this sugary thing; you put it in your mouth and you suck on someone else's body. And in this way, my work becomes part of so many other people's bodies. It's very hot. For just a few seconds, I have put something sweet in someone's mouth and that is very sexy."[125]

Thus, though it is rarely explicitly visible, the traces of the body can be felt everywhere in Gonzalez-Torres' work. In pieces which reflected Gonzalez-Torres's over exposure to the medical regimens of the AIDS patient, plastic bead curtains hanging from a door were color-coded white and red to represent blood cells, or blue and green to represent the chemicals used in blood therapies. Similarly, in *Untitled" (31 Days of Bloodworks)*, an apparently minimalist set of grid drawings are based on charts of the AIDS infected body's declining resistance to infections.

But not all Gonzalez-Torres' works were about death and mourning. While pursuing his own work, he was also a member of Group Material, an activist art group which during the 1980s and early 90s undertook to challenge the political quietude and right wing drift of the Reagan and Bush years with exhibitions, broadsides, public forums and guerilla actions. Similar political convictions underlie many of Gonzalez-Torres' individual works. His stacks of printed paper, like the candy spills, were meant to be taken away by visitors and replenished when they disappeared. Some of the images in the stacks were lyrical, depicting nearly empty vistas of sky or sea. Others were unmistakably political. In some stacks, large sheets of paper containing tiny news clips exposed the hypocrisy of the political right. One provided a gridded representation of the names and faces of all the 464 Americans shot dead spanning one week. Most pessimistically, a funereal black bordered sheet was laconically entitled *Untitled (Republican Years)*.

And even the more personal works carried political resonances. The billboard of the unmade bed was, on one level, a meditation on love and intimacy and, among other things, a reference to the loss of his lover. But as the artist made clear to interviewers, it was also a reflection on Bower vs. Hardwick, the 1986 Supreme Court case that determined that the constitutional right to privacy doesn't extend to homosexual "sodomy." Placing the beds on very public billboards throughout the city, Gonzalez-Torres made the point that for homosexuals, the supposed line between public and private life no longer seemed to exist.

Gonzalez-Torres' recurring commentaries on the pleasure of homosexual love, the bankruptcy of the government's AIDS policy and indifference of American politicians to human need and suffering would seem likely to make him a target of the moral gatekeepers who had so vociferously pursued Mapplethorpe and Wojnarowciz. However, even when Gonzalez-Torres was the subject of a 1994 museum exhibition in Washington DC at the height of the frenzy over culture war, he escaped censure. As he impishly told an interviewer, "When I had a show at the Hirshhorn, Senator Stevens, who is one of the most homophobic anti-art senators, said he was going to come to the opening and I thought he's going to have a really hard time explaining to his constituency how pornographic and how homoerotic two clocks side-by side are. He came there looking for dicks and asses. There was nothing like that. Now you try to see homoeroticism in that piece."[126]

Like Wojnarowicz, Gonzalez-Torres' work was imbued with a sense of loss, and like Mapplethorpe, it seduced the viewer with an appeal to beauty. Though apparently less troubled by his early religious training than either of them, an incarnational consciousness nevertheless underlay his approach to art. Writer Lewis Baltz suggests that one way to think about Gonzalez-Torres' work is to consider its connection to the Christian concept of grace. He says, "The celebrated paper stacks and the arrangements of candy, from which the visitor was invited to take one (or more) elements, are described by the artist as having an 'ideal' height or weight, to be replenished as necessary from an 'endless' supply, function as symbolic generosity while alluding to another, impossible, generosity; the hope of the endless renewal, like divine grace. This is the language of prayer, and the gesture of trans-substantiation, but, like the wily priest, Gonzalez-Torres' gifts create obligations." [127]

Those obligations were social as well as spiritual. Gonzalez-Torres powerfully held political convictions, along with his belief in art as a force for change allowed him to redirect the essential carnality of the Catholic Imagination into coded representations that merged the individual body with the body politic. Reconciling the two, he evaded the frustrations inherent in Catholicism's contradictory messages about homosexuality.

For the artists in this chapter, death was a constant presence, thrust into their lives by the devastations of the AIDS crises. But an immersion in death and mortality is also part of a more general experience of the incarnational consciousness. In the next chapter, we will see how Catholic morbidity enfolds death into the meaning of life.

* * *

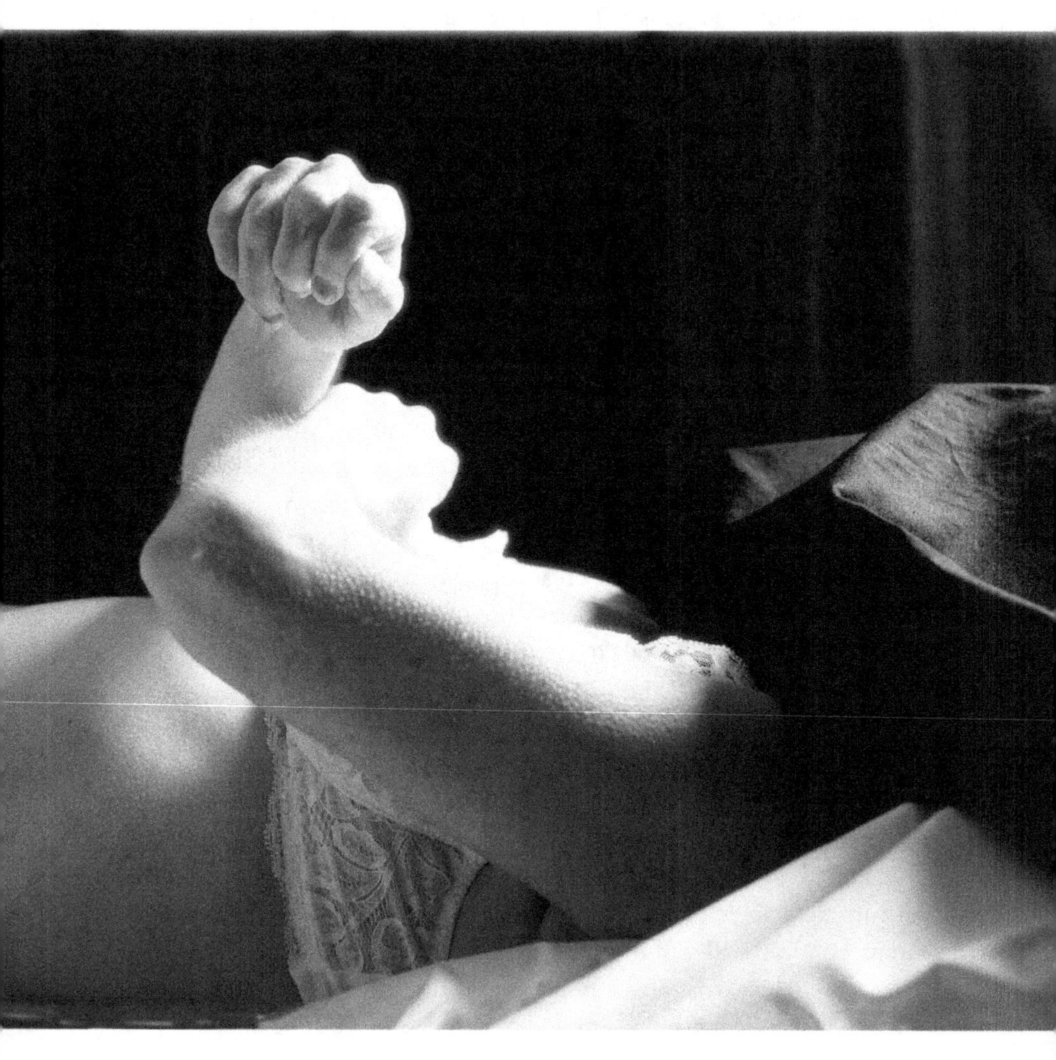

Andres Serrano, *Morgue (Rat Poison Suicide)*, 1992

© Andres Serrano, Courtesy of the artist

CHAPTER 5

CORRUPTABLE BODIES: CATHOLIC MORBIDITY

Death is the mother of beauty; hence from her,
Alone, shall come fulfillment to our dreams
And our desires.

–Wallace Stevens, *Sunday Morning*

Wallace Steven's great poem *Sunday Morning* is essentially a conversation about the meaning of death and the nature of Paradise. Couched as a dialogue between two voices, it lays out a pair of arguments that take us to the heart of our modern ambivalence about mortality.

The poem sets the stage with a description of a dreamy Sunday morning as the unnamed female interlocutor drifts from the comforts of her immediate surrounds to a meditation on the religious meanings of the day. Rebelling against the Christian preoccupation with death, she offers a counterproposition: Invoking the beauties of nature she declares, "Divinity must live within herself." Not one of the religion's trappings of shroud and spirit "has endured/ As April's green endures; or will endure/ like her remembrance of awakened birds, Or her desire for June and evening . . ." Thinking further, however, she notes that this proposition is not wholly satisfying: "But in contentment I still feel the need of some imperishable bliss".

Her conundrum is addressed by an omniscient voice that makes the case for the inseparability of death and life. Declaring, "Death is the mother of beauty," this voice invokes the pathos of a paradise without death, where ripe fruit never falls and perfection abolishes all change. Instead, the voice suggests, what makes life precious is the presence of death in our midst. Casting back to the theological speculations that open the poem, the female interlocutor finally understands the Christian fixation on mortality: "She hears, upon that water without sound,/ A voice that cries, "The Tomb in Palestine/Is not the porch of spirits lingering./ It is the grave of Jesus, where he lay."

Sunday Morning beautifully captures the tension in Western culture between our fear and our fascination with death, and links this dilemma to the legacy of Christianity. In Chapter 1 we noted how the embrace of the doctrine of the Resurrection of the Body in medieval Christianity lead to what today we might deem a fetishization of dead bodies and body parts. Among its manifestations were the preservation of relics, the accumulation and display of corpses in charnel houses and the creation of graphic, even grisly images of martyred saints and the dead Christ. In more recent times, American Christianity (this includes both Protestant sects and even post Vatican II Catholicism) has downplayed what Stevens refers to as "the domain of blood and sepulchre" in favor of an emphasis on spiritual rebirth. In his lively book on the religions born on American soil, Harold Bloom notes, "the

American religion takes up the cross only as the emblem of the risen God, not of the crucified man, if indeed it takes up the cross at all...”[128] And yet as Stevens suggests in *Sunday Morning*, modern Christianity has not so much banished death as driven it underground. Periodically Catholic morbidity bursts back to the surface to remind us what we really are.

In his monumental study, *The Hour of our Death*, Philippe Aries takes on Western culture's changing attitudes toward death.[129] He describes a medieval world in which death is an incident in a larger vision of life that begins with birth and ends with the reunion of body and soul at the end of time. He notes the shift from a pre-Christian and Jewish tendency to view the dead as unclean and to keep them at a distance from the living to the view that the presence of the dead sacralizes the spaces of life. In the early Christian era, keeping with this new sensibility, burials moved into the city where churches and graveyards became centers of social life.

Later, around the fourteenth century, beliefs about the nature of death changed again. No longer a sleep shared by all until the Last Judgment at the end of time, death, defined as the moment the soul leaves the body, became a moment of truth in which one's salvation or damnation was determined. This led to a new anxiety about death that manifested itself in a covering of the corpse and a remarkable flowering of artistic representations of the macabre.

Medieval art from the fourteenth to the sixteenth century reflects a consciousness of death as the fearsome moment when one's eternal fate is decided. The tradition of the 'vanitas' or 'memento mori' incorporated symbols of death and decay into representations of earthly abundance. 'Transi' sculptures lovingly reproduced the half decomposed corpse in all its gruesome detail. Prayer books were full of tableaux in which God and Satan vie for the soul of a dying person. Also popular were images of the Danse Macabre in which the dead and living dance together as rotting mummies taking the hands of robust men and women. Similar representations live on today in Mexican celebrations of the Day of the Dead.

The new reform movements that followed the Reformation tended to view the pre-Reformation focus on dead bodies as morbid and unhealthy. Aries quotes New England Puritan leader Increase Mather, “When the soul departs this life, it carries nothing away with it but grace, God's Favor, and good conscience."[130] The body, once viewed as an indivisible feature of human identity, becomes for Mather simply a useless shell to be disposed of without ceremony once it has served its earthly function. He notes, "The body, when the soul is gone, will be a horror to all that behold it, a most loathsome and abhorred spectacle. Those that loved it most cannot now find in their hearts to look on it, by reason of the griefly deformedness which death will put upon it. Down it must into a pit of carrions and confusion, covered with worms, not able to wag so much as a little finger, to remove the vermin that feed and gnaw upon its flesh."[131]

Aries charts a general post-Reformation trend away from a preoccupation with physical death. Images like those above were seen as gruesome and distracting; "vain fantasies" in the words of John Calvin.[132] The Catholic sacrament of Extreme Unction, or Last Rites, in which a sinner could be absolved of all sin on his deathbed was anathema to Luther. So was the Catholic concept of Purgatory, that intermediate state between heaven and hell from which souls of sinners can be released to heaven through the prayers of the living. Instead of worrying about death and the long process of negotiating one's fate after death, the faithful were enjoined to focus on life.

The dethroning of death accelerated in the twentieth century when death left the home and became ensconced in the sterile impersonality of the hospital. As a result, death largely disappeared from sight. Survivors were counseled to "move on" and avoid morbid attachments to the dead. But, as Aries notes, the attempt to 'modernize' attitudes toward death by banishing fear, superstition and fatalism simply made it unmentionable. By 1969, in her groundbreaking book *On Death and Dying*, Elisabeth Kubler-Ross could write that death is a "dreaded and unspeakable issue to be avoided by every means possible in modern society."[133]

Despite a Protestant tendency to associate the cult of death with Catholicism, seeing morbidity as a residue of Papism, Aries notes that these attitude changes engulfed Catholics and Protestants alike. However, he concedes that residues of medieval beliefs about death retain a powerful hold on the modern psyche. Indeed, many of the practices decried by Protestants and downplayed by the Catholic Church were very much a part of my pre-Vatican II Catholic childhood. I remember wearing scapulars, cloth badges which were said to insure the wearer against unexpected death. I recall reciting prayers and novenas that, my prayer book promised me, would relieve a designated number of years in purgatory. Like a bank account, these could be redeemed for oneself or transferred to a soul currently languishing in Purgatory. The assumption was that this grateful soul would later intercede for its deliverer at the time of one's death. These practices disappeared with the modernization of the Catholic Church in the 1960s. However, In Latin cultures and in parts of the United States with large Latin populations, the cult of death survives in such rituals as the celebration of the Day of the Dead and the cult of Sacred Heart.

But the contemporary aversion to death is countered by an equally powerful pop culture fascination with morbid and gruesome images of death. The loving recreation of flying body parts and blood drenched corpses in films by such popular directors as Quentin Tarantino and Wes Craven reveal a willingness to embrace the spectacle of death as mass entertainment. Another case in point: the success of HBO's series *Six Feet Under* which takes place in a funeral home in which dead bodies laid out on gurneys serve as background props for the unraveling of characters' convoluted personal dramas. Further evidence of the seductions of the morbid can be found in the enormous crowds who flocked to *Body Worlds*, an anatomical exhibition that appeared in London in 2002 and featured dozens of real flayed bodies stiffened with plasticine and arranged in lifelike poses. After weathering a court challenge, the exhibition drew blockbuster-sized crowds before culminating in a televised live autopsy carried out by its impresario, the German doctor Gunther von Hagens.

Located at a safe psychological distance, death makes for pleasant diversion. But when it comes closer to home, it has clearly not lost its sting. Following the attack on and collapse of the World Trade Towers in 2001, photographs of people jumping to their deaths from the burning Trade Towers were quickly removed from print and broadcast view. In the subsequent wars in Afghanistan and Iraq, American photographers found themselves following an unspoken code that forbade the depiction of actual bodies or body parts. In a war diary report aired on National Public Radio on April 15, 2003, photographer David Leeson explained the dilemma. "Photographing the dead is very difficult," he reported. "Today, when I approached this man in his vehicle with the intention to photograph a civilian casualty, [I] couldn't quite do it... This man had been shot behind the wheel of his car and when I got to the car he had no face. So, it was entirely too sad and too gruesome at the same time. It just didn't seem fitting for human life to be photographed in that state. So, I just didn't do it. I walked away from it, went and found something else to photograph."

Thus while graphic images of military and civilian deaths were released by news outlets in Europe and the Middle East, American audiences rarely saw them. One cannot help wondering about the extent to which this unspoken interdiction against explicit representations of war's carnage helped keep American support high during the conflict.

Such contradictory attitudes toward death formed the subtext of a court case in 2002 that sent a young Cincinnati artist named Thomas Condon to prison for six months. During the course of his trial and imprisonment, Condon became known as the "morgue artist" for a series of photographs he had taken of cadavers at the city morgue. Believing he had secured permission to pursue this private art project in the course of negotiations with the coroner's office about making a training film for employees, Condon photographed corpses juxtaposed with various objects meant to signify the cycle of life and death, among them shells, toy ladders and sheet music. He planned to crop the photographs to hide the identity of his subjects.

However, when he sent several sets of negatives to be developed commercially, the developer, alarmed at the content of the pictures, passed the negatives to the police. They promptly arrested Condon and seized his photographic equipment. The negatives then were mysteriously leaked to the press, where they were printed in local tabloids and reproduced on local television news stations. Although Condon had intended to crop the photographs to obscure the identity of the bodies, these leaked images contained clearly identifiable features, stirring understandable outrage among the relatives of the deceased.

The result was a predictable media circus in which local pundits denounced Mr. Condon's project as "sick" and "repulsive," demanding his incarceration. After considering various charges, among them breaking and entering and pandering obscenity, the prosecutors eventually indicted Condon for corpse abuse, a charge which carried a salacious odor of necrophilia and body snatching. After a brief trial overshadowed by a heavy media focus on the anguish of the families of the deceased, Condon was convicted and imprisoned for six months in the spring and summer 2002, after which he was released pending appeal.

The legal issues were complicated, involving issues of permission, ethics and the definition of "corpse abuse." The situation was further complicated by the general atmosphere of Cincinnati, a city with a long and litigious relationship to avant-garde art. It was in Cincinnati that the Mapplethorpe controversy came to a head, when local prosecutors tried Dennis Barrie, then the director of the Contemporary Arts Center, on obscenity charges for presenting the artist's retrospective. Five years later, the city prosecuted the Pink Pyramid bookshop for renting out a video of Passolini's *Salò:120 Days of Sodom.* The Condon case was also aggravated by a simmering feud between the coroner's office and the county prosecutor that involved several cases in which bodies had been mixed up and improperly disposed of.

But one thing that emerged clearly from the murk was the ease with which the public's discomfort with death could be manipulated by an unscrupulous media. After all, Condon is hardly the first artist to use photographic images of dead bodies in his work. His direct inspiration was Andres Serrano's 1992 *Morgue Series.* He also was following in the wake of artists like Jeffrey Silverthorne who created a series of photographs that overlaid images of the living and the dead to suggest the continuity of life and death. (Silverthorne wisely secured permission for his project from the Attorney General of Rhode Island where the morgue in question was located. He made sure that his images were not exhibited locally.) Going farther back in time, one could cite the mangled bodies in the appropriated disaster photographs of Andy Warhol discussed in Chapter 2, as well as the now classic images by the photojournalist Weegee of the gory aftermath of gangland shootouts and grisly murders.

Such precedents carried no weight in Condon's trial. Underlying the official outrage was the assumption that the depiction of dead bodies in and of itself is somehow obscene and that people need to be protected from a direct visual contact with death. Condon's photographic project ran counter to the unspoken cultural taboo against the unvarnished depiction of dead bodies. As Cincinnati Coroner Carl Parrott told the *Cincinnati Enquirer* "Not only is it probably illegal, it's immoral."[134]

Raised Catholic, Condon evidences a more accepting attitude toward representations of our mortal remains. Noting that, "In these photographs, people have just come from death," he explains. "I wanted to show the split second fragility of life." He adds, "I wanted to help people come to an acceptance that this is what the body is. The body represents a life lived. It's a road map to the person's life. When the body is opened up and exposed this way, its a very beautiful thing."[135]

In this Condon echoes the sentiments of Andres Serrano, an artist whose work was an important influence on him. Serrano is best known to the public for *Piss Christ*, the photograph immortalized in the mass media as "the crucifix dipped in urine." The brouhaha which ensued when this work was included in a traveling exhibition partly paid for by the NEA in 1989 obscured the fact that *Piss Christ* is part of Serrano's ongoing exploration of the spiritual dimensions of base matter. Over the years he has explored this theme through a succession of photographic series that lets him frame overtly allegorical works using animal parts and costumed models to a set of more abstract "immersion" works of which *Piss Christ* is one. In these works symbolic objects have been photographed through various body fluids. The fluid photographs were followed in 1990 by portraits of such diverse groups as New York homeless people, Ku Klux Klansmen and members of the Catholic clergy.

Serrano's *Morgue Series* consists of photographs taken in an undisclosed morgue of bodies awaiting autopsies or removal to funeral homes. Many had come to the morgue as a result of violent and unexpected deaths. Serrano noted this in titles like *The Morgue (Rat Poison Suicide)*, *The Morgue (Knifed to Death)* and *The Morgue (Death by Drowning)*. These wrenching titles provided a disturbing counterpart to the ravishing beauty of the images themselves. Using dramatic lighting, zeroing in on telling details and carefully cropping out identifying characteristics, he maintained the corpses' anonymity. Losing their specificity, they were transformed into studies reminiscent of Renaissance religious themes like the Nativity or the Deposition of Christ. *The Morgue (Fatal Meningitis II)* presents the head of a child whose lower features are covered with a white cloth, bringing to mind traditional depictions of the swaddled Christ Child. *The Morgue (Knifed to Death I and II)* is a diptych of a pair of hands, fingers blackened with ink for fingerprinting and wrists punctured with the coroner's scalpel. Serrano presents the outstretched hands so that they face each other, echoing the touch of God and man in the Creation panel of Michelangelo's Sistine Chapel. Another work *The Morgue (Rat Poison Suicide)* focuses on the stiffened arms of a woman who died of ingesting rat poison. Her arms are raised in a defensive gesture as if, in the artist's words, "she is fighting off demons."[136]

Thus, despite the often-grisly circumstances of death, Serrano invests these images with a luminous beauty that reminds us that in the Christian tradition, death is simply a threshold between two states of being. Like Condon, he presents them redeemed by beauty. Serrano has said of this series, "I never saw the bodies as cadavers or corpses. I called them my models, my subjects. I was interested in the way they still had a human presence, that something of their soul was intact."[137]

The *Morgue Series* is an extension of Serrano's preoccupation with beauty as a manifestation of the divine on earth. As he once noted, "You can't have the sacred without the profane . . . What is wrong is to make something that isn't beautiful."[138] What makes his work both provocative and profound is the way he creates this beauty from raw materials that are conventionally considered disgusting or sordid. Dead bodies certainly fall under that rubric. So do body fluids like blood, milk, semen, and urine that form the basis of the *Immersion* series to which the much-maligned *Piss Christ* belongs.

In Chapter 3, we noted how body fluids play an important role in Catholicism's incarnational consciousness. The blood of Christ that flows from his battered body during the Crucifixion is physical evidence that he has carried out his act of sacrificial redemption. Mary's milk is not only the human substance that sustains the infant Jesus, but it serves in religious art as a symbol of the sustaining power of God's grace.

In similar fashion, Serrano's body fluids operate on multiple levels. On one hand, they provided him with a unique artistic material. In the beginning, he photographed the fluids themselves after confining them into symbolically shaped containers. One of the first of this series is *Blood Cross* in which the red liquid is seeping through the corners of an imperfectly made plexiglass form, while another resembles a Malevich painting composed of flat squares of red blood and white milk. He discovered that the fluids provided a striking palette: blood created a flat crimson ground, while milk suggested a white, undefiled purity.

He originally began to employ urine because of the radiant amber glow that resulted when it was lit from behind.

These works were followed by a series that involved photographing symbolic objects, typically religious or classical statuettes, through films of various fluids. He also began to blend liquids in more abstract ways, in the process discovering that blood mixes with blood while urine and blood stay separate. He added other liquids. When he immersed a black statuette of Leonardo's *Last Supper* in sparkling water tiny light filled bubbles attached to the figures like encrusted jewels or barnacles. For his *Ejaculation Series*, Serrano shot streams of semen across a dark background, creating a torquing form that has something of the purity and motion of Brancusi's *Bird in Space*. As recounted in Chapter 1, while *Piss Christ* was the work that landed him in trouble with America's religious right, the ejaculation photographs were the works that gave the official Catholic Church pause, due to concerns about the "unnecessary spilling of seed."[139]

But if the fluids made for a beautiful, and at times even ethereal light, they also comprise, as he put it, "life's vital fluids."[140] In this their employment served as a deliberate effort to subvert contemporary society's denial of the body's physicality. *Piss Christ*, which was read literally by its critics to mean "piss on Christ," was actually a celebration of the human body. The yellow-orange radiance that surrounds the cheap dime store crucifix is made possible by the medium of urine through which it has been photographed. As a result, the work redeems this socially unacceptable substance. Serrano told interviewer Derek Guthrie, "I've completely aestheticized this very base material and in my pictures, piss is not something repugnant, its something very beautiful, it's a beautiful glowing light."[141] He added, "It's waste, and I think it's seen as something repugnant, but I think this aversion to piss probably has more to do with the aversion we have to our own bodies..."

The elevation of the lowly is a recurrent theme in Serrano's work. Following the fluid works, he created the *Nomads*, a series based on hard-core homeless individuals in New York. Using a portable studio, he photographed street dwellers in heroic poses that recall Edward Curtis's 19th century photographs of the vanishing American Indians. Simultaneously with these works, he created the *Klan Series* in which he photographed leaders of the Georgia Ku Klux Klan in their robes. It was a paradoxical project, since Serrano is Hispanic, thus representing an ethnic group officially denounced by the Klan. In fact, in gaining the confidence of figures with imposing titles like Imperial Wizard and Grand Kaliff, he discovered they were often desperately poor individuals, whose extreme prejudice stemmed from their desperation. His images of them, like those of the homeless, are strangely sympathetic. Rims of troubled eyes peer from the stitched holes in their coarse homemade robes and hoods.

In such works, Serrano rediscovers the humanity of the dispossessed and despised. In this he recalls Christ's willingness to associate with beggars, tax collectors and adulterers, the most detested classes of his time. But the transforming beauty of the *Klan* and *Nomad* photographs, like that of his *Morgue* and *Fluid* works, converges as well with Catholic emphasis on transformation, transfiguration and transubstantiation. As the mortal body is glorified at the end of time, the simple substances of bread and wine changed into the body and blood of Christ in the Catholic mass, so Serrano takes raw materials normally considered vile, be they urine, corpses, homeless people, or Klansmen, consecrates and ennobles them by the beauty of art. As a result, his works have an almost sacramental quality.

Serrano's preoccupation with these kinds of transmutations is rooted in his personal history. Born to an African Cuban mother and a Honduran father who abandoned the family soon after his birth, he grew up in Williamsburg, Brooklyn. Raised Catholic, he initially rejected his faith as a young man, lured by the seductions of the street. After a bout as a drug addict, he "found" himself through art. In 1993 he told an interviewer, "I am drawn to subjects that border on the unacceptable, because I lived an unacceptable life for so long."[142]

He studied photography at the Brooklyn Museum School and began to photograph tableaux that drew on Catholicism, surrealism and dada. He told critic Lucy Lippard, "I just felt like I wanted to take the pictures in my head, and I started to do setups with raw meat. I felt the connection to death, and the meat images were living and dead at the same time. I'd been doing religious pictures for two or three years before I realized I had done a lot of religious pictures!"[143]

Serrano remains disturbed about official policies of the Catholic Church, particularly with respect to the status of women and its failure to carry out its mission to aid the poor and oppressed. Nevertheless he remains deeply attached to the spirituality inculcated during his childhood. He told interviewer Marcia Tucker, "There's a lot of irony in my work, but it's not sacrilegious. I've always thought that you feel God inside you; I have no problem with God: my issue is with the Church, with the dogma and confusion, a perversion of the actual teaching, that seems to have failed Christianity." [144]

Serrano's focus on degradation echoes that of Joel Peter Witkin, another artist with a conflicted personal history. However while Serrano deals with "subjects that border on the unacceptable," Witkin exalts and beautifies them. He traffics in images of the dead and the dispossessed, but his approach is quite different. In Witkin's photographs, dead bodies are clearly, often gruesomely dead, their exposed entrails visible, their limbs bloated or stiffened in rigor mortis, their skulls cracked and limbs severed. In one image, a decapitated cadaver sits on a chair. In another a decaying head of an old man has been sliced and rearranged so that his profiles fuse and join lips in a gesture that recalls Brancusi's *Kiss*. In yet a third, a massive masked nude woman lies in a pose reminiscent of Caravaggio's *Bacchus* grasping three preserved fetuses.

While Witkin's most notorious photographs use dead bodies or body parts, he does not limit himself to that subject. An ad placed at the end of one of his books contains a plea for models which solicits, among others: "pinheads, dwarfs, giants, hunchbacks, pre-op transsexuals, bearded women... twins joined at the foreheads, anyone with a parasitic twin, people with tails, horns, wings, fins, claws, reversed feet or hands, elephantine limbs . . . Anyone born without arms, legs, eyes, breasts, genitals, ears, nose, lips. All people with unusually large genitals... hermaphrodites and teratoids (alive and dead). A young blonde girl with two faces. Any living myth. Anyone bearing the wounds of Christ." [145]

These models become elements in carefully constructed photographic tableaux that inhabit a bizarre territory that is part Bosch, part Coney Island. They include still lifes which mingle organic produce and body parts, 'freak show' imagery (in one, a man's testicles are stretched by a device attached to a pulley which threatens to drop a heavy weight on his face; in another a pair of masked twins conjoined at the head gently cradle a dove and a bouquet of flowers), and demented restaging of famous paintings. In Witkin's works hermaphrodites pose as classical gods and goddesses, people with deformed limbs are outfitted with wings to play the role of angels, and severed heads are served up on platters a la John the Baptist.

Curiously, given the potentially inflammatory nature of his photographs, Witkin has never been the subject of a full-fledged controversy despite having received NEA grants and major museum exhibitions. The closest he has come to Serrano or Mapplethorpe type dustup came in 1993 when NEA foes featured his print of the testicle-stretching figure in some anti NEA literature. It is possible that his work has evaded right wing scrutiny because his photographic technique makes it difficult to discern how much is real and how much the result of postproduction manipulation. Witkin always photographs in black and white, and often scratches his negatives and then prints them through tissue paper to slightly blur details. He completes them by mounting them on aluminum, applying pigments and covering the whole with polished beeswax. The photographs that result have a faded daguerreotype quality whose illusion of temporal distance helps aestheticize their admittedly shocking subject matter.

Although evangelist Pat Robertson has denounced him as a Satanist, Witkin himself declares that he is a practicing Catholic. At a conference I attended in Arizona, he noted that he sees his work as a sacred act. He prays over his subjects, dead and alive, before he photographs them.[146] Some commentators have seen this confession of faith as a cynical effort to cultivate a perverse public persona, but his history suggests a genuine spiritual search.

He and his brother Jerome (himself a painter of the bizarre and grotesque) are identical twins, and were born after their mother miscarried a third child who would have been their triplet. Their mother was a Roman Catholic and their father an Orthodox Jew. The parents separated when the boys were three; they were raised by their mother and grandmother. In a dramatic and perhaps somewhat overheated account of his life written for his masters thesis at the University of New Mexico in Albuquerque, Witkin reports that his first memory is of witnessing a three car accident during which a little girl's severed head rolled by his feet. Witkin offers this story as the genesis of his artistic career. "Out of it I see many roots extending to my visual work in my use of severed heads, masks and my concern with violence, pain and death."[147] (A reporter for *Vanity Fair* checked out the story with Witkin's mother and reports that while there was a bad accident in which a girl was killed, no one else remembers a rolling head).[148]

Witkin's unusual preoccupations manifested themselves in other ways. He recounts a youthful visit to photograph *The Rabbi who Saw God*. However, instead of an instrument of the divine, he found "a tired, sleeping old man sitting in a corner of a large dusty study."[149] But despite this disappointment, he notes, he still believed "that the sight of God would give life reality and purpose." This autobiography is full of feverish tales of Witkin's spiritual struggles. Witkin notes that he spent three years working as a combat photographer documenting "forms of death," explaining that an early series entitled *Contemporary Images of Christ* was an attempt to "bring God down to earth."[150]

By the time he completed graduate school at University of New Mexico at age 37, Witkin was already well on his way to his current aesthetic. He concluded his thesis by remarking, "I agreed to photograph my potential models only after they understood that in my images I would deny, as I always have denied, the individual character and reality of models. There were the visual symbols of my thoughts."[151]

The willingness of individuals who are deformed, maimed, or suffering from obscure illnesses to serve as Witkin's models probably stems from this realization. Witkin uses them essentially as props in narratives that obsessively return to the notion of thresholds. He focuses on individuals and scenes that represent border states: hermaphrodites, transsexuals, cadavers (many obtained from morgues in Mexico where permission requirements are less stringent), twins, people with AIDS, the blind or the masked, pregnant women and others who inhabit multiple states. His scenarios are equally hybrid. He frequently represents angels as agents of intercourse between earth and heaven, or sets up interactions between animals and humans, the living and the dead, the sacred and the profane.

In this context, death remains the ultimate border. He has remarked, "I wanted my photographs to be as powerful as the last thing a person sees or remembers before death."[152] Witkin's still lifes in particular take the logic of the 'memento mori,' with its stark reminder of the presence of death in life, to its logical extreme. In his *Feast of Fools*, a dead baby and several severed feet and hands coexist with grapes, shellfish and pomegranates. In *The Result of War: Cornucopian Dog* a cornucopia of fruits and vegetables spill from the chest cavity of a dead dog. In an often shockingly graphic manner (but perhaps no more explicit than the medieval 'Transi' sculptures of worm infested corpses), such works thrust our mortality back into view.

Is Witkin, as some have charged, just a pervert taking cover under art and religion? He emphatically denies this. He told Aperture magazine, "I want to be remembered as an American Christian artist. I think of myself as a devout Catholic." He added, "They say that the saints need to go back into the darkness to bring the darkness to the light and back again. I'm no saint but I try to do the same thing in my work."[153]

Witkin's own rhetoric tends to obscure an important aspect of his work: its humor. Witkin reports that photo sessions with live models are full of jokes and buffoonery.[154] If one can get beyond the grisly details, his photographs are marked by an absurdist sensibility that comes close to a quality described by literary critic Mikhail Bakhtin as the "carnivalesque." Taking his cue from the folk culture of the medieval carnival, Bakhtin posited the notion of a subversive humor in which all hierarchies and official orders are temporarily suspended. In their place, he maintained, was a liberating chaos in which different spheres were fused, normally hidden sexual and scatological body functions like farting, defecation, and copulation were put on public display and death became a joke instead of a threat. This, he declared, was "carnivalesque."[155]

Critic Wayne Booth summarizes Bakhtin's influential idea thus: "Carnival laughter, the intrusion of everything forbidden or slanderous or joyfully blasphemous into the purified domains of officialdom, expressed a complex sense that the material body was not unequivocally base: every death contains within it the meaning of rebirth, every birth comes from the same region of the body as does the excremental. And the excremental is itself a source of regeneration: it manures life... References to the lower body were... used to produce a regenerative, an affirmative, a healing... finally a politically progressive laughter."[156]

In Bakhtin's view, this emancipating frivolity has largely disappeared from an overly atomized and individualistic society. He remarks, "It must be recalled that the image of death in medieval and Renaissance grotesque (and in painting, also in Holbein's or Durer's *Dance of Death*) is a more or less funny monstrosity. In the ages that followed, especially in the nineteenth century, the public at large almost completely forgot the principle of laughter presented in macabre images."[157]

From this perspective, Witkin can be seen as a purveyor of a kind of transformative laughter that subverts boundaries in order to bring us back to our essential humanness. This playful attitude toward death remains visible today in the Mexican celebration of the Day of the Dead and in the idea of Halloween, its Anglo counterpart. While Halloween has largely become a means of acting out fantasies, the Day of the Dead remains tied to the idea of the dead among us. It is an occasion for festive interaction between the living and dead, marked by the preparation of meals for the dead, the exchange of special foods like sugar skulls, chocolate skeletons, and special Bread of the Dead which is ornamented with bone motifs, and in some locations processions in which townspeople dress up as ghouls and carry an open coffin with a smiling "corpse" within.

The raucous embrace of death represented by the Day of the Dead points to an important aspect of contemporary Catholic flirtations with the macabre. This fixation tends to persist most powerfully in Latin versions of Catholicism, which were shaped by the meeting of the medieval Catholic morbidity of the Spanish conquerors with the death cults of the Aztecs and other indigenous American peoples. In some cases, the fusion of the two consciousnesses was quite deliberate, as when Spanish priests moved the Aztec celebration of Miccailhuitontli, dedicated to the goddess Mictecacihuatl ("Lady of the Dead"), to the first two days of November so that they coincided with the Catholic observance of the All Saints and All Souls Day. (These latter were the days the faithful honored the saints who had been accepted into heaven and prayed for the souls of those still waiting release from purgatory).

Such religious fusions reinforced tendencies toward the embrace of death that, as Aries points out, were beginning to wane even among Roman Catholics in post-reformation Europe. The blending of pre and post Colonial religion remains powerful in the culture of Mexico and Latin America to this day, finding manifestation in the merging of Aztec goddess Tonantzintla with the Virgin Mary in the figure of the Virgin of Guadalupe (see next chapter) and the incorporation of undercurrents of the Aztec ritual of human sacrifice with the sacrificial death of Christ on the Cross. From this perspective, as Shifra Goldman points out, the playful skeletons of the Day of the Dead have antecedents in the pre-Columbian belief in the duality of life and death.[158] Another sign of this convergence is the popularity of the folk cult of the Sacred

Heart, which involves the adoration of Christ's pierced and bleeding heart, while pointing back to the culminating moment in Aztec sacrifice when the victim's still pulsing heart was lifted to the gods.[159]

Thus, it should come as no surprise to realize that many of the contemporary artists most deeply involved in the imagery of death have Latin roots or connections. Serrano comes from a mixed Afro-Cuban and Honduran background. He is somewhat ambivalent about his Hispanic identity, happy to embrace it, but unwilling to be pigeonholed as a Hispanic artist. He describes his obsession with religious imagery thus, "It's a Latino thing, but it's also a European thing."[160]

Witkin is not ethnically Latin. However his long residence in New Mexico, where the Hispanic influence is particularly acute, has clearly reinforced his natural penchant for the morbid. Some of his works make explicit reference to this influence. For example, his photograph "Penitente, New Mexico", depicts a masked, body pierced and hand-less nude figure on a cross, flanked by a pair of crucified dead rhesus monkeys. The work's title makes reference to the Penitente Brotherhood, a survival of a medieval Catholic cult which still endures in New Mexico and whose observances include self-flagellation and a reenactment of the Crucifixion each Good Friday.

Witkin's embrace of the more macabre aspects of Hispanic culture takes place in the context of his private search for God. However, Michael Tracy, another Anglo who has immersed himself in the Latin cult of the dead, does so, at least in part, in the service of a political agenda.

Tracy received a fairly conventional Catholic education. He was an Irish Catholic altar boy in Cleveland, Ohio. He attended Saint Edwards University, a Catholic college in Austin, Texas. It wasn't until he entered the graduate art program at the University of Texas in Austin that his future interests began to manifest themselves. Critic Thomas McEvilley reports in the catalogue of his first major retrospective that during his time there he was production designer for a play written by a friend that focused on the ninth century Pope Formosis, who was brutally murdered by his bishops for making overtures to the Eastern Church. Tracy created a sanctuary like set with a ziggurat stage. The inherent violence of the story was accentuated by the costumes of the actors, who were bound in sheets of foam rubber covered with liturgical symbols.[161]

After graduation, Tracy traveled throughout Europe, Egypt and Greece before resettling in Texas. In 1978 after a number of trips to Mexico he landed in San Ygnacio, Texas, a dusty border town that is the only place this side of the Rio Grande where penitents relive the Passion of Christ every Good Friday. Tracy has lived in San Ygnacio ever since, immersed in a culture where remnants of Spanish colonialism mingle freely with elements of pre Columbian consciousness. In the process, he has evolved a unique body of work in which references to Crucifixion, blood ritual and sacrifice take on a second meaning as reminders of the political atrocities enacted against the populations of Mexico and Latin America in both the colonial and contemporary eras. He has declared, rather histrionically, "Mexico is the cross I want to be, am nailed upon. It is the final result of my life."[162]

To this end, Tracy has employed performance, installation and sculpture. These works mingle materials that signify the excess of baroque religious art: gold leaf, bronze and wood with organic matter, flowers, hair and body fluids like blood, semen and urine. He creates paintings encrusted with gold leaf and dried blood and constructs crosses and icons pierced with bronze spikes, knives, bones and shards of glass. At times his works evoke holy relics, their bits of human matter bearing witness to the never-ending saga of human suffering. Over the years he has orchestrated several elaborate quasi-religious ceremonies, one of which culminated in the ritual murder of one of his most important paintings by stabbing and immolation.

In such works, the cross and the canvas serve as surrogates for the broken and martyred human body. Often they have specific political subtexts. For example *Cruz to Oscar Romero, Martyr of El Salvador* (1981-82), is homage to Archbishop Romero, a Salvadoran cleric who was gunned down by Salvadoran right wing death squads as he celebrated mass in a hospice for cancer patients. The work consists of a huge processional cross, embedded with bull's horns. Its carrying handles have been wrapped with a fabric that calls to mind Bishop's robes. Flowers are scattered at the bottom of the cross along with two photographs, one of Romero and the other of Alexander Haig, then U. S. Secretary of State and architect of America's destructive policy toward El Salvador. Ironically, Haig is pictured as he receives communion.

Thus, this work seamlessly mingles ecclesiastical and political symbols, infusing it with the ethos of "liberation theology" a Roman

Catholic movement that pursues liberation of the poor through social action in the Third World. A statement accompanying the piece makes this connection explicit. Tracy notes, "This work was dedicated to my brothers and sisters in Central America as they entered the horror of the eighties. Experiencing the daily madness of terror and the insane waste of war. What happened to them as their heads were cut off, their feet beaten and their bones smashed was also mystically happening to all of us. Our government supported and quietly supports today the cause of their dark and constant pain."[163]

The statement ends with a note of exalted rhetoric, "Baptism by blood then, by fire by bullets. A sacramental death, Holy Life! A life of suffering… to find the body and blood of Christ ineffably and ironically is our body and our blood."[164]

Tracy has frequently returned to this identification of religious and political violence. In a sculptural triptych entitled *Triptico Para Los Desparecidos (Triptych for the Disappeared Ones)* from 1982-83, he pays homage to the thousands of victims of El Salvador's death squads. Here the three panels are riddled with knives, swords and a machete, as well as surrogate torture devices like knitting needles and shards of broken glass.

At Artspace in San Francisco he created *Santuarios* (1989), remaking the gallery into a chapel dedicated to both the recent war dead of Nicaragua and El Salvador and the continuing plight of Mexican 'mojados' or wetbacks who die in their efforts to cross the border into the United States. In this work, a selection of ritual objects, cruciform assemblages, blood encrusted shrines and paintings, were set off against gridded wooden chairs and partitions meant to evoke the confessional. During the run of the exhibition, Mass was held twice in this space, once for the local community and once to pray for the victims of AIDS.

But perhaps Tracy's most spectacular sacrificial ritual took place on the Rio Grande River outside San Ygnacio on Good Friday, 1990. This is the day that the town's populace traditionally restages the Stations of the Cross, the path taken by the bloodied Jesus Christ on his way to his Crucifixion. Tracy's *The River Pierce: Sacrifice II, 13.4.90* also took the form of a Stations of the Cross procession, but the object to be sacrificed was one of his largest sculptural crosses, a ten foot high accretion of horns, 'milagros,' crosses, mud and flowers. Carried on a horse drawn cart and accompanied by a train of invited clergy, artists and select townspeople, it was carried to the edge of the river, set afire and pushed by the wind to the Mexican side of the river.

Tracy dedicated this ritual to the River Grande itself, which he sees as a victim of the environmental indifference of the Mexican and American governments. The work also celebrates the River as the lifeline that connects two countries across a difficult and contested border. The sacrifice of this cross, like the sacrifice of Christ, was offered up for the redemption of an entity that seemed otherwise condemned to death.

In a book chronicling this performance, Tracy wrote, "I'm not interested in the same old Catholic line of do it for Jesus, the Madonna or Love. Not just do it. I don't expect resurrection, ultimate union with God. I'll take my chances with a god from here - or forgiveness. I like the social aspect. The popular conscience of human injustice. But really I guess I've always felt more Roman. I rather like the idea - none of us is getting out of this alive. So we better make the best of it."[165]

Over the years, Tracy's works have often taken the qualities of shrines and memorials. Their explicit references to blood, broken bones and instruments of torture evoke traditional rituals for the veneration of Christ and the martyrs who died for the faith. But they also turn our attention to the continuing horrors of social injustice. Thus the Catholic language of death becomes a means to espouse a politics of life.

Catholic morbidity takes on a female coloration in the work of Ana Mendieta. In what became a cause célèbre, dividing the art world into hostile camps, Mendieta died at age thirty-six when she plunged from a window in her Soho loft after an altercation with her husband, the well-known minimalist sculptor Carl Andre. At issue was whether she was pushed or fell, a controversy that did not die down even after Andre was acquitted of her murder after a highly publicized trial.

Many saw an irony in Mendieta's early death. A Cuban-American, her work involved symbolic burials and blood based rituals, which she herself maintained were at least partially inspired by the Afro-Cuban religion of Santeria. Santeria fuses the African religions of the slaves imported to the Americas with elements of Catholicism (some of them adopted as a kind of camouflage behind which adherents could continue to practice forbidden rituals). It is an animistic religion, based on a principle of universal energy. Adherents follow such traditional practices as sacred drumming and dance, trance possession as a means to communicate with the ancestors and deities, and animal sacrifice.

Today Santeria claims many adherents of Hispanic and Caribbean descent who also count themselves as Catholics.

Mendieta was exposed to Santeria during her childhood in Cuba. (Her sister recalls that, while her parents looked down on Santeria as superstition, the two girls learned about it from the family's servants). However, it did not become important to Mendieta until much later, when as an adult she began to confront the enormous chasm that divided her childhood in Cuba from her later adulthood. The chasm opened up when, at age thirteen, Mendieta and her sister Raquelin were sent to Iowa without their parents as part of Pedro Pan Operation. This program, initiated by the Cuban Catholic Church, was designed to preserve the Catholicism of young Cubans in the wake of the Communist Revolution. Mendieta was not to return to Cuba for twenty years, by which time she had become an established artist.

Mendieta's art education, which took place in the years 1969-1973 at the University of Iowa, introduced her to the American art world at a moment of tremendous ferment. Among the artists who visited the department during her time there were such heavyweights as Vito Acconci, Carolee Schneemann, Bruce Nauman, Hans Haacke and Robert Smithson. From them she imbibed the avant-garde gospel of the time, with its emphasis on rejection of the object, viewer interaction and subversion of all forms of authority. Her early performances have elements that echo the experimental body art being practiced by many artists of the day. She transferred mustache hair from a male friend to her face, distorted her features by smashing her face into a nylon stocking, and pressed her naked body against a pane of glass.

Such works made it clear that Mendieta was interested in gender issues at this early stage. But she also began to employ more shocking elements of blood and bone that pointed back to her ethnic and religious roots. In a performance entitled *Sweating Blood* she was filmed with her eyes closed as blood trickled down her face. In *Blood Writing* she pushed herself against a wall and slowly sank down, leaving a blood trail as her hands drag against the surface. In an untitled performance from 1972, a naked Mendieta embraced a skeleton, breathing life into its mouth and covering it with her body in a movement that was at once sexual and protective. In *Death of a Chicken* (1972), she made explicit reference to Santeria, as she stood naked holding a beheaded chicken as its blood spurted over her body.

Such works suggest that Mendieta was seeking a way to reconnect with a heritage from which she had been forcibly separated. Looking back on her student days, she later told Judith Wilson, "I started thinking I would have to act it out and work from my own experiences, my own sources, I started immediately using blood. I guess because I think it's a very powerful, magical thing. I don't see it as a negative source." [166]

Given the enormity of the breech in her life, it seems safe to say that Mendieta's 'Cubanisima' was as much constructed as discovered. A great deal has been written about her work as a manifestation of the trauma of exile. But for our purposes, the interesting thing is how this longing brought her back to themes of death and resurrection. In a posthumously published interview, she told Linda Montano, "I don't think you can separate Death and Life. All my work is about these two things, about Eros and Life/Death." [167]

Mendieta is best known for a series of works entitled *Siluetas* (Spanish for silhouette). In these works, which exist today only as photographs or films, she pressed her body onto the landscape and marked the shape with a variety of symbolic and evocative materials. The first work in this series was executed in a Zapota tomb in Oaxaca (Zapotas were a Mesoamerican people who resisted the Aztecs). For this work she climbed naked into the shallow rock cavity and covered her body with long stems and white flowers. The photograph that records this work is hauntingly beautiful. Her body seems literally in the process of disintegrating into a cloud of white and green foliage.

The presence of a physical body is unusual in this series. More commonly, the *Siluetas* present the female form as a void, cut into earth or sand and filled with moss, water, flowers, blood or mounds of rocks. One, entitled "Anima" and recorded in a short film, consists of a female outline formed of ignited fireworks, which gradually burn out, leaving nothing but ashes. The *Siluetas* are canny celebrations of death and rebirth. The figural cavity is at once a womb and a grave, and the elements that fill it become surrogate souls whose natural processes point to the cycle of decay and rebirth.

Mendieta followed the *Siluetas* with a related series, the *Fetishes*. These consisted of bodies molded from earth and penetrated in various more or less violent ways. The *Fetishes* were marked with blood, branded with an iron, or pierced with sticks. Thus, their implied anger at female victimization suggests a more overt feminism than is found in the *Siluetas*.

One of Mendieta's last series of works, the *Rupestrian Sculptures*, marked her return to Cuba after twenty years. For these works, she carved relief forms that suggested primitive fertility figures into the wall of a cave in Cuba. These works were influenced by her self-conscious identification with the pre-Columbian peoples displaced and destroyed by the Spanish conquerors.

Art historian Miwon Kim has pointed out that Mendieta's use of her body almost always involved some form of erasure or negation.[168] Though her body was the initial reference, it constantly disappeared, to be replaced by a surrogate of earth, fire, rock or flora. Thus, in marked contrast to the death related work of Serrano, Witkin and Tracy, her works are as imbued with a sense that rebirth is inseparable from death. She was fond of a quote by Octavio Paz that appears in one of her artist statements. It says, "Our cult of death is also a cult of life in the same way that love is a hunger for life and a longing for death. Our fondness for self-destruction derives not from our masochistic tendencies but also from a certain variety of religious emotion."[169]

Unlike Serrano, Witkin and Tracy, Mendieta internalized death, using her own body to evoke its constant presence in our lives. In the process, she gives the idea of death and resurrection a decidedly female spin. Mother Earth is both our origin and our destination. The blood of birth and the blood of death commingle, placing us in a never-ending cycle of dissolution and regeneration. In the process death loses its horror and menace, and becomes instead, as Stevens suggests, the lair "in whose bosom we devise/ our earthly mothers waiting, sleeplessly."

Mendieta's tendency to internalize Catholicism's psychic truths is a quality that recurs continuously in the work of women artists from Catholic backgrounds. As we shall see in the next chapter, this gives a very different inflection to works that reflect a female view of the incarnational consciousness.

* * *

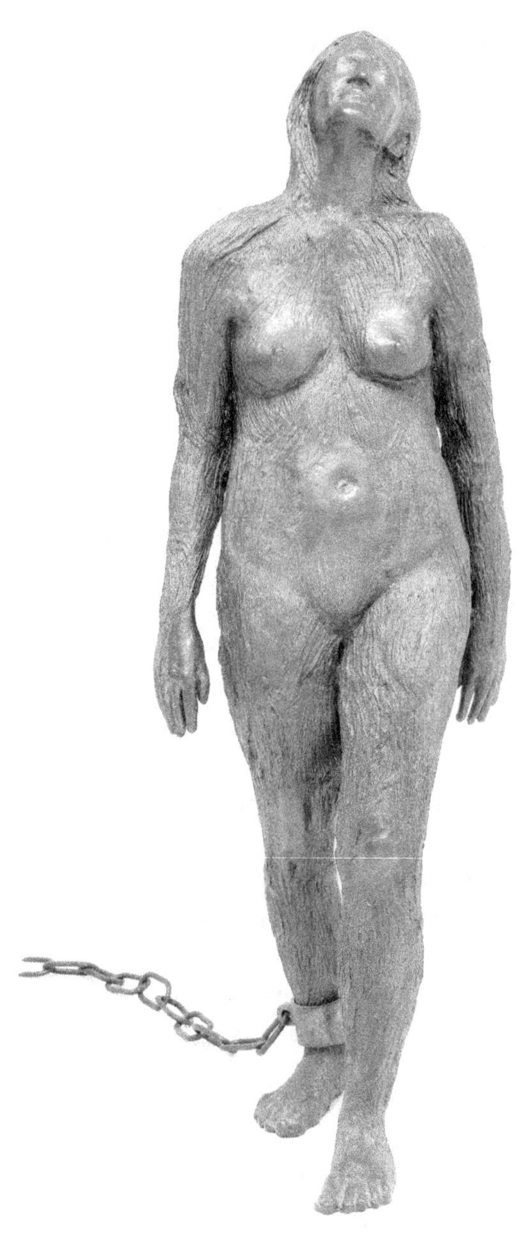

Kiki Smith, *Mary Magdalene*, 1994

© Kiki Smith, courtesy Pace Gallery

CHAPTER 6

KNOWLEDGE THROUGH THE BODY: THE FEMALE PERSPECTIVE

Interviewer:

Isn't it true that growing up Catholic you're cursed with the view of women either as virgins or whores?

Madonna:

I was certainly aware of it, but I couldn't understand why you couldn't be both.[170]

Mariology - the veneration of the Virgin Mary - is one of the points of doctrine that most clearly separates Protestants and Catholics. While Protestants tend to downplay Mary's role, seeing her simply as an exemplary woman, for Catholics she performs multiple functions. She is the embodiment of perfect motherhood, the compassionate intermediary with God (Bernard of Clairvaux wrote: "If you fear the Father, go to the Son, if you fear the Son, go to the Mother"), Queen of heaven and hence bride of Christ (a pair of functions which would seem to be in conflict with her role as Christ's mother), champion of the oppressed, protector of the church and worker of miracles. She is revered in the latter capacity by Pope John Paul II who credits her with thwarting the attempt on his life in 1981 which, it turns out took place on the anniversary of her appearance to a group of Portuguese children in Fatima in 1917.

But if Mary is the ultimate heroine to some, for others she is a symbol of the Catholic Church's archaic attitude toward women. A crucial part of her persona is her purity. This manifests itself in her lifelong virginity and her Immaculate Conception, the miraculous circumstance by which she was born without the stain of sin that infects the soul of all other humans born since the original transgression of Adam and Eve. By denying Mary a sexual nature, many modern commentators believe that the Catholic Church has seized upon a doctrinal justification for its refusal to deal honestly with female equality and human sexuality.

In her magisterial study of the evolution of the cult of the Virgin Mary, historian Marina Warner concludes that Mary has been transformed from a real woman who is barely mentioned in the Bible into a symbol of unattainable female perfection. This idea of perfection Warner notes is, "built on the equivalence between goodness, motherhood, purity, gentleness and submission."[171] Hardly a set of attributes likely to help the modern woman make her way in the male dominated world. Further, the myth is built on an irresolvable contradiction: Mary establishes motherhood as woman's highest destiny while valorizing the state of virginity that would prevent ordinary women from achieving that destiny. Thus, Warner concludes, "The Virgin Mary is not the innate archetype of female nature, the dream incarnate; she is the instrument of a dynamic argument from the Catholic Church about the structure of society, presented as a God-given code."[172]

Garry Wills takes similar aim at the doctrine of Mary's virginity, seeing in it the roots of what he believes are the Church's wrongheaded positions on contraception, female clergy and priestly celibacy. Like Warner, he argues that these doctrines have the effect of perpetuating women's inferior status within the Church. He quotes Catholic novelist Mary Gordon, "In my day, Mary was a stick to beat smart girls with. Her example was held up constantly, an example of silence, of subordination, of the pleasure of taking the back seat... For women like me, it was necessary to reject that image of Mary in order to hold onto the fragile hope of intellectual achievement, independence of identity, sexual fulfillment. Yet we were offered no alternative to this Marian image; hence we were denied a potent female image whose application was universal."[173]

Countering these voices are other commentators who argue that it's a mistake to reduce Mary to an argument for virginity. Seeking a more layered understanding of Mary, poet Kathleen Norris celebrates her symbolic status, "... if we insist too much on a literal Mary, encasing her too firmly in the dress of a first century peasant, we risk losing her as a living symbol."[174] She suggests we think of virginity more as a state of mind, a way of assenting to a new un-self centered identity. This idea reemerges in a surprising place, when the Virgin Mary's namesake, the Pop star Madonna, takes on the persona of a sexually experienced woman in her music video "Like a Virgin." Wearing a white wedding dress, she croons to her new lover, "You make me feel like a virgin, touched for the very first time."

Meanwhile, in other circles Mary has become a political symbol. In the guise of the Virgin of Guadalupe, she appeared near Mexico City as a woman of mixed race to a native Mexican peasant named Juan Diego in the sixteenth century. From then on she has come to stand for ethnic pride and postcolonial resistance. Mexican American writer Richard Rodriquez asserts, "The faith that Europe imposed in the sixteenth century was, by virtue of Guadalupe, embraced by the Indian. Catholicism has become an Indian religion. By the twenty-first century, the locus of the Catholic Church, by virtue of numbers, will be Latin America by which time Catholicism itself will have assumed the aspect of the Virgin of Guadalupe. Brown skin."[175]

Yet for others, she is the promise of infinite mercy. This Mary surfaces in the Beatles secular hymn *Let it Be*, where she offers balm to the troubled soul. Drawing its refrain from the words with which Mary accepted her awesome role, the song offers the consoling message, "When I find myself in times of trouble, Mother Mary comes to me, speaking words of wisdom, 'Let it be, Let it be.'"

In these contradictory readings, Mary serves as symbol of fecundity, an emblem of sterility, the embodiment of passivity, a standard bearer of resistance, as scourge of Catholic schoolgirls and font of infinite mother love. Her complex persona reflects Catholicism's tendency to absorb and incorporate aspects of the religions into whose regions it has been transplanted. Thus there are traces in Mary of the fertility goddesses of the Near East: Diana the Roman's Virgin goddess and the lunar deities who in ancient Greece controlled women's menstrual cycles, hence female fecundity. In more recent history the Virgin of Guadalupe's native antecedents are traced to the Aztec snake mother goddess Tonantzin. Meanwhile, the Afro Caribbean religions that developed with the conversion of African slaves in the New World melded Mary with Jemanja, goddess of the waters.

In yet another clash between official policy and incarnational consciousness, these undercurrents play against the Church doctrines that lay such stress on Mary's virginity and exclusion from Original Sin. Thus, while such Church teachings have historically contributed to Western culture's devaluation of active female sexuality, justifying women's exclusion from full participation in the Catholic Church, the figure of Mary has also played an important role in feminizing the Church, softening the hard edges of divine justice. For many of us her role as Intercessor and Queen of Heaven, she offers a model of female strength and power.

The debate over Mary thus offers insight into Catholicism's ambiguous relationship to female sexuality. Perhaps nowhere do the contradictions become clearer than in Bernard of Clairvaux' twelfth century sermon on the *Song of Songs*, the Old Testament's paean to the beauties of married love. Historically, the *Song of Songs* has served as a metaphor, first for God's covenant with Israel, then for Christ's relationship to his Church. Bernard, the founder of the Cistercian Order, took an almost Calvinist position toward Church ornament and visual pomp. Yet in his sermons, Bernard revels in the unabashedly erotic imagery of this psalm, from which he constructs a complex argument about the nature of Christ's love for his Church.

In Bernard's schema, the bride of the verse stands both for the community of the faithful and for the individual soul. She also melds with the figure of the Virgin Mary who, assumed bodily into heaven, there embraced by Christ her son/bridegroom, prefigures the Church's future glory and the soul's promised union with Christ. In twelfth century coronation tableaux and mosaics inspired by Bernard's writings, Mary becomes a radiant young woman being crowned by Christ.

In Bernard's sermons, the bride is embraced by Christ the bridegroom whose kiss, symbol of the Holy Spirit, brings her a mystical understanding of God's love. The language is startlingly earthy to modern ears accustomed to more disembodied descriptions of Divine Love. Describing the bride's desire, he says, "And she asks him for a kiss? Is she drunk? Indeed she is! And perhaps then when she burst forth thus she had come out of the wine cellar."[176] The bridegroom, meanwhile, appears to the bride in various guises. As well as bridegroom, he is physician for the sick soul, travel companion, wealthy father and powerful king because the soul's desires are so various that, "it is essential that the taste of God's presence be varied too and that the infused flavor of Divine delight should titillate in manifold ways the palate of the soul that seeks him."[177]

Bernard defends this eroticized language in terms that echo Saint Augustine. He maintains, "The spiritual creature which we are has a body which is necessary to it and without which it cannot reach that knowledge which is the only way to knowledge the blessed have." But despite such imagery, Bernard is quick to clarify that the bride… "loves in a holy way, because she does not love in fleshly desire but in purity of spirit."[178]

This mixed message about the value of the body and sexuality (especially female sexuality) lies at the heart of the female version of the incarnational consciousness. The full-figured nursing Mary radiates physicality and heady sensuality. In her role as Queen of Heaven she is a commanding presence who is the object of Christ's desire. But she is also the eternal Virgin, whose physicality is compromised by her sexless conception and her special status as the only human after Adam and Eve born without sin.

The female Catholic imagination is further complicated by the prominent role in religious art and literature of the figure of Mary Magdalene who serves in many ways as the Virgin Mary's alter ego.

Mary Magdalene actually appears by name in the Bible only a few times. She is one of Christ's female followers who, "had been healed of evil spirits and infirmities." She is witness to the crucifixion and she is the first person to encounter the resurrected Christ. However, she has been conflated in popular tradition with an unnamed adulteress who was saved from stoning by Christ. Mary Magdalene sat with Mary of Bethany at Christ's feet to learn while her sister Martha went about her domestic chores. She was there with Martha witnessing their brother Lazarus' miraculous resurrection.

Thus has grown up the myth of Mary Magdalene as the repentant prostitute and assertive acolyte who in some versions of popular culture (for example Martin Scorsese's *Last Temptation of Christ* and the Nikos Kazantzakis novel which inspired it) is the unconsummated love interest of Jesus. She is also the author of one of the unofficial Gnostic gospels rediscovered after nearly 2000 years in 1945. In this gospel, Mary Magdalene receives private information from Jesus that she shares with his discouraged disciples in the dark days after his departure from earth.

Artistic representations of Mary Magdalene tend to stress her unfettered eroticism. While the Virgin Mary tends to be depicted fully dressed, except when she matter-of-factly offers her bare breast to her child, Mary Magdalene provided artists the opportunity to dwell on the charms of a fully sexual woman. Even after her conversion, she is depicted with the flowing hair with which she is said to have washed Christ's feet. Frequently her long hair is her only adornment. Even when she is clothed, her breasts and full figure are clearly visible beneath her garments. A rare and striking exception to this voluptuous version of the Magdalene is Donatello's bronze sculpture that depicts her after her self imposed thirty-year exile in the desert. Gaunt, wild eyed and draped with wild animal skins, she seems to have abandoned her civilized demeanor for the life of a wild beast.

In Catholic art, popular narratives and poetry, women's roles exist within a continuum suggested by Mary the Virgin Mother at one extreme and Mary Magdalene the redeemed seductress on the other. As might be expected, this creates a set of meanings for the female body in Catholicism that contrasts sharply with those attached to the male body. Medieval scholar Caroline Walker Bynum points out that male and female bodies play very different roles in medieval theology.

She cites the medieval mantra that, "spirit is to flesh as male is to female."[179] To modern ears this would seem to be a restatement of tired justifications for the inferiority of women in the Christian order. But, while acknowledging the long-standing tradition that associated women with lust, physical weakness and irrationality, Bynum argues that it would be a mistake to read the equating of woman and body too simply. She invokes the Incarnation to suggest that woman's association with the physical in the medieval world also gave her a privileged position.

Bynum argues, "Medieval men and women did not take the equation of woman with body merely as the basis for misogyny. They also extrapolated from it to an association of woman with the body or humanity of Christ. Indeed, they often went so far as to treat Christ's flesh as female, at least in certain of its salvific functions, especially its bleeding and nurturing. This fact helps us to understand why it was women more than men who imitated Christ bodily, especially in stigmata."[180] As evidence she cites the existence of gender bending images of a female Christ on the cross, the tendency of mystics and devotional writers to speak of Christ in female terms as mother and the association in texts and images of the blood shed in Christ's Passion with women's monthly bleeding.

Eschewing the separation of body and soul that is one of the legacies of the Reformation, medieval Christians saw them as an indivisible unity. Body was, from one perspective, a source of the temptations that lead to sin. But it was also, through its association with the body of Christ, the key to salvation and hence a means of access to the Divine. And as symbol of body, especially Christ's body, 'Woman' harbors humanity's potential for salvation.

The positive connotations of the female body in medieval theology resonate powerfully with contemporary feminism's emphasis on the idea of knowledge gained through the body. In the 1960s and 70s, feminist theorists drew on such diverse sources as psychoanalysis, literature, history and political theory to challenge the Western tradition's long-standing embrace of the mind/body split that formed the core of Cartesian rationalism. They noted that assumptions of female inferiority were grounded in the ancient association of women with nature and body and in the persona of Eve with sin. By contrast, male superiority drew on the connection of the male with culture, mind and spirit. Rather than deny this breakdown, many of the most vocal feminist art writers chose to turn it around, and celebrate the positive aspects of the female half of the equation.

Early feminist art theory is full of provocative ideas which range from the persuasive to the preposterous. Interest soared in goddess cults, prehistoric matriarchal societies, and all-female communities. Feminist critics called for the return of a body consciousness in art and decried "masculinist" notions of high culture that undervalued female-associated activities like craft, storytelling and decoration. Women artists acknowledged their uniquely female experiences, made art that incorporated elements like menstrual blood and placentas, stripped naked to celebrate their ownership of their own sexuality and explored motifs and media that had long been invisible in a male dominated art world.

As might be expected, however, feminists did not speak with a single voice. In fact, feminism has proved as contentious in its own way as Christianity. By the eighties it was marked by the emergence of an iconoclastic split which in some ways echoes the divisions created by the Reformation when it sundered the Christian world into Catholic and Protestant camps.

At issue were the meanings of gender and the political implications of the representation of the female body. While the so called 'essentialists' sought to establish the existence of a distinctive female nature grounded in women's unique relationship to her body, the 'deconstructionists' argued that gender was simply a social construct. The assertion of a unique female identity actually reinforces social conventions that contribute to societal convictions of female inferiority.

The fault lines were particularly clear over the issue of female representation. Essentialists encouraged the celebration of female sexuality through positive images of the female body created by female artists, while deconstructionists believed that the naked female body is inevitably subject to the male gaze, thus playing into the culture's objectification of women. On one side were artists like Hannah Wilke, who posed naked in flirtatious poses while cautioning her viewers to, "Beware of Feminist Fascism." On the other were artists like Barbara Kruger who emblazoned the warning "Your Body is a Battleground" over an image of a woman borrowed from a 1950s era magazine.

For women artists from Catholic backgrounds, feminist debates over the rhetorical meaning of the female body are complicated by Catholic tradition's ambiguous messages about female sexuality.

Working their way through these complexities, such artists exhibit a version of the Catholic Imagination that is distinctly female. The political and social uses of icons like the Virgin Mary and Mary Magdalene, theological debates over the meaning of Mary's virginity and purity and Catholicism's celebration of Mary's maternity, compassion and strength are all raw materials from which artists create personal visions of female identity and female sexuality. The internal contradictions evident in the Catholic version of femininity frequently serve as points of departure for profound and multi-layered works of art.

The divergence between male and female versions of the Catholic imagination is well illustrated by several recent art controversies that erupted over the artistic use of the image of the Virgin Mary. Two of the art works were created by male artists; two by female artists. Though the shape of the uproars themselves was discouragingly similar, the differences in the artists' approaches to their subject are highly instructive.

Chris Ofili's painting *The Holy Virgin Mary* came to national attention in 1999 when it was included in *Sensation*, an exhibition at the Brooklyn Museum that featured a group of young British artists from the collection of British art collector and advertising magnate Charles Saatchi. Ofili, an English born artist of Nigerian ancestry, represented the Virgin in a stylized and African manner employing vibrant layers of dots inspired by the artist's trip to the ancient caves of Zimbabwe. Adapting a motif he has used in other paintings with secular subjects, he attached several balls of a rhinestone studded black substance identified in the catalogue as elephant dung.

The show might have proceeded without official notice if the museum, hoping to boost attendance by capitalizing on the notoriety which some of these artists had achieved in England, had not mounted an advertising campaign which emphasized the potentially shocking nature of some of the works. Alas, the strategy backfired when New York Mayor Rudolph Giuliani, searching for an issue in his upcoming Senate campaign, was handed a copy of the catalogue. Noting that the Brooklyn Museum received a good portion of its operating funds from the City of New York, Giuliani decided to make a particular issue of *The Holy Virgin Mary*, which he derided as "sick stuff" designed to denigrate the Catholic Church.[181]

For several months, the city of New York was treated to a political sideshow as the Mayor threatened to close down the Museum if it refused to remove the offending painting. Spurred by the publicity, protesters (most of whom, like the Mayor, never actually set eyes on the work) appeared daily outside the Museum in a face off with the record numbers of visitors who came to see what the fuss was about. One visitor, a fervent Catholic no doubt, emboldened by the Mayor's attacks threw paint on the work. From then on it had to be protected by guards and a plexiglass screen. After a long and costly court battle, the city was ordered to restore the canceled funding and was restrained from further punishing the Museum financially at a later date.

There were a number of interesting things about this incident. First was the Mayor's decision to direct his outrage at the Ofili painting while passing over a number of other potentially offensive artworks. These included a bisected pig carcass encased in plastic, a cow's head being consumed by maggots and a graphic three dimensional reconstruction of one of the most gruesome images in Goya's etching series *The Disasters of War* which features the dismembered and decomposing corpses of three naked war victims hanging from a tree. If the Mayor was seeking specifically religious insults, he might also have fixated on a photographic tableau of the Last Supper by female artist Sam Taylor Wood that placed the naked artist in the central Christ position. (Interestingly, a year later a very similar work by a black woman artist became the centerpiece of the Mayor's renewed attack on the Brooklyn Museum).

It appears that Giuliani zeroed in on *The Holy Virgin Mary* because the painting offered him the opportunity to revisit the *Piss Christ* controversy that played so well during the right wing attack on the National Endowment for the Arts ten years earlier. Substituting dung for the offending urine of the earlier scenario, Giuliani was able to play on the American disgust for body fluids and excretory functions. Throughout the media, the work became known as "the Madonna splattered with dung". (An alternative description had her "smeared" instead.) In fact, the dung was confined to three discrete rhinestone dotted balls, two serving as props at the bottom of the painting and the third affixed like a breast to the Virgin's chest. The painting's defenders attempted without too much success to point out that Ofili was a practicing Catholic, that the dung, which he employed as well in other non religious works, was part of his interest in exploring his African heritage. By explanation, in many African countries dung, far from being a loathsome material, is a construction material and a symbol of fertility.

Equally interesting was the fact that Giuliani passed over what might have been expected to be the most offensive feature of the painting. Floating over the Virgin's blue robe and gold background in a manner that clearly referenced the ubiquitous putti of traditional Madonna paintings were small photographic images collaged on the canvas. On closer inspection, these were revealed to be representations of splayed buttocks cut from porn magazines. Perhaps Giuliani found excrement more offensive than pornography. More likely the catalogue reproduction on which he based his protests was too small for this detail to be clearly visible. Many commentators also detected a veiled racism in his rejection of a Madonna with black features, a charge bolstered by his objections a year later to Renee Cox's all black Last Supper.

Nevertheless, Ofili's addition of the pornographic putti moves his image beyond the celebration of fecundity that has become standard features of representations of the Virgin Mother. While there is nothing erotic about Ofili's Madonna, the floating buttocks make witty reference to the thorny question of her virginity and the nature of her possible sexual experiences.

Charges of desecration also lay behind the controversy that developed in 1997 over an untitled installation by sculptor Robert Gober. An American artist well known for his meticulous recreations of both ordinary domestic objects like sinks, cribs, chairs and urinals and of wittily distorted human body parts, Gober had never before overtly referred to his Catholic upbringing until he was commissioned to create an installation by the Museum of Contemporary Art in Los Angeles. Gober's original idea was to create a three-story house structure that would reflect upon the process of leaving home and developing an identity. Gradually this evolved into a shrine that incorporated a complex arrangement of symbolic objects that made reference to the religious concepts of heaven and earth. Paul Schimmel, the curator who oversaw this project, reports that Gober did not decide until nearly the last minute to include a six foot tall white Madonna whose mid section was pierced by an aluminum culvert pipe.[182]

This figure became the focus of controversy when representatives of the Los Angeles Roman Catholic Archdiocese and William Donohue's Catholic League read a favorable review of the show in a local newspaper. Sight unseen, they loudly denounced Gober's treatment of the Virgin Mary. In the media blitz that followed, she quickly became, "the Madonna impaled on a pipe," and the latest evidence of the art world's unrelenting hostility toward religion.[183]

In fact, the work was a complex and thoughtful meditation on the dualities at the heart of the Catholic religion, the meaning of redemption and the place of sensate experiences and the human body in our understanding of the Divine. Though not a practicing Catholic, Gober told an interviewer, "I have no problems with Catholicism in terms of faith, I just object to the way it's taught. I wanted to ventilate that and complicate that, in terms of life."[184]

Gober is a gay man whose work has often used objects associated with purification, disease and death to deal with the tragedy of AIDS. Here the idea of purification took on a religious overtone. There were two levels to the installation. Viewers entering the space found themselves in an austere, nearly empty room with light gray walls. The six-foot Virgin with the pipe dominated the room. On the floor on either side of her were a pair of open suitcases while at the far end of the room, one could make out a wooden staircase leading up and down to undisclosed locations. The sound of rushing water filled the room, and it was quickly evident that it was flowing down the wooden steps.

Approaching the Virgin, one realized that the pipe was set at eye level to provide a more focused view of the stairs cut into the back wall. The Virgin herself was placed over an open storm drain that afforded a view of a strikingly different environment beneath her feet. The rushing water here flowed over an Edenic tide pool populated by waving aquatic plants. Moving to the suitcases, which were also situated over drains, one glimpsed an even more surprising sight - a pair of legs, one belonging to a man, the other to an infant whom seemed on the verge of dipping into the water.

The work is rife with associations: the culvert pipe which pierces the Virgin's abdomen, replacing her womb, can be seen, as various commentators have pointed out, as a conduit for grace which, through the conception of her child, reconnects man to God. In this it recalls the symbolic figure used by Bernard of Clairvaux to compare the Virgin to an aqueduct that brings the grace of God coursing down through the city of the faithful. The water that pours down the stairs and into the subterranean grotto recalls the redemptive powers of Baptism, an association strengthened by the pair of legs that seem themselves in the process of rebirth through baptismal immersion. Suitcases, of course, are symbols of passage and transformation.

Meanwhile, the structure of the installation as a whole seems to offer a comment on alternative visions of heaven. The sterility of the upper room, evoking the white clapboard austerity of a Congregational church, contrasts with the underground world below where, in the sphere usually reserved for hell, Eden is reborn in all its luxuriant abundance. Playing with the dualism which permeates Christian thought, Gober takes what we might see as the very Catholic position that we have misplaced our emphasis on spirit over body and hence our sense of the source of God's redemptive power.

In these works, Gober and Ofili touch on the Virgin Mary's problematic role in Catholic doctrine. Ofili's putti make sly reference to official denials of Mary's sexual nature, while the placement of Gober's Virgin suggests that her purity need not be synonymous with sterility. Despite these doctrinal difficulties, each artist also celebrates the positive attributes that have made Mary an enduring symbol. For Ofili she is the fecund earth mother; for Gober she becomes the selfless intermediary between heaven and earth. But at the same time, both maintain a certain distance from the Virgin as a symbol. In neither case is there any question of the artists' identification with the Virgin. If anything, commentators have seen the two male figures in Gober's subterranean grotto as the artist's alter egos.

This is in striking contrast to the two works inspired by the Virgin Mary to which we now turn. Again, these works were the subject of controversies in which the artists were accused of desecrating Mary's image and fomenting anti-Catholicism. Again the artists were Catholics dealing with the complexities of Mary's role in the Church. However, a closer analysis suggests that there are marked differences in the way these artists, both women, approached their subject.

The first incident took place in late 1996 when Pennsylvania State University art student Christine Enedy provoked controversy with a pair of works exhibited on campus under the auspices of the art department. The first, which was her part of her senior project, was a grotto in the form of a red vagina lined with black fur and holding a statue of the Virgin Mary. Though it remained only briefly on view, the work sparked a controversy among local Catholics as to whether the

University ought to instate a policy against public desecration of religious symbols. The A.P. wire picked up discussions of the incident in the local paper where they came to the attention of the Catholic League's director William Donohue. Not content with reports that the artist herself after consultation with the campus chaplain had removed the work, Donohue sent out a missive asking the Catholic League's 250,000 members to write the University demanding that Christine Enedy be punished.

Enedy, a practicing Catholic, maintained in the numerous newspaper interviews that followed, "this work was in no way intended as a slur against Catholicism." She was quoted in the campus paper, "It was never an issue of me against the Catholic Church. I was just trying to portray an image of the oppression of women in the church and the oppression of women in general."[185]

A few months later, Enedy presented another work in a student show on campus entitled *Twenty-five years of Virginity . . . A Self Portrait.* It comprised a quilt made of twenty-five pairs of women's panties, each with a red cross stitched on the crotch. Enedy saw this work as an opportunity to explain her self and the previous work, and to celebrate her hard-maintained virginity in the face of a campus culture that had little sympathy for her traditional Catholic values. Instead, this work simply reignited the controversy. It moved into the political arena when a Pennsylvania State representative threatened to vote to withhold state subsidies to the University unless the work was removed from view. While the University administration refused to bend to this intimidation, the controversy became the occasion for a set of new guidelines urging greater dialogue among students and teachers with regard to the display of potentially controversial student art.

Again Enedy insisted that her work was being misrepresented. Noting her desire to create a personal work, she told a local reporter, "In olden times, women would take fabric from garments worn by their family members to make their quilts more personal. The first thing that came into my mind was my underwear. Because it's very personal. The cross represents a chastity belt, something sacred."[186] To another reporter she said, "All I wanted to do was something that pertained to me and would tell them who I am as a person. I am a Catholic and I am a virgin and that's that."[187]

At issue here is not the quality of either work. They were after all student works created in a university setting where explorations of identity issues and the testing of limits is the norm. Rather, what interests us are the kinds of meanings which the artist attached to the Virgin Mary, her celebrated virginity and to her perception of the relationship of that idealized icon to real women in the real world.

For Enedy, the Virgin Mary was first and foremost a woman with whom she could identify. She told an interviewer that the Virgin statue had in fact come from her mother's lawn and that she intended to connect memories of prayer trips she had taken with her mother to her frustration over the oppression of women by the Catholic Church, "I thought of it as a woman-empowering grotto,"[188] she said.

To another reporter Enedy noted that she meant the work to bring together her sense of Catholicism and feminism. "Also on my mind were women's issues, things I've seen that have gone on like women not being able to be priests. I wanted to merge these two issues, being a woman and being Catholic, in my art."[189]

Placing the Virgin in a vaginal grotto, she hoped to bring together potent symbols of religion and feminism in order to suggest the Church's need to take more seriously the power embedded in its most beloved female symbol. When this work was so totally misconstrued and was read instead as pornographic, sacrilegious and offensively anti-Catholic, Enedy attempted to clarify her message with the second work. One of the ironies of this controversy is the fact that the works under fire took the position of affirming the Catholic Church's valorization of virginity. The reaction against *Twenty Five Years of Virginity* included charges that it ridiculed the cross, allowed "blasphemy to masquerade as art,"[190] and that it was "a mockery of Christianity."[191] These positions suggest that any mention of the reality of female sexuality in connection with religion is apparently incendiary, even when it conforms to the Church's much criticized position on virginity and celibacy.

The second in this pair of controversies involves a Chicano artist named Alma Lopez who contributed a work entitled *Our Lady* to a spring 2001 exhibition at the Museum of International Folk Art in Santa Fe, New Mexico. Lopez' work is a computerized photo-collage which depicts the Virgin of Guadalupe as an exuberant modern woman wearing a bathing suit of roses. She is held aloft by a buxom, bare-breasted angel. Local Catholic officials, quickly seconded by the Catholic League's William Donohue, demanded that this, "repulsive, insulting and even sacrilegious," work be removed. Donahue also stated that the director of the Folk Art museum and the director of the Museum of New Mexico of which it is a branch, tender their resignations. The Archbishop Michael Sheehan was particularly pointed in his criticism. Maintaining that the work was an, "insult to the religious beliefs of a very large number of people that look at the Virgin Mary as being very holy." He reported in a sound bite that become ubiquitous in the local press, "She is depicted in a floral bikini as if she were a tart." [192]

The controversy spread to the local government, where nine Santa Fe legislators sent an angry letter to the Museum threatening future cuts in funding. After a public hearing in which passionate arguments on both sides of the issue were aired, the Museum officials stood firm, and refused to remove the work, though the run of the exhibition was shortened.

Again, it quickly emerged that the artist was a practicing Catholic who was drawing on a symbol that she, as a Chicana, felt was rightfully hers to appropriate. In response to the Irish archbishop's complaint that, "I wish those who want to paint controversial art would find their own symbols to trash," Lopez pointed out that, as a Chicana, she had every right to depict the Virgin. As she told a reporter, "I have a relationship with the Virgin of Guadalupe since I was born in Mexico, baptized Catholic and grew up in East L.A. with the Virgin in my home and community." [193]

One of the salient points in this controversy is the status of the Virgin of Guadalupe as an icon of liberty and liberation for Mexican and Chicano Catholics. The legend of the Virgin of Guadalupe dates back to the period shortly after the Spanish Conquest of Mexico during the height of the missionary effort to convert the native populace to Catholicism. In 1531 a converted Indian named Juan Diego had a vision of the Virgin Mary on a hilltop. She appeared to him as a beautiful, dark complexioned woman with garments "shining like the sun" and surmounted by a rainbow that, "clothed the land so that the cactus and other things that grew there seemed like celestial plants, their leaves and thorns shining like gold in her presence." The Virgin instructed Diego to build a church in her honor on the spot. He ran into understandable opposition from the local Church authorities until the Virgin presented him with a sign of her authenticity. Instructed to climb a mountain in late December, Diego discovered roses blooming miraculously in the dead of winter. He gathered these in his mantle and brought them back to the Bishop. When he unrolled the mantle, it was imprinted with the image of the Virgin of Guadalupe surrounded by an aura of sunrays that has now become her emblem.

At first, Spanish authorities tried to suppress the growing cult of the "Indian Virgin" but eventually they also embraced her as an important tool in the Christianization of Mexico. She was declared the patroness of Mexico in 1754 and of the Americas in 1910. During the Mexican Revolution, the Independents marched under her banner. More recently, political activists have unofficially adopted her as the symbol of resistance. The Virgin of Guadalupe also has become a central feature in the popular culture of Mexico and the southwestern states with a heavy Chicano population. She is the ubiquitous icon whose image appears on everything from car dashboards and amulets to tattoos, low rider cars, air fresheners and tee shirts.

Contemporary artists have extensively appropriated the Virgin of Guadalupe. Lopez' rose clad Virgin is not the first such adaptation to engender controversy. In 1987, protests erupted in Mexico City over a montage created by artist Rolando de la Rosa that laid Marilyn Monroe's face and bare breasts over an image of the Virgin. Protesters denounced the work as an emblem of "satanic blasphemy" while the artist argued that he was merely intending to demonstrate, "how our consumer society uses religious and sacred symbols for commercial ends."[194]

Chicana artists, meanwhile, are more likely to adopt the Virgin as a strong female role model who provides a counterweight to the macho excesses of Latino culture. In an incident which echoes the Alma Lopez controversy, the artist Yolanda Lopez received a bomb threat in 1984 when *Fem,* a Mexican feminist magazine, featured her image of the Virgin in a short skirt and high heels on its cover. Defending this and other works in which she portrayed the Virgin as a contemporary Chicana, Yolanda Lopez remarked, "Because I feel living, breathing woman also deserve the respect and love lavished on Guadalupe, I have chosen to transform the image. Taking symbols of her power and virtue, I have transferred them to women I know. My hope in creating these alternative role models is to work with the viewer in a reconsideration of how we as Chicanas portray ourselves. It is questioning the idealized stereotype we as women are assumed to attempt to emulate."[195]

Consciously working in the same vein, Alma Lopez argued that she was drawing on the tradition of the Virgin of Guadalupe as an emblem of liberty and equality. In a statement issued at the height of the controversy she noted, "I see Chicanas creating a deep and meaningful connection to this revolutionary cultural female image that appeared to an indigenous person at a time of genocide; and an inspiration during liberation struggles such as the Mexican Revolution and the Chicano Civil Rights Movement." Further she questioned the motives of her critics in political terms maintaining, "I feel that if my work is removed it means that I have no right to express myself as an artist and a woman. It means that as Chicanas we can only be sexualized or only be virgins. It means that we cannot look upon the Virgin and relate to her personally."[196]

This quartet of controversies reveals the very different dynamic that underlies male and female approaches to the Virgin Mary. While male artists deal with her in a detached manner, playing off the various associations she provides as a cultural symbol, women artists have clearly forged a far more personal relationship. For them, the Virgin is a role model whose eternal virginity presents a challenge or a problem. She is also a partner in their battle for female equality. Enedy and Lopez are not alone in internalizing the mixed signals the Virgin Mary transmits about purity, female strength and compassion. In their works, they clearly feel compelled to reinterpret her in ways that help them resolve their conflicts about their own sexuality and social role. As these controversies suggest, women artists also slip more easily from the personal to the political, seeing Mary as a powerful instrument in the battle against female oppression.

Similarly conflicting emotions lie behind the work of Renee Cox, who unintentionally became the star of Act II of Rudy Giuliani's battle against the Brooklyn Museum. Cox is a striking African American woman of Jamaican descent who uses her own often-naked body in photographic tableaux that celebrate female power and eroticism. In the persona of her comic strip alter ego Raje, she depicts herself as Wonder Woman's Black Amazon sister who does battle with western stereotypes of African American women. Provocatively dressed in a revealing Jamaican tricolor super heroine outfit, she has liberated the Aunt Jemima and Uncle Ben from their slave based identities, snarled Times Square traffic in order to prevent taxis from speeding by African American customers and challenged Nazis, the Ku Klux Klan and other groups implicated in racism against her people.

Cox has also created a number of works that rework traditional religious themes in ways that question society's commitment to gender and racial equality. For *And They Shall Be Named,* which was included in *Black Male,* an exhibition at the Whitney Museum devoted to American society's negative stereotypes about black men, Cox created a photograph of a black man hanging from a cross. A poignant image of the victimization of the African American male, it was also designed to draw attention to the participation of Christian slave owners in the institution of slavery. A similar message resonated in her reworking of the Pieta, with herself as a partially draped Virgin Mary holding the naked body of a supine black man. In her version of the Madonna and Child, she stands proudly naked, holding her own two year old son, intentionally confounding the official denial of the Virgin's, and hence motherhood's, sexual side.

Yo Mama's Last Supper, the work included in the Brooklyn Museum's survey of the work of Black photographers, is in a similar vein. This five-panel photographic work recreates Leonardo da Vinci's *Last Supper* with an all black cast. In the center is Cox herself, taking Christ's position and holding her arms out in a benedictory gesture as she stands facing us in the nude. For Cox, the work was meant to challenge the way that both women and people of color have been written out of both the visual representations and the power structure of the Catholic Church.

Cox was not the first to create a feminist reworking of da Vinci's *Last Supper.* In the 1970s artist Mary Beth Edelson recreated the image using collaged faces of prominent women artists. And in the Brooklyn Museum's *Sensation* show, which the year before brought the wrath of Giuliani on Chris Ofili's *The Holy Virgin Mary,* British artist Sam Taylor Wood presented Leonardo's tableau as a drunken revel with herself presiding bare breasted over the melee. As a number of commentators pointed out, this white female Christ apparently escaped the Mayor's notice during his excoriations of the Brooklyn museum's "anti-Catholicism."

Cox, however, immediately became a magnet for criticism, as the Mayor's office, William Donohue's Catholic League and local officials of the Catholic Church joined forces in condemning the work as, "a vulgar display of anti-Christian sentiment."[197] The Jamaican born artist, who was raised Catholic in Scarsdale, New York, decided that she had nothing to lose in challenging her attackers. In numerous newspaper and television interviews, including a face-off with Donohue sponsored by the First Amendment Center in New York, she defended her position. She insisted, "There are plenty of images of a nude Christ... My guess after all of this hoopla is that it is a question of race. People have a problem with the fact that it's an African American woman at the head of the dinner table."[198] She added," I don't think its anti-Catholic at all. I grew up Catholic."[199] And she pointed out, the work was first exhibited in the Oratorio di San Ludovico, a seventeenth century Catholic Church, as part of the 1999 Venice Biennale, where its proximity to the Vatican caused no outcry.

For Cox, the issues raised by this and her other work revolve around the hypocrisy of the Catholic Church whose message of love and mercy is belied by its treatment of women and people of color. More so American culture's puritanical attitude toward the female body, especially when that body is black. She says, "I see it as, black women have been told, you're not 'it.' You're not supposed to be like yourself, you should be getting your hair straightened to appeal to a Caucasian standard of beauty. I try to say 'No, you don't have to be that. It's a state of mind. Engage in self love.'" Regarding her own eroticized presentation of herself, she maintains, "I generate this imagery, I wasn't told to do this by some man. I derive pleasure from it. But when an African American woman does this there seems to be huge resistance. It's almost like you've committed a sin."[200]

In her desire to derive pleasure from her body, Cox takes issue with the current American church establishment's official discomfort with female eroticism. Inscribing herself into time honored religious tableaux, she draws attention to the sensuality and sexuality that permeates the western tradition of religious art. She notes, "Christ on the crucifix and the Virgin Mary were the first images I saw. But I never found them inclusive of who I was as an African American woman of Jamaican descent. Mary is always about purity and trust, about the powerlessness of woman. So I wondered, how do I flip that? How do I inject what I want to say?"[201]

She solves the problem by representing Christ as a full-breasted female, a conception not without precedent in medieval art. Similarly she enacts the Madonna's loving relationship with her child in a way that does not deny her own sexuality. The female incarnational imagination allows her to declare, "I can be as sexual as I want and as powerful."[202]

Even in the absence of controversy, this battle cry resonates for women artists raised as Catholics. Take, for instance, Kiki Smith, one of the most prominent artists on the contemporary scene. Smith has long acknowledged the influence of Catholicism on her creative imagination. She notes, "I was very influenced by the lives of the saints when I was a kid. You have a body with attributes and artifacts evoked by a sort of magic. Catholicism has these ideas of the host, of eating the body, drinking the body, ingesting a soul or spirit; and then of the reliquary, like a chop shop of bodies. Catholicism is always involved in physical manifestation of physical conditions, always taking inanimate objects and attributing meaning to them. In a way its compatible with art."[203]

Much of Smith's art centers on the human body. She notes that she has moved from the inside out, beginning with explorations of birth imagery, moving through evocations of body fluids and internal organs and finally representing skin, muscles and then the entire human body. Working in a variety of media ranging from glass, paper, wax, and bronze and encompassing sculpture, installation, drawings and prints, she has long been preoccupied with the beauty of the purely physical aspects of the human body. She has created exquisite glass stomachs and sperm, red stained paper skin and rolled paper umbilical cords, terra cotta rib cages, ceramic hearts, and bronze uteruses.

Smith's work directly challenges the revulsion that contemporary Americans feel toward the body and its processes. Life-size figures with trains of yellow glass urine or red glass menstrual blood trailing from their bodies deal directly with body fluids and excretion. Of these, *Tale* is particularly unsettling. It consists of a naked female figure on all fours excreting a long trail of feces. Such works are meant to embody psychological conditions; the feeling of loss of control or of being unable to escape one's mental baggage.

While all of her work manifests a powerfully female incarnational consciousness, exemplifying Smith's sense that, "… women don't separate their identity of self from their identity of themselves as bodies," she has also directly addressed her Catholic consciousness. A series of sculptures deal with the Virgin Mary in her various manifestations. On one hand, Smith sees the Virgin Mary as "powerful female goddess figure."[204] But she is also deeply aware of the ambiguous messages Mary conveys about female sexuality. In particular, she was troubled about the submissive posture conventionally attributed to the Virgin. She told an interviewer, "The Virgin Mary always extends her arms, making the body vulnerable. Vulnerable and compassionate, but to be vulnerable is to lose insight. It makes you exposed. For me, to be that vulnerable, I think you could lose all your insides, losing yourself. I am angry that the Virgin Mary pays for her compassion by being neutered. The position of the Virgin robs you of your femininity and sex."[205]

Smith created several works dealing with this situation. To suggest how Mary had essentially given up her carnal nature for God, she created a full-size sculpture of the Virgin Mary, first out of pigmented wax and then in bronze, in which she appears flayed. In both works Mary's skin has been removed to expose the red tissue and veins beneath. Smith highlighted Mary's vulnerability with a paper sculpture in which a chain of paper intestines spilled from the Virgin's torso.

Indirectly, Smith referred to the Virgin in a related work called *Mother* in which, recalling the nursing breasts of innumerable paintings of the Madonna and Child, rivulets of paper flowed like milk from a woman's swollen breasts. A crouching white wax figure with abnormally extended arms is part curtseying debutante, part Virgin Mary "with her arms open, but here they're extended. It's like she's asking to be walked on."[206]

In contrast to these representations of female vulnerability, Smith has also paid homage to the Virgin's pagan origins. She conflates her with such other female goddess figures as Shela-na-Gig, a Celtic goddess who, in Smith's representation bends over to flaunt her vagina; Nuit, Egyptian goddess of the sky who is literally all arms and legs in Smith's version and Daphne, the Greek nymph who escaped Apollo's unwanted advances by being transformed into a laurel tree. Through these transformations, Mary regains the sexuality and fecundity denied her by the Christian tradition.

Smith has also created a memorable sculpture of Mary Magdalene, the Virgin Mary's alter ego. Depicting the Magdalene as a wild, almost animal-like creature in her later years as a hermit in the desert, Smith pays homage to Donatello's famous version of this subject. However, while Donatello dresses Mary Magdalene in animal skins which hang loosely over her emaciated body, Smith depicts her naked, with a hairy voluptuous body, as if she had become re-sexualized by her return to an animal state. When Smith first exhibited this work she accentuated the contrast between Catholicism's two versions of female nature. She placed it looking up at a sculpture of the Virgin Mary.

Sculptor Janine Antoni shares Smith's preoccupation with the body as a source of knowledge. Like Smith, she wants to understand the body from the inside out. However her mode of exploration involves performance. Going back to the endurance artists of the 1970s, she relies on ritualized and often painful actions that allow her, as she says, "to get back inside the body."[207] She translates traditional artistic activities into body processes - making reference to the wildly abandoned brush work of the Abstract Expressionists in a work in which she paints the floor with her long hair dipped in hair dye, creating sculptures by chiseling large chunks of chocolate with her teeth and molding lard into soap to wash her body, making a delicate drawing by beating her mascara loaded eyelashes against pieces of paper.

There are many ways to interpret Antoni's work. Commentators have linked it to feminism, to the magical transformations found in traditional fairy tales, to the social pathology of bulimia and to psychoanalytic concepts of the self's passage from the Imaginary realm into the Symbolic Order.

However, one of the most powerful readings of Antoni's works results when it is interpreted from the perspective of the Catholic imagination. This is a reading Antoni heartily endorses, and in fact the company that she formed to pursue her art projects is called "Immaculate Conception, Inc." Reviewing some of the modes she has used to shape her materials, she notes, "I like the idea of eating, the notion of incorporation and for that matter, communion. Then there is the washing, which brings us to Baptism and holy water, not to mention Mary Magdalene drying the feet of Christ with her hair."[208]

Born in Freeport, Bahamas, Antoni attended Catholic School through high school and confesses that in second grade she wanted to be a nun. Her work returns obsessively to the themes of birth, motherhood and transformation. Frequently these are understood with reference to Catholic doctrines like the Incarnation, Immaculate Conception and the Transubstantiation of the Eucharist from bread and wine into the body and blood of Christ. On occasion Antoni borrows directly from traditional religious art, adapting well-known images or motifs to suit her own purposes.

For instance, *Momme* from 1995 is a photograph of an attractive middle-aged woman in a long white dress sitting quietly on a sofa beside a window that is flooded with light. Despite the serenity of the image, a disparate element interrupts its ordinariness. This is an anomalous third foot that emerges from beneath the hem of the long dress between the woman's two bare feet. Looking more closely, we realize this foot belongs to another hidden figure who is nestled around her waist beneath the voluminous white dress.

Antoni notes that she was thinking about the eerie stillness of Vermeer's interiors when she made this image. But even more, it is her version of the Annunciation. The woman, in fact Antoni's own mother, sits bathed in an almost unearthly light, pregnant with another person who is in fact Antoni herself. On a table beside her mother is a framed photograph of Antoni's grandmother, completing the matrilineal line that is represented in the traditional Annunciation story by Mary and her mother Anne.

A similar adaptation appears in *Coddle* (1998). This photograph suggests a traditional painting of Madonna and Child, or alternately, a Pieta, in which the Virgin Mary cradles the dead body of her son after his Crucifixion. In Antoni's version, the artist poses as the Virgin, her long hair falling over a face nearly lost in the shadows. The light instead picks out the center of the scene, where her hands gently hold, not a child or man, but her own bare leg. This disconcerting image is open to a variety of interpretations. From one perspective, the child is missing and has been transformed into a phantom limb by a mother who cannot endure her loss. Or, less tragically, the image reminds us that the child who emerges from its mother's womb is still, literally, a part of the mother's body.

Both photographs use the language of religious art to deal with the meaning of mother love and the mysterious link between mother and child. Both in their own way deal with the idea of Incarnation; bringing it back into the human realm, where we are asked to consider how each of us is, like Christ, a spirit made flesh.

Antoni is best known for her works involving lard and chocolate. The materials themselves are rife with potentially religious associations. Lard is white and chocolate is dark, raising the specter of Christian dualities of purity and defilement, sacred and profane, heaven and earth. Antoni is also interested in them for their relationship to the body. Both are composed of largely or wholly of fat, one of the body's major components. Chocolate, when ingested, returns to the body as fat, while lard is the fat used to create soap that washes the body.

Antoni's works with these materials involve transformations, or to use the more religiously loaded term that she prefers, transubstantiations. For *Gnaw*, (1992), she laboriously chewed a large cube of chocolate and a large cube of soap until their tops and corners were worn away with her teeth marks. She shaped the chewed residue into 24 chocolate boxes and three hundred lipsticks, which were then displayed in a kiosk made up to look like a department store display. Critics seized on the work as a commentary on bulimia, then a hot topic on the self-help circuit.

In fact, Antoni's concerns were more metaphysical. Drawing on her interest in the origin of these substances as fat, she saw this work as an investigation of cyclicality. The transformation of soap and chocolate into lipstick and candy boxes suggest how things which came from the body could be reshaped by a body process and returned to the body as decoration or food. Further, she notes, the action of chewing was important because it allowed her to connect with her materials in a deeply physical way, not unlike the way the Catholic believer becomes one with Christ by eating his body.

The next year, Antoni returned to soap and chocolate for *Lick and Lather*. For this work, she used her own head as the mold for a set of casts in lard and chocolate. Then she proceeded to erode them by licking the chocolate and washing the bust. When the features had been largely worn away, she displayed the busts on pedestals facing each other. Again, she was interested in the cycle of bodily activity, in coming into intimate contact with an image of herself through the actions of licking and lathering.

However, the work that speaks most dramatically to the idea of transformation and rebirth is *Eureka*, also from 1993. The title of this work refers to the discovery of displacement of matter by the ancient Greek mathematician Archimedes. The story goes that Archimedes was asked by the king to measure how much gold was in his crown. He puzzled over this problem, even taking it with him to his bath, whereupon he was suddenly struck with the answer. Just as his body displaced an equal mass of water, so the gold in the crown could be measured by the amount of water it displaced. Shouting "Eureka" he leaped from his tub and ran naked through the city streets.

In Antoni's version, water is replaced by lard. Lowering herself into a bathtub filled with 400 pounds of lard, she extracted an amount equal to her body mass and turned it into a cube of soap with which she proceeded to wash herself until the edges were soft. Again, the work deals with the washing of body with body. It is also a striking image of rebirth. Antoni has remarked, "I think of the tub of lard as a womb image because lard is a material of the body."[209] In this, it also references resurrection. When displayed, the work consists of the lard filled tub in which the impression left by Antoni's body is still evident, along with the cube of worn soap made from the displaced materials. The body has been transformed, reshaped and reborn in the form of a soap cube, recalling the reunion with their glorified bodies that the faithful will experience at the end of time.

Historian Marina Warner has pointed out that one of the most important aspects of Antoni's work is the way it challenges the traditional hierarchy of the senses.[210] While western culture tends to privilege knowledge gained through the eyes, associating it with rationality, science, objectivity (and of course, maleness), Antoni turns to the more female associated senses of taste, smell, sound and touch. Her focus on the bond between mother and child reminds us that the child's first connection to the mother's body, and hence to the outside world, is through non-visual sensations: touching, suckling and smelling. Antoni's work is in large measure an effort to return to this kind of knowing, a knowing through the body that is a reflection of her incarnational consciousness.

The Virgin Mary is also deeply implicated in sculptor Petah Coyne's conception of femininity. Recalling her introduction to the ideals of womanhood inculcated in Catholic school, Coyne remarks, "When I look at the Virgin, I see the nuns. The nuns told us that the Virgin was epitome of perfect womanhood. I thought that's what we would move into. I thought perfection was our given right. When I grew up, of course, I was bitterly disappointed."[211]

Like many of the artists in this book, she grew up to become an artist without reflecting deeply on her Catholic origins. Only later, in mid-life, did the subterranean Catholic motifs and themes that had always been there rise to the surface. Coyne's work essentially deals with the beauty of decay and imperfection. She first gained widespread notice with oddly beautiful black sculptures composed of pods of wire coated with black casting sand that hung like mutant growths from the gallery ceiling. They had an unsettling animate appearance, halfway between plant and animal, and also seemed to speak, in some melancholy way, of death and loss.

These works, which Coyne began to call her "girls", were soon joined by white wax sculptures, equally amorphous in form which were embedded with stuffed birds, artificial flowers and ribbons, often so deeply covered in wax as to be almost invisible. Commentators compared them to melting chandeliers and invoked Charles Dickens' Miss Havisham, who, on being jilted on her wedding day, spent the rest of her life enclosed in a room with her decaying cake and slowly disintegrating wedding dress.

Coyne was taken aback when a critic referred to the "Catholic sensibility" in her work. In retrospect there is clearly much justification for such a description: the dualism of black and white, the flesh like surface of the work, the preoccupation with death and decay, the use of birds, Christian symbols of the Spirit and Fish, Christian symbol of Christ. There was as well the relic-like preservation of dead animals and artificial flowers. Coyne told an interviewer in 1988, "This is the residue of life, discarded things. I'm trying to give them a second life. That means, I guess, that I believe in heaven and hell."[212]

However, it wasn't until 1999 that the Catholic references in Coyne's work became explicit. In a series of sculptures created in the aftermath of the death of her brother to whom she had been extremely close, Coyne began to incorporate standing plaster figures of the Madonna.

Like the other found objects that had made their way into her work, these had a poignant history. The plaster Madonnas came from a company that made religious statuary. When Coyne inquired whether they had any that were damaged or imperfect which she might buy at a discount, she was shown a room full of discarded Virgins. She bought the whole lot and proceeded to use them in her work.

The first works that used these elements combined the figures with horsehair given to Coyne by artist Ann Hamilton. The Madonnas are placed against walls, their faces hidden and almost lost in the piles of coarse black hair. Coyne notes that she was thinking about a Japanese folk story about women who donated their hair to the temple, where it was woven into ropes that were at once dangerous and alluring. Here, the hair sexualizes the otherwise Virginal figures while also giving them a mournful, even elegiac aspect.

In subsequent sculptures, Coyne covered the Madonna statues with layers of dripping wax and unlighted candles, making them into votive objects. She also began to set them into freestanding partitions, so that they had a dual aspect. From the front, one could see only the outlines of the Virgin's back, curdled with layers of soft white wax. Mingled in the translucent material were flowers, birds and even piles of white pillows. These latter bring to mind the billowing clouds upon which the Virgin is often seen floating in representations of her many apparitions. From the other side, one glimpsed the Virgin's plaster face peering though a hole in the wall. When these partitions were propped against the gallery wall, this latter aspect became almost secret, to be discovered only by the intrepid viewer willing to slip into the narrow space between partition and wall.

Thus Coyne was able to express her sense of the ambiguity of the female role. "Once I put them in the walls, what was behind became interesting," she remarks, "it was like the confessional. The backside is what the work really is. It's like a woman, where the outside is ornamental, but the real part is the inside which is not accessible."[213]

As Coyne's pre-Madonna work demonstrates, the incarnational imagination need not manifest itself in obvious Catholic imagery. In fact, it may be powerfully present in work that seems on the surface to be the antithesis of religious imagery. This is the case with the work of Lisa Yuskavage, who gained notoriety in the late 1990s as part of the so-called Bad Girl phenomena. As christened by the art press, the Bad Girls were younger women artists who seemed to have discarded the iconoclasm of their feminist foremothers, creating work that exulted in raunchy, titillating and unabashedly pre-feminist depictions of female sexuality.

In her oil paintings, Yuskavage created overt images of budding female sexuality. Her pouting, barely pubescent girls fondle their swelling breasts and upturned nipples with unabashed pleasure. They are lovingly painted in layers of translucent oil paint that gives their skin and surroundings a luminous glow. Often they are painted in settings that play on the traditional conventions of eroticism, among them glowing sunsets, beads, flowers, pillows. At the same time there is something unsettling about these voluptuous maids. The lush brushwork and translucent light can't camouflage the fact that they seem to have more in common with Keene paintings or romance novel cover art than with nineteenth century odalisques. Yuskavage's apparently un-ironic celebration of kitsch and her recourse to the tropes of low rent seduction have made many critics uncomfortable. Deeming her creations bimbos, nymphets, or Barbies, they debate whether the artist is exploding or reinforcing oppressive female stereotypes.

But in fact, Yuskavage had something very different in mind. She remarks that if she had not turned to the tradition of the female nude, she would have painted religious themes. The product of a close-knit Catholic family who count priests and nuns among her immediate relatives, Yuskavage sees these works as homages to the great traditions of Western art. "I'm not trying to piss people off," she says, noting that her work grows out of her intense respect for the authority of tradition. She is particularly interested in the way that the old masters used light as a metaphor for the divine. In her own work, she remarks, "Light is the presence of goodness."[214]

At the same time, she acknowledges that her versions of the grand themes are deliberately "flatfooted." The sexuality of her nudes is exaggerated. They are endowed with impossibly enlarged breasts, nipples and buttocks. But running counter to these cultural symbols of eroticism is a sense of inner life that is essentially inaccessible to the viewer. In a very different way than Antoni or Smith, they also defer to the idea of knowledge gained through the body rather than the intellect. From another perspective, Yuskavage's paintings illuminate the degree to which the language of popular devotional art resembles that of popular seduction. Soft focus representations of Christ with blond curls and bleeding heart evoke scenarios of desire, love and willing submission remarkably similar to those exhibited by soft focus romance novel heroines wrestling with overwhelming passion

Yuskavage says she does not draw directly from Catholic kitsch, but acknowledges its pull on her. "Kitschy things are something I feel a great deal of compassion towards. People that I love have mirrored walls and plastic slipcovers. Their velvet lampshades and statues of the Sacred Heart of Jesus glow with manufactured spirit. I want to combine that nostalgia with my painting knowledge and not judge one as better than the other."[215]

As these artists demonstrate, incarnational thinking provides a fruitful way for Catholic women artists to explore the dilemmas posed by contemporary feminism. In some cases, Catholicism's conflicts mirror societal ones. In others, Catholicism provides a visual language for reimagining oppressive roles and assumptions. Antoni talks about her concern that she was somehow betraying her belief in female equality when she created works that included Catholic inflected elements of submission and endurance or when she immersed herself too deeply in the comfort of the mother-daughter relationship. Smith admits that she was long reluctant to talk about her attraction to Catholic motifs for fear that her work would be dismissed by members of the art establishment who equated religion with superstition and political reaction. Enedy was astonished that her statement about female oppression was read as virulent anti-Catholicism. Coyne sees her work as a rebellion against perfectionism and the demands it places on women in both its earthly and spiritual manifestations. Cox works out her anger at sexism and racial prejudice by reinventing traditional religious images in her own image. Yuskavage, less militant about feminism, struggles against ideological readings of her work that negate its spirituality or condemn its "politically incorrect" view of sexuality.

In Catholicism, the female body is less a battlefield than a minefield, intimately bound up with doctrinal and political struggles over contraception, abortion, virginity and the nature and origin of sin. But, as the artists discussed here demonstrate, it is also a remarkable source of inspiration. Providing an alternative to starkly rationalist views about the separation of mind and body, female incarnational thinking offers a model for other forms of knowledge that do less violence to our sensate, feeling selves. Knowledge through the body, as both feminists and female Catholics concur, is knowledge that celebrates our sexual, sensual nature.

* * *

POSTSCRIPT

When I first began thinking about this book in the mid 1990s, the bitterest battles of the so called "Culture War" - the Mapplethorpe trial, the demonizing of Andres Serrano and the NEA four, the battle over the NEA "decency pledge" - were still playing themselves out in the courts and in the field of public opinion. The religious right, in alliance with political conservatives, was pursuing an agenda whose major initiatives included the dismantling of the NEA, the promotion of prayer in public schools and opposition to abortion. Recurring controversies over the use of taxpayer funds to support "anti-Christian," obscene, or otherwise degenerate art revealed that this group saw artists as useful scapegoats in their battle to de-secularize American society.

Since September 11, 2001, the focus of the Culture War has shifted in ominous directions. The deaths of over 3000 people in New York and Washington have empowered a divisive black and white vision of public morality. The tragedy also set the stage for a revival of the ugliest aspects of American nationalism. In the immediate aftermath of the attacks, Moral Majority founder Jerry Falwell suggested in an interview with Pat Robertson that September 11 was retribution for America's slide into godless liberalism. "What we saw on Tuesday, as terrible as it is, could be minuscule if, in fact, God continues to lift the curtain and allow the enemies of America to give us what we probably deserve," he opined. He went on to list the specific agents of America's moral decay, among them the ACLU, abortionists, feminists, gays and People for the American Way.[216]

In the media firestorm that followed both men were forced to retract this outrageous assertion. However, the related notion that liberalism's philosophy of cultural relativism had somehow contributed to America's vulnerability to foreign attacks gained considerable currency in conservative circles. In the New York Times, cultural critic Edward Rothstein declared, "This destruction seems to cry out for a transcendent ethical perspective. And even mild relativism seems troubling in contrast."[217] Meanwhile a report entitled *Defending Civilization: How Our Universities are Failing America and What Can Be Done About It,* published in November of 2001 deemed college professors, "the weak link in America's response to the attack." Produced by the ultra conservative American Council of Trustees and Alumni (ACTA), it purported to demonstrate the dangerously anti-American tendencies of the liberal academic cabal that supposedly runs our nation's universities. *Defending Civilization* ferreted out examples of university professors calling for tolerance of Islam, understanding of third world grievances and international cooperation in the wake of the September 11 attacks. In expressing such sentiments, the report charged, leftist academia pointed, "accusing fingers, not at terrorists, but at America itself."[218]

In the months following September 11, the notion of evil that had lost much of its mainstream currency in the years since Ronald Reagan's "Evil Empire" collapsed of its own weight, was suddenly everywhere. In declaring a "War on Terror," President George W. Bush promised to ferret out "evildoers" everywhere. Later he identified a specific "Axis of Evil" embodied by the governments of Iraq, Iran and North Korea. In the conservative cable news networks and popular press, figures of "evil" multiplied, as the term was attached to the 9/11 hijackers and their ringleader Osama bin laden, to Islamic fundamentalists generally, to Saddam Hussein and (most ominously,) to any who opposed United States foreign policies. "You are with us or you are with the terrorists," as President Bush famously warned.

As the nation rushed toward war, first in Afghanistan and then in Iraq, it became increasingly difficult to disentangle political and moral justifications for action. Religious conservatives issued inflammatory statements, equating Muslims with Nazis (Pat Robertson), describing Mohammed as a "terrorist" (Jerry Falwell) and designating Islam an, "a very evil and wicked religion" (Franklin Graham, son of Billy Graham).[219] In his first major speech after the attacks of September 11, President Bush maintained, "Freedom and fear, justice and cruelty, have always been at war, and we know that God is not neutral between them."[220] In his 2003 State of the Union Address, he elaborated, "We do not claim to know all the ways of Providence, yet we can trust in them, placing our confidence in the loving God behind all of life, and all of history."[221] For many Americans, as the "War on Terror" accelerated, so did the conviction that God was on our side.

However, this belief was not universal. On the eve of the Iraq invasion, former President Jimmy Carter, himself a born-again Christian, (but of a very different stripe than his successor) warned against relying on religious justifications for a preemptive strike, "As a Christian and as a President who was severely provoked by international crises, I became thoroughly familiar with the principles of a just war, and it is clear that a substantially unilateral attack on Iraq does not meet these standards. This is an almost universal conviction of religious leaders, with the most notable exception of a few spokesmen of the Southern Baptist Convention who are greatly influenced by their commitment to Israel based on eschatological, or final days, theology."[222]

President Bush's decision to go ahead, despite such resistance could be understood, Garry Wills argued, in light of his belief that he is an instrument of Divine Providence. "Many have wondered," Wills writes, "how the President can so readily tear down whole structures of international cooperation at a time when, in the fight against terrorism, we need them most. His calm assurance that most of the world and much of the nation is wrong comes from an apparent certainty that is hard to justify in terms of geopolitical calculus. It helps, in making the leap, to be assured that God is on your side."[223]

As Wills points out, the obvious consequence of this is that those who oppose him are not simply misguided, "Question the policy, and you no longer believe in evil, which in this context, is not believing in God. That is the religious test on which our president is grading us."[224]

And yet, it should not be forgotten that the September 11 hijackers were also on a mission from God, and that they were equally as convinced of the righteousness of their cause and the wickedness of their enemies. Furthermore, on the eve of the Iraq War, Saddam Hussein rallied his country with assurances of God's blessing that eerily echoed those of President Bush. "The enemy will fall on his face," he declared, "despised, condemned and defeated, while your banner, the banner of God is Great, will continue to fly high on its nest, dignified and honorable."[225]

Thus, rather than creating a map of the world starkly divided into the righteous and the evildoers, the brave new post 911 world reveals the danger of any kind of fundamentalist certainty, whatever its religious origin. In 1835, Alexis De Tocqueville argued that America's devotion to religion was inseparable from its devotion to equality and democracy. In public discussion today, religion is more likely to be attached to a harsh, exclusionary and elitist vision of society that is the antithesis of those ideals.

This is apparent on many fronts. As I write this conclusion in the summer of 2003, debate rages over the morality of gay marriage and the justness of the Supreme Court's divided decision to strike down Texas' antiquated sodomy law. Astonishingly, conservatives mounted a spirited opposition to the notion that the state has no right to enter the bedrooms of Americans, if those Americans happen to be homosexual. One of the most pugnacious spokespersons for this view was Republican Senator Rick Santorum who defined the decriminalization of sodomy as a grave moral issue that would lead inevitably to a social embrace of bigamy, polygamy, adultery and incest.

Meanwhile one of the comic sideshows of this otherwise troubled summer involved the exposure of conservative spokesperson William Bennett as a high stakes gambler. The author of *The Book of Virtues*, a best selling tome which preaches a morality based on personal responsibility, argued that his habit was a victimless pastime since he never threatened his family's well being. While conservatives were discomfited and liberals gleeful about Bennett's revelations, few bothered to question whether it was seemly, if not immoral, for a self proclaimed moralist to throw away over eight million dollars at the gaming tables at a time when unemployment was at an all time high and severe limitations on welfare were creating legions of homeless families.

Such developments suggest that the issues raised by this book are even more urgent now than when I first began writing seven years ago. Religion is at the core of nearly every international and domestic debate; from the Middle East conflict which has provided much of the fuel for the growing power of Islamic fundamentalism, to debates over government funding for faith-based initiatives, the social acceptance of homosexuality, the state's responsibility to its citizens and the proper content of public education.

The time would seem to be ripe for an open and spirited debate about what religion can and cannot be expected to accomplish in a democratic society. Is religion, as conservative politicians and religious leaders contend, a bulwark against the anti-social behavior prompted by too many material and social choices? Or do it's more extreme manifestations, as other writers have suggested, pose a threat to our civil liberties and our belief in individual self determination? Is religion a force for tolerance or a breeding ground for intolerance? Does it offer solutions or compound the problems?

And yet, such debate rarely takes place. Instead, like much of the political debate over where we should be heading as a nation, it is choked before it can begin by heavy-handed tactics of intimidation. To question current American policies is to be branded "unpatriotic" and to question the prevailing gospel of "family values" is to be labeled degenerate or immoral.

Can we afford to leave definitions of morality to the religious right? I have argued against a narrow definition of Catholicism precisely because such exclusionary tactics impoverish us as both spiritual and social beings. The "postmodern heretics" discussed here enlarge our definitions of religion and its meaning in people's lives. Looking at their work in the context of Catholicism often reveals surprising things. For instance, some of the most apparently virulently anti-Catholic artists discussed above, among them, Karen Finley, Renee Cox and David Wojnarowicz, are in fact taking aim at present day moralists who distance themselves from the real message of Jesus and his gospel of love and tolerance. Similarly, other artists here exhibit a refreshing openness to other systems of belief. This category includes Ana Mendieta, who melded Catholicism with the animism of Santeria, Linda Montano, who combines her childhood faith with the spiritual practice of yoga and Kiki Smith who describes her beliefs as a mixture of Catholicism and Hinduism. Such a spirit of ecumenism is of great value during this era of divisive and bloody religious conflict.

Though the Catholicism of these artists manifests itself in unique and often startlingly divergent ways, each is grounded in some way in the body, its processes, its pleasures and its pains. By bringing the body into the equation, they all acknowledge a continuum between the spiritual and physical worlds, and hence between the supposedly distinct realms of the sacred and profane. This could not be further from the perfectionist views of religious conservatives who divide the world into the saved and the damned; making rigid oppositions between good and evil, body and soul, sacred and profane. By labeling many human behaviors deviant, regarding physical urges and experiences primarily as impulses to be suppressed or mastered, often rejecting the visible and sensual world as a mere distraction from the "real world" to come, they promote a utopian vision of society which is counter to human nature.

In his scathing indictment of fundamentalism, which he terms "legalistic Christianity," journalist Bruce Bawer points out how this belief system creates a psychology of hypocrisy and deception.[226] In most evangelical denominations, he notes, salvation is a matter of election or of being born again. Heaven is reserved for those who have accepted Christ as their savior through some kind of officially sanctioned profession of faith. Those who simply focus on good works, moral choices, and love for others are not guaranteed salvation. The need to "witness," to demonstrate to the world that one is among the saved means that any evidence to the contrary must be suppressed. This engenders a tremendous anxiety about the real and normal vicissitudes of life.

Bawer quotes several former fundamentalists: "Everything they do is for show, or, as they would say, a good witness," one says. "No one asks for help because it would blow their cover."[227] Says another, "I think we were actually taught not to love. The liberals were always talking about love and the social gospel, so it was probably a reaction. It was almost is if our fundamentalist elders were saying, "We will preach truth. To hell with love."[228]

By contrast, the artists here, drawing on an incarnational consciousness rooted in their Catholic backgrounds, offer an essentially anti-utopian vision that celebrates human imperfection and impurity. The Andy Warhol seen here is neither saint nor Satan, but a flawed human being struggling with the contradictory messages conveyed by his religion and his culture. Andres Serrano exalts the debased and beautifies the corrupt, creating a visual equivalent of the transforming power of grace. Similarly, in the face of AIDS, death and loss, Felix Gonzales-Torres' work is a gesture of generosity and love.

In the work of our Postmodern Heretics, knowledge, transcendence and redemption are possible only through the medium of the imperfect human body. For so-called endurance artists, an embrace of pain and vulnerability leads to a higher consciousness of self and others. For women artists struggling with mixed messages about sex and spirituality, the body and its physical processes become instruments for the exploration of the contradictory roles thrust upon them in contemporary society. For artists like Joel Peter Witkin and Ana Mendieta, death, blood and decay serve as necessary stages in the eternal cycle of life.

Thus, these artists remind us that it is precisely the most human elements of our nature that also give us the capacity to be spiritual. Even Robert Mapplethorpe - the "baddest of the bad" - appears here as a tormented soul whose natural longings for transcendence and sublimity were redirected by the social denunciation of his sexual impulses.

As Bawer points out, Jesus felt far more comfortable in the company of social outcasts and 'perverts' than with the self proclaimed righteousness of learned churchmen.[229] Embedded in the incarnational consciousness is a vision of religion that is generous, inclusive, forgiving and accepting of human imperfection. It is a vision that is better suited to our pluralistic society and our multi-dimensional world than the cold moral calculus that is more commonly in evidence in our public policies and debate.

While working on this book, I frequently presented versions of the ideas here in lectures at universities, art museums and even on occasion, religious institutions. I have been greatly heartened by the responses I have received. Many of the artists I deal with level powerful criticisms of Catholic orthodoxy. The first time I laid out my ideas before a crowd which contained a significant numbers of priests and nuns, I was nervous about how the work of artists like Mapplethorpe, Serrano, Witkin and Gober would be received. During the question and answer period at the end, it was clear that I shouldn't have worried. Rather than condemn my postmodern heretics for their unorthodoxies, my educated, literate audience was clearly delighted to find connections between contemporary art and religion. In fact, at one Catholic college, the museum director who had invited me later wrote to report that my lecture and exhibition spurred one of best discussions he had ever witnessed at the school about the essence of Catholicism.

What does it mean to be a Catholic? Mapplethorpe's conflicted relationship to his childhood religion is at the far end of the spectrum from Serrano's serene acceptance or Gober's nuanced embrace of the duality of heaven and earth. Michael Tracy's social consciousness contrasts with the more inward spirituality of Kiki Smith or Janine Antoni. Witkin's subversive humor is part of a private search for God, while Karen Finley and David Wojnarowicz demand that the Catholic establishment make a public accounting of its self. Is one of these approaches more valid than another? Or do they join together to provide a nuanced, layered picture of Catholicism in contemporary America?

In a society where belief is forever being challenged by secular skepticism, where knowledge of the oppressive history of religion coexists with recognition of its liberating potential, and where body and spirit exist in tumultuous relationship, such reactions are all valid responses to the challenge of faith in a secular age. Works by artists like these reveal that, far from being adversaries, art and religion are inextricably linked together, joined by an incarnational consciousness that enriches both. Without taking the complexities explored here into account, we will fail to understand the deepest aspects of both Catholic spirituality and contemporary art.

* * *

ENDNOTES

1. Quoted in Charles Scribner III, *Bernini* New York: Harry N. Abrams, 1991, p. 92,
2. ibid.
3. Richard Bolton, editor, *Culture Wars*. New York: New Press, 1992, p 27.
4. ibid.
5. "New McNally Play cancelled After Protests and Threats" *New York Times*, May 23, 1998. B9.
6. Don Barry and Carol Vogel, "Giuliani Vows to Cut Subsidy over 'Sick' Art" *New York Times*. September 23, 1999, A1.
7. Steven Dubin, *Arresting Images: Impolitic Art and Uncivil Actions* New York: Routledge, 199, p. 127.
8. Dubin, p. 32.
9. Bolton, p. 228.
10. Leo Steinberg, *The Sexuality of Christ in Renaissance Art and in Modern Oblivion.* Chicago: University of Chicago Press, 1996, p.121.
11. Andrew Greeley, *The Catholic Imagination.* Berkeley: University of California Press, 2000, p. 6.
12. ibid.
13. David Tracy, *The Analogical Imagination* New York: Crossroads, 1982.
14. All from "Bill Moyers in conversation with Sister Wendy" WGBH Boston, Mass. Air date October 6, 1997 at 10 pm.
15. Steinberg, p. 120.
16. Caroline Walker Bynum, *The Resurrection of the Body* New York: Columbia University Press, 1995, p. 97.
17. Steinberg, p. 71.
18. Steinberg, p. 21
19. ibid.
20. Jane Allen Addams, "The Sacred and The Profane," *New Art Examiner* Summer 1990, p. 18.
21. John Dillenberger, *The Visual Arts and Christianity in America.* New York: Crossroad, 1988 p. 71.
22. On Fundamentalism, see: Bruce Bawer, *Stealing Jesus: How Fundamentalism Betrays Christianity.* New York: Three Rivers Press, 1997; Harold Bloom, *The American Religion: The Emergence of the Post-Christian Nation.* New York: Touchstone, 1992; Robert Fuller, *Naming the Antichrist. The History of an American Obsession.* Oxford: Oxford University Press, 1995 and George Marsden, *Understanding Fundamentalism and Evangelicism.* Grand Rapids: William B. Eerdmans Publishing Company, 1991.
23. Catholic League for Religious and Civil Rights. *Catalyst Magazine,* online publication. url: www. catholicleague.org/catalyst. html.
24. Robert Lockwood, "PAPAL SIN IS PALPABLE NONSENSE", *Catalyst Magazine,* May 07, 2001.
25. Laura Miller, "The new victimology: The Catholic League depicts critics as prejudiced and their ideas as hate crimes" *Salon,* Feb. 17, 2001. (Online publication).
26. George Marsden, "Religious Americans and the Arts in the 1990s" in Alberta Arthurs and Glenn Wallach, eds. *Crossroads: Art and Religion in American Life* New York: The New Press, 2001, pp. 71-102.
27. Andrew Greeley, *The Catholic Myth: Behavior and Beliefs of American Catholics.* New York: Charles Scribner's Sons, 1990, pp. 77-78.
28. Elaine Pagels, *The Gnostic Gospels* New York: Vintage Books: 1989.
29. Quoted in Robert Hughes, "The Rise of Andy Warhol" *The New York Review of Books,* February 18, 1982, p. 7.
30. ibid.
31. See roundtable discussion in Gary Garrels, *The Work of Andy Warhol* Seattle: Bay Press, 1989, pp.124-139.
32. Thomas Crow," Saturday Disasters: Trace and Reference in Early Warhol", *Art in America,* May 1987, pp. 128 -137.
33. Trevor Fairbrother, "Skulls," in Gary Garrels, ed, *The Work of Andy Warhol.* Seattle: Bay Press, 1989, p. 94.
34. Kenneth E. Silver, "Modes of Disclosure: The Construction of Gay Identity and the Rise of Pop Art" in Russell Ferguson, ed. *Hand-Painted Pop: American Art in Transition, 1955-62* Los Angeles: Museum of Contemporary Art, 1992. pp. 179-294.
35. Simon Watney, "Queer Andy" in Jennifer Doyle, Jonathan Flatley & Jose Esteban Munoz, eds. *Pop Out: Queer Warhol.* Durham: Duke University Press, 1996, pp. 20-30.
36. Hughes, p. 47.
37. "Eulogy for Andy Warhol by John Richardson", in Jane Daggett Dillenberger, *The Religious Art of Andy Warhol.* New York: Continuum, 1998, p.13.
38. Jane Daggett Dillenberger, p. 117.
39. Andy Warhol and Pat Hackett, *POPism: The Warhol 60s* New York: Harcourt Brace Jovanovich, 1980, p. 3.
40. Quoted in G.R. Swenson, "What is Pop Art? Answers from Painters, Part I" *Artnews,* November 1963, p. 26.
41. ibid.
42. Crow, p. 135.
43. Swenson, p. 60.
44. Rainer Crone, *Andy Warhol* New York: Praeger, 1970, p. 30.
45. Fairbrother, p. 94.
46. ibid.
47. Carter Ratcliff, *Andy Warhol.* New York: Abbeville Press, 1983, p. 52.
48. Jane Daggett Dillenberger, p. 35.
49. See Jennifer Doyle, Jonathan Flatley, & Jose Esteban Munoz, *Pop Out: Queer Warhol* Durham: Duke University Press, 1996.
50. Warhol. *Popism,* p. 294
51. Quoted in Jonathan Fineberg, *Art since 1940: Strategies of Being*

Englewood Cliffs: Prentice Hall, 1995, p. 342.

52. "ABC Art" reprinted in Barbara Rose, *Autocritique: Essays on Art and Anti-Art 1963-1987* New York: Weidenfeld & Nicolson, 1988, p. 55.

53. Michael Fried," Art and Objecthood". *Artforum* June 1967, pp. 12-23.

54. Quoted in Kathy O'Dell, *Contract with the Skin: Masochism, Performance Art and the 1970s* Minneapolis: University of Minnesota Press, 1998, p. 40.

55. Theodor Reik, *Masochism in Modern Man*. New York: Farrar Straus, 1949.

56. Reik, p. 358.

57. Donald Kuspit, "Chris Burden, The Feel of Power" in Anne Ayers and Paul Schimmel, eds. *Chris Burden: A Twenty Year Survey Newport* Beach, Calif: Newport Harbor Art Museum, 1988.

58. Amelia Jones, *Body Art/ Performing the Subject* Minneapolis: University of Minnesota Press, p. 229.

59. Pagels, p. 82.

60. O'Dell.

61. ibid, p. 13.

62. Hermann Nitsch, "The Theater of Orgies and Mysteries" reprinted in Michael Rush, ed, *Gunter Brus, Hermann Nitsch*, catalogue for exhibition at White Box, New York, Nov-Dec. 1999, p. 31

63. Rush, p. 13

64. Interview with the author, January 5, 2000.

65. ibid.

66. ibid.

67. Interview with the author, February 6, 2000.

68. ibid.

69. Jones, p. 134-35.

70. Interview with the author.

71. ibid.

72. Linda Montano, *Art in Everyday Life,* New York: Astro Arts/18th Street Complex, 1981

73. Dubin, pp .149-50.

74. Karen Finley, *A Different Kind of Intimacy: the Collected Writings of Karen Finley* New York: Thunder's Mouth Press, 2000, p. 84.

75. ibid.

76. Linda Greenhouse.

"Justices Uphold Decency Test in Awarding Arts Grants, Backing Subjective Judgments" *New York Times*. June 26, 1998, A 17.

77. Finley, p. 126.

78. Finley, p. 72.

79. Bill Stamets, "Randolph Street Gallery: Chicago: Performance". *New Art Examiner*. Summer 1993, p. 46.

80. Jurij V Krpan, Interview with Ron Athey, *Virus Magazine* , January 1997.

81. Bob Flanagan, "Bob Flanagan: Supermasochist", *RE/Search People Series: Volume one,* 1993, p. 47.

82. Flanagan, p. 75.

83. Visiting Hours, 1993-1994 exhibition co-organized by the New Museum of Contemporary Art in New York and the Santa Monica Museum of Art in Santa Monica, California.

84. Flanagan, p. 47.

85. ibid, p. 90.

86. ibid.

87. Elaine Scarry, *The Body in Pain: The Making and Unmaking of the World* Oxford: Oxford University Press, 1985, p. 199.

88. Tim Miller, "Jesus and The Queer Performance Artist", *Amazing Grace: Stories of Lesbian and Gay Faith,* The Crossing Press, 1991.

89. Patrick Buchanan, "Where a Wall is Needed", *Washington Times*, November 22, 1989, reprinted in Richard Bolton, ed. *Culture Wars*. New York: New Press, 1992, p. 138.

90. Garry Wills, *Papal Sin: Structures of Deceit* New York: Doubleday, 2000, p. 194.

91. Eve Kosofsky Sedgwick, *Epistemology of the Closet*, Berkeley: University of California Press, 1990, p. 140.

92. Mark D. Jordan, *The Silence of Sodom*, Chicago: University of Chicago Press, 2000, p. 8.

93. Dubin, p. 159.

94. Dubin, p. 150.

95. Michael Anft, *NEA-Disapproved Holly Hughes Takes on the Supreme Court,* Baltimore City Paper, February 2, 2000.

96. Email to the author, October 12, 2001.

97. Miller.

98. Terrence McNally, *Corpus Christi,* script published by Dramatists Play Service, Inc. 1999, p. 56.

99. ibid, p. 48.

100. "New McNally Play Cancelled After Protests and Threats". *New York Times*. May 23, 1998. B9.

101. Catholic League for Religious and Civil Rights," CORPUS CHRISTI" IS GAY HATE SPEECH" *Catalyst Magazine,* Nov 1998 (online publication)

102. Dubin, p. 172.

103. Arthur Danto, *Playing with the Edge,* Berkeley: University of California Press, 1996, p. 89.

104. ibid, p. 90.

105. Janet Kardon, *Robert Mapplethorpe: The Perfect Moment* Philadelphia: Institute of Contemporary Art, 1988, p. 11

106. ibid, p. 25.

107. Patricia Morrisroe, *Mapplethorpe: A Biography* New York: Da Capo Press, 1997.

108. Morrisroe, p. 230.

109. Allen Ellenzwig, and George Stambolian, *The Homoerotic Photograph* New York: Columbia University Press, 1992, p. 132.

110. Morrisroe, p. 235.

111. Danto, *Playing with the Edge,* p. 25.

112. ibid, p. 90.

113. Susan Sontag, "The Pornographic Imagination" reprinted as an introduction to Georges Bataille, *Story of the Eye*, London: Penguin Books, 1982, p. 115.

114. See Ellis Hanson, *Decadence and Catholicism*. Cambridge: Harvard University Press, 1997.

115. See Ellenzwig.

116. Morrisroe, p. 140.

117. David Wojnarowicz, "Post Cards from America: X-Rays from Hell" reprinted in Blinderman, Barry. *David Wojnarowicz: Tongues of Flame*, Normal, Illinois: University Galleries, Illinois State University, 1990, p. 106.

118. Dubin, p. 213.

119. Dubin, p. 216

120. Lippard, "Passages in the Shadows", p. 8.

121. Lippard. "Out of the Safety Zone", p.182.

122. David Cole, "David Wojnarowicz", *Aperture*. Fall 1994, p. 37.

123. Lippard. "Out of the Safety Zone", p. 136.

124. Tim Rollins, "Interview with Felix Gonzales-Torres", in William s. Bartman, ed., *Felix Gonzalez-Torres*, Los Angeles: A.R.T. Press, 1993, p. 23.

125. Nancy Spector, *Felix Gonzalez-Torres*, New York: Guggenheim Museum, 1995, p. 17.

126. Robert Storr, "Interview with Felix Gonzalez-Torres" *ArtPress*, January 1995, p. 30.

127. Lewis Baltz, "Felix Gonzalez-Torres". *L'Architecture D'Aujour'hui* September 1996, p 15.

128. Harold Bloom, *The American Religion: The Emergence of the Post-Christian Nation* New York: Touchstone, 1992, p. 264

129. Philippe Aries, *The Hour of Our Death* New York: Alfred A. Knopf, 1981.

130. Aries, p. 342.

131. ibid.

132. Aries, p. 300.

133. Elisabeth Kubler-Ross, *On Death and Dying*, New York: Macmillan, 1970, p. 14.

134. Dan Horn, "While county considers charges, others defend artistic motivation" *The Cincinnati Enquirer* February 4, 2001, p. 1.

135. Eleanor Heartney, "Is the body more beautiful when it's dead?" *New York Times*. June 1, 2003, Arts and Leisure, p. 37.

136. Robert Hobbs, "Andres Serrano: The Body Politic" in Patrick T. Murphy, *Andres Serrano: Works 1983-1993*, Philadelphia: Institute of Contemporary Art, University of Pennsylvania, 1994, p. 42.

137. Eleanor Heartney," Postmodern Heretics". *Art in America*, February 1997, p. 32.

138. Celia McGee. *New York Times*. "A Personal Vision of the Sacred and Profane", Jan 22, 1995, Arts and Leisure, p.35.

139. Heartney. "Postmodern Heretics, p. 35.

140. Simon Watney. *Talking Art!* London: Institute of Contemporary Art, 1993.

141. Derek Guthrie, "Taboo Artist: Serrano Speaks" *New Art Examiner*. September 1989, p. 45.

142. Hobbs, p. 17

143. Lucy Lippard. "Andres Serrano: The Spirit and the Letter." *Art in America*. April 1990, p. 241.

144. Marcia Tucker. "Andres Serrano: Retrospect" in Patrick T. Murphy. *Andres Serrano: Works 1983-1993*, philadelphia: Institute of Contemporary Art, University of Pennsylvania, 1994, p. 100.

145. Richard Woodward. "Joel Peter Witkin: An eye for the forbidden" *Vanity Fair*, April 1993, p. 192.

146. "Ethics and the Arts", Lincoln Center for Applied Ethics, Arizona State University, Tempe Arizona, October 28, 2001.

147. Joel Peter Witkin. "Revolt Against the Mystical." reprinted in Germano Celant, *Joel Peter Witkin*. Zurich: Scalo, 1995, p. 49.

148. Woodward, p. 217

149. Witkin. *Revolt*, p. 50

150. Witkin. *Revolt*, p. 52.

151. Witkin, *Revolt*, p. 62.

152. Witkin, *Revolt*, p. 62.

153. Joel Peter Witkin. "Danse Macabre". *Aperture*. Fall, 1997, p. 37.

154. Chris Buck and Christine Alevizakis, "Popped: Joel Peter Witkin", photographerinterviews. com (online publication) February 2, 1989.

155. Mikhail Bakhtin, *Rabelais and his World*. translated by Helene Iswolsky, Bloomington: Indiana University Press, 1984.

156. Wayne Booth. "Freedom of Interpretation". In *Bakhtin: Essays and Dialogue on His Work,* edited by Gary Saul Morson. Chicago: University of Chicago Press, 1986. p. 161-162.

157. Bakhtin, p. 50.

158. Shifra Goldman. "The Heart of Mexican Art: Image, Myth and Ideology" *New Art Examiner*. December 1993, p. 14.

159. See Olivier Debroise, Elizabeth Sussman and Matthew Teitelbaum. *The Bleeding Heart* Boston: The Institute of Contemporary Art, and Seattle: The University of Washington Press, 1991.

160. Lippard, "Andres Serrano: The Spirit and the Letter", p. 241.

161. Thomas McEvilley. "Your Flowers as my Hair: The Art of Michael Tracy" in Edward Leffingwell, *Terminal Privileges"* New York: P.S.1 Institute for Art and Urban Resources, Inc. 1987, p.34.

162. McEvilley, p. 51

163. Leffingwell. *Terminal Privileges*, p. 31.

164. ibid.

165. Michael Tracy, *The River Pierce: Sacrifice II, 13.4.90*. San Ygnacio: The River Pierce Foundation, 1990, p. 40.

166. Judith Wilson. "Ana Mendieta plants her garden". *Village Voice*. August 13, 1980.

167. Linda Montano. "An Interview with Ana Mendieta", *Sulfer 8*, no.1 (Spring 1988), p. 66.

168. Miwon Kwon, "Bloody Valentines: Afterimages by Ana Mendieta" in *Inside the Visible*, edited by Catherine M. De Zegher. Cambridge Mass: MIT Press, 1996, pp. 167-68.

169. Unpublished artist statement, quotes Octavio Paz, *The Labyrinth of Solitude*, New York: Grove, 1961, p. 23.

170. "Confessions of a Catholic Girl". Interview of Madonna by Becky Johnston, in *The Madonna Companion*, edited by Carol Benson and Allan Metz., New York: Schirmer Books, 1999. p 69.

171. Marina Warner, Alone *of All Her Sex, the Myth and the Cult of the Virgin Mary, New* York: Vintage Books, 198, p. 335.

172. ibid.

173. Garry Wills, *Papal Sin: Structures of Deceit*, New York: Doubleday, 2000, p. 204

174. Kathleen Norris, *Meditations on Mary*, New York: Viking

Studio, 1999, p. 17.

175. Richard Rodriquez, "India" in *Goddess of the Americas: Writing on the Virgin of Guadalupe,* edited by Ana Castillo, New York: Putnam Publishing Group, 1996, p. 24.

176. Bernard of Clairvaux, "Sermon 7", in *Bernard of Clairvaux: Selected Works,* edited and translated by G. R. Evans. New York: Paulist Press, 1987, p. 232.

177. Bernard of Clairvaux, "Sermon 31" p. 267.

178. Bernard of Clairvaux, "Sermon 5" p. 227.

179. Caroline Walker Bynum, *Fragmentation and Redemption* New York: Zone Books, 1992, p. 206.

180. ibid, p. 204.

181. Dan Barry and Carol Vogel. "Giuliani vows to Cut Subsidy Over 'Sick' Art", *New York Times.* September 23, 1999, A1.

182. Paul Schimmel, *Robert Gober,* catalogue for exhibition organized by the Museum of Contemporary Art, Los Angeles. Zurich-Berlin-New York: Scalo, 1997

183. Erika Doss, "Robert Gober's 'Virgin' Installation: Issues of Spirituality in Contemporary American Art", *The Visual Culture of American Religions,* edited by David Morgan and Sally M. Promey Morgan. Berkeley: University of California Press, 2001.

184. Doss, p. 142.

185. "Virgin Mary Sculpture Controversy Continues". *Daily Collegian.* Feb 7, 1997, p. 9.

186. Vicki Cheng, "Student's art prompts controversy, new guidelines". *Centre Daily Times,* March 9, 1997, p.1.

187. Michael Raphael, "Some have heated reaction to Penn State art student's quilt." *Philadelphia Inquirer,* March 12, 1997, p B3.

188. Monica Yanst, "Aiming for the personal, artist got provocative", *Philadelphia Inquirer,* March 23, 1997, B1, B7.

189. Kate Miller, and Hutton Wilson, "Censors Target Art Education", *Voices of Central Pennsylvania,* April 10, 1997, p. 19.

190. "The Art of Insulting the State's Catholics" *The Catholic Standard and Times.* March 3, 1997, p.10.

191. John A. Lawless, Pennsylvania State Representative, Letter to the Editor, *Philadelphia Inquirer,* March 26, 1997, p. 11.

192. "Museum Board to consider withdrawing controversial icon" *Santa Fe New Mexican,* April 9, 2001, p. 1

193. "Work not meant to offend, L.A. Artist says" *Sante Fe New Mexican,* March 24, 2001, p. 1.

194. Lucy Lippard, *Mixed Blessings* New York: Pantheon Books, 1990, p. 43.

195. ibid.

196. "Sante Fe Madonna Sparks Firestorm" *Art in America.* June 2001, p 23.

197. David Schwartz, and Laruen Rubin, "Cardinal Draws Art Line" *New York Daily News,* March 3, 2001, p. 3.

198. Karen Croft, "Using Her Body". Interview with Renee Cox in Salon.com, Feb 22, 2001, (online publication).

199. Interview with the author, July 2001.

200. ibid.

201. ibid.

202. ibid.

203. David Frankel, "In Her Own Words", interview with Kiki Smith in *Kiki Smith,* edited by Helene Posner, New York: Bullfinch Press, 1998, p. 38.

204. Interview with the author, September 1996.

205. Claudia Gould, interview with Kiki Smith in *Kiki Smith,* catalogue for Williams College Museum of Art, Williamstown, Mass, 1992, p.3

206. Frankel, p. 39.

207. Interview with the author. July 2001.

208. Sarah Bayless, "The 24 Hour a Day Artist" *Artnews.* Nov 1999, p 164.

209. Amy Cappellazzo, "Mother Lode", *Janine Antoni,* edited by Janine Antoni, Kusnacht, Germany: Ink Tree Editions, 2000, p. 113.

210. Marina Warner, "Child's Play" in *Janine Antoni,* edited by Janine Antoni, Kusnacht, Germany: Ink Tree Editions, 2000, p. 80-89

211. Interview with the author, July 2001.

212. Judith H. Dobrzynski, "Petah Coyne's Art Strategy has its Scary Moments" *New York Times,* October 6, 1998, p. 1.

213. interview with the author, August 2001.

214. Interview with the author. August 2001.

215. Chuck Close, interview with Lisa Yuskavage in Faye Hirsch, *Lisa Yusakavage,* New York: Smart Art Press, 1996, p. 6.

216. Gustav Niebuher. "U.S. 'Secular Groups Set Tone for Terror Attacks, Falwell Says". *New York Times.* Sept 14, 2001. A1.

217. Edward Rothstein. "Attacks on U.S. Challenge the Perspectives of Postmodern True Believers". *New York Times.* Sept 22, 2001. A 17.

218. Emily Eakin, "On the Lookout for Political Incorrectness" *New York Times.* Nov 24, 2001, A 15.

219. "Seeing Islam as 'Evil' faith, Evangelists Seek Converts" *New York Times May* 27, 2003, A1.

220. "Bush leads Prayers, Visits Aid Crews", *New York Times,* September 15, 2001, A1

221. "President's State of the Union Message to Congress and Nation", *New York Times,* January 29, 2003. A12.

222. Jimmy Carter," Just War - Or a Just War". *New York Times.* March 9, 2003, A24.

223. Garry Wills. "With God on His Side". *New York Times Magazine.* March 30, 2003.

224. ibid.

225. John Burns," War Looms but God is with us, Hussein tells Iraqis" *The New York Times* Oct 12, 2003, A11.

226. Bruce Bawer, *Stealing Jesus: How Fundamentalism Betrays Christianity,* New York: Three Rivers Press, 1997

227. Bawer, p. 230.

228. Bawer, p. 243.

229. Bawer, p. 245.

SELECTED BIBLIOGRAPHY

Adams, James Luther and Yates, Wilson, eds. *The Grotesque in Art and Literature: Theological Reflections.* Cambridge, UK: William B. Eerdmans Publishing Company, 1997.

Allen, Jane Addams. "The Sacred and The Profane," *New Art Examiner* Summer 1990, pp. 18-22.

Anft, Michael. "NEA-Disapproved Holly Hughes Takes on the Supreme Court", *Baltimore City Paper,* February 23, 2000.

Antoni, Janine, ed. *Janine Antoni.* Kusnacht, Germany: Ink Tree Editions, 2000.

Aries, Philippe. *The Hour of Our Death.* New York: Alfred A. Knopf, 1981.

Arthurs, Alberta and Wallach, Glenn, eds. *Crossroads: Art and Religion in American Life.* New York: The New Press, 2001.

Ayers, Anne, and Schimmel, Paul, eds. *Chris Burden: A Twenty Year Survey.* Newport Beach, Calif: Newport Harbor Art Museum, 1988.

Bakhtin, Mikhail. Trans. By Helene Iswolsky. *Rabelais and his World.* Bloomington: Indiana University Press, 1984

Baltz, Lewis. "Felix Gonzalez-Torres". *L'Architecture D'Aujour'hui* September 1996, pp. 12-16.

Bartman, William S., ed., *Felix Gonzales-Torres,* Los Angeles: A.R.T. Press, 1993, p. 23.

Bayless, Sarah. "The 24 Hour a Day Artist". *Artnews,* November 1999.

Bawer, Bruce. *Stealing Jesus: How Fundamentalism Betrays Christianity.* New York: Three Rivers Press, 1997.

Bernard of Clairvaux, "Sermon 7", in *Bernard of Clairvaux: Selected Works.* Edited and translated by G. R. Evans. New York: Paulist Press, 1987.

Bloom, Harold. *The American Religion: The Emergence of the Post-Christian Nation.* New York: Touchstone, 1992.

Blinderman, Barry. *David Wojnarowicz: Tongues of Flame,* Normal, Illinois: University Galleries, Illinois State University, 1990.

Bolton, Richard, ed. *Culture Wars.* New York: New Press, 1992

Booth, Wayne. "Freedom of Interpretation". In *Bakhtin: Essays and Dialogue on His Work.* Ed, Gary Saul Morson. Chicago: University of Chicago Press, 1986.

Bynum, Caroline Walker. *Fragmentation and Redemption.* New York: Zone Books, 1992.

Bynum, Caroline Walker. *The Resurrection of the Body.* New York: Columbia University Press, 1995.

Castillo, Ana, ed. *Goddess of the Americas: Writing on the Virgin of Guadalupe.* New York: Putnam Publishing Group, 1996.

Catholic League for Religious and Civil Rights, *Catalyst Magazine,* online publication. Url: www.catholicleague.org/catalyst.html.

Celant, Germano. *Joe-Peter Witkin.* Zurich: Scalo, 1995.

Cole, David, "David Wojnarowicz", *Aperture*. Fall 1994. p. 36-37.

Close, Chuck. Interview with Lisa Yuskavage in Faye Hirsch *Lisa Yuskavage*. New York: Smart Art Press, 1996.

Croft, Karen. "Using Her Body". Interview with Renee Cox in Salon.com, Feb 22, 2001.

Crone, Rainer, *Andy Warhol*. New York: Praeger, 1970.

Crow, Thomas. "Saturday Disasters: Trace and Reference in Early Warhol". *Art in America*, May 1987. p. 128-136.

Danto, Arthur. *Playing with the Edge*, Berkeley: University of California Press, 1996.

Danto, Arthur. "Robert Mapplethorpe". *The Nation*. September 26, 1988.

Debroise, Olivier, Sussman, Elizabeth and Teitelbaum, Matthew. *The Bleeding Heart*. Boston: The Institute of Contemporary Art, and Seattle: The University of Washington Press, 1991.

Dillenberger, John. *The Visual Arts and Christianity in America*. New York: Crossroad, 1988.

Dillenberger, Jane Dagget. *The Religious Art of Andy Warhol*. New York: Continuum, 1998.

Doss, Erika. "Robert Gober's 'Virgin' Installation: Issues of Spirituality in Contemporary American Art". *The Visual Culture of American Religions*. Edited by David Morgan and Sally M. Promey.

Berkeley: University of California Press, 2001. P 129-145.

Doyle, Jennifer; Flatley, Jonathan & Munoz, Jose Esteban. *Pop Out: Queer Warhol*. Durham: Duke University Press, 1996.

Dubin, Steven. *Arresting Images: Impolitic Art and Uncivil Actions*. New York: Routledge, 1992.

Duncan, Michael. "Tracing Mendieta". *Art in America*. April 1999, pp. 110-113, 154.

Ellenzwig, Allen and Stambolian, George. *The Homoerotic Photograph*. New York: Columbia University Press, 1992.

Evans, G. R., ed and trans. *Bernard of Clairvaux: Selected Works*. (New York: Paulist Press, 1987.

Fairbrother, Trevor. "Skulls," in Garrels, Gary, *"The Work of Andy Warhol* . Seattle: Bay Press, 1989.

Fineberg, Jonathan. *Art since 1940: Strategies of Being*. Englewood Cliffs: Prentice Hall, 1995.

Finley, Karen. *A Different Kind of Intimacy: the Collected Writings of Karen Finley*. New York: Thunder's Mouth Press, 2000.

Flanagan, Bob. "Bob Flanagan: Supermasochist", *RE/Search People Series: Volume one*. 1993.

Fried, Michael. "Art and Objecthood". *Artforum*. June 1967 pp. 12-23.

Fuller, Robert. *Naming the Antichrist. The History of an American. Obsession*. Oxford: Oxford University Press, 1995.

Gould, Claudia, interview with Kiki Smith in *Kiki Smith,* catalogue for Williams College Museum of Art, Williamstown, Mass, 1992.

Goldman, Shifra. "The Heart of Mexican Art: Image, Myth and Ideology". *New Art Examiner.* December 1993, pp. 12-15, 44, 45.

Greeley, Andrew. *The Catholic Imagination.* Berkeley: University of California Press, 2000.

Greeley, Andrew. *The Catholic Myth: Behavior and Beliefs of American Catholics.* New York: Charles Scribner's Sons, 1990.

Guthrie, Derek. "Taboo Artist: Serrano Speaks", *New Art Examiner.* September 1989, pp 45-46.

Hanson, Ellis, *Decadence and Catholicism.* Cambridge: Harvard University Press, 1997.

Haskins, Susan. *Mary Magdalene: Myth and Metaphor.* New York: Harcourt Brace & Co., 1993.

Heartney, Eleanor. "Is the body more beautiful when it's dead?" *New York Times.* Arts and Leisure. June 1, 2003.

Heartney, Eleanor. "Postmodern Heretics". *Art in America.* February 1997.

Hirsch, Faye. *Lisa Yuskavage.* New York: Smart Art Press, 1996.

Hughes, Robert. *The Rise of Andy Warhol.* The New York Review of Books, February 18, 1982, pp. 6-10.

Jones, Amelia, *Body Art/Performing the Subject.* Minneapolis: University of Minnesota Press, 1998.

Jordon, Mark D. *The Silence of Sodom,* Chicago: University of Chicago Press, 2000.

Kardon, Janet. *Robert Mapplethorpe: The Perfect Moment.* Philadelphia: Institute of Contemporary Art, 1988.

Kwon, Miwon. "Bloody Valentines: Afterimages by Ana Mendieta". In *Inside the Visible.* Edited by Catherine M. De Zegher. Cambridge Mass: MIT Press, 1996.

Krpan, Jurij V. Interview with Ron Athey, *Intersections #2.* Online publication. Url: mindlounge.mayancaper.net/intersections/ron_athey.html

Leffingwell, Edward. *Terminal Privileges".* New York: P.S.1 Institute for Art and Urban Resources, Inc. 1987.

Lippard, Lucy, "Andres Serrano: The Spirit and the Letter." *Art in America* April 1990, pp. 238-45.

Lippard, Lucy, "Passage in the Shadows", *Aperture.* Fall 199, p. 6-25.

Lippard, Lucy, "Out of the Safety Zone", *Art in America,* December 1990, pp. 130-139, 182, 186.

Lovelace, Carey. "Lisa Yuskavage: Fleshed Out". *Art in America,* July 2001.

Lyon, Christopher. "Kiki Smith: Body and Soul". *Artforum ,* February 1990.

Marsden, George. *Understanding Fundamentalism and Evangelicism.* Grand Rapids: William B. Eerdmans Publishing Company, 1991.

Marshall, Richard. *Robert Mapplethorpe.* New York: Whitney Museum of Art, 1988.

McGee, Celia, *New York Times.* Jan 22, 1995, Arts and Leisure Section, p. 35.

McNally, Terrence, *Corpus Christi.* Script published by Dramatists Play Service, Inc. 1999.

McShine, Kynaston, ed. *Andy Warhol: A Retrospective.* New York: Thames and Hudson, 1989.

Miller, Tim. "Jesus and The Queer Performance Artist", *Amazing Grace: Stories of Lesbian and Gay Faith,* Berkeley: The Crossing Press, 1991.

Montano, Linda. *Art in Everyday Life.* Barrytown: Station Hill, 1981.

Montano, Linda. "Interview with Ana Mendieta". *Sulfer,* Spring 1988.

Morgan, David and Promey, Sally M. Eds. *The Visual Culture of American Religions.* Berkeley: University of California Press, 2001.

Morrisroe, Patricia. *Mapplethorpe: A Biography.* New York: Da Capo Press, 1997.

Moyers, Bill in conversation with Sister Wendy. WGBH Boston Mass. Air date October 6, 2000.

Murphy, Patrick T. *Andres Serrano: Works 1983-1993.* Philadelphia: Institute of Contemporary Art, University of Pennsylvania, 1994.

Norris, Kathleen. *Meditations on Mary.* New York: Viking Studio, 1999.

O'Dell, Kathy. *Contract with the Skin: Masochism, Performance Art and the 1970s.* Minneapolis: University of Minnesota Press, 1998.

Pagels, Elaine. *Adam, Eve and the Serpent .* New York: Vintage Books, 1989.

Pagels, Elaine. *The Gnostic Gospels.* New York: Vintage Books:1989.

Posner, Helene. *Kiki Smith,* New York: Bullfinch Press, 1998.

Princenthal, Nancy. "Janine Antoni: Mother's Milk". *Art in America,* September 2001.

Ratcliff, Carter. *Andy Warhol.* New York: Abbeville Press, 1983.

Reik, Theodor, *Masochism in Modern Man.* New York: Farrar Straus, 1949.

Rodriquez, Richard. "India" in *Goddess of the Americas: Writing on the Virgin of Guadalupe.* Edited by Ana Castillo, New York: Putnam Publishing Group, 1996.

Rose, Barbara, "ABC Art" reprinted in Barbara Rose, *Autocritique: Essays on Art and Anti-Art 1963-1987.* New York: Weidenfeld & Nicolson, 1988. Pp. 55-72.

Rush, Michael, *Gunter Brus.* Palm Beach, Florida: Palm Beach Institute of Contemporary Art. 2002.

Scarry, Elaine. *The Body in Pain: The Making and Unmaking of the World.* Oxford: Oxford University Press. 1985.

Schleifer, Kristen Brooke "Inside & Out: An Interview with Kiki Smith". *Print Collector's Newsletter* 22 July/August 1991.

Scribner, Charles III. *Bernini.* New York: Harry N. Abrams, 1991.

Shearer, Linda and Gould, Claudia, *Kiki Smith.* Williamstown, Mass: Williams College Museum of Art, 1992.

Schimmel, Paul. *Robert Gober.* Catalogue for exhibition organized by the Museum of Contemporary Art, Los Angeles. Zurich-Berlin-New York: Scalo.

Siegel, Katy. "Blond Ambition". *Artforum* May 2000.

Silver, Kenneth E. "Modes of Disclosure: The Construction of Gay Identity and the Rise of Pop Art" in Ferguson, Russell, ed. *Hand-Painted Pop: American Art in Transition, 1955-62.* Los Angeles: Museum of Contemporary Art, 1992, pp. 179-204.

Sultan, Terrie. *Petah Coyne: black/white/ black".* Washington DC: The Corcoran Gallery of Art, 1996.

Sontag, Susan. "The Pornographic Imagination" reprinted as an introduction to Georges Bataille, *Story of the Eye*, London: Penguin Books, 1982.

Spector, Nancy, *Felix Gonzalez-Torres*, New York: Guggenheim Museum, 1995.

Spector, Nancy, "Felix Gonzales-Torres: Travelogue", *Parkett*, no 39, 1994 p .24-26.

Storr, Robert. Interview with Felix Gonzalez-Torres. *ArtPress*, January 1995, pp. 24 -32

Storr, Robert. "Setting Traps for the Mind and Heart". *Art in America*, January 1996.

Steinberg, Leo. *The Sexuality of Christ in Renaissance Art and in Modern Oblivion*. Chicago: University of Chicago Press, 1996.

Sedgwick, Eve Kosofsky. *Epistemology of the Closet*, Berkeley: University of California Press, 1990.

Swenson, G. R. "What is Pop Art?: Answers from Painters, Part I" *Artnews*, November 1963.

Tallman, Susan. "Kiki Smith, Anatomy Lessons". *Art in America*. April 1992.

Tracy, David. *The Analogical Imagination*. New York: Crossroads, 1982.

Warhol, Andy and Hackett, Pat. *POPism: The Warhol 60s*. New York: Harcourt Brace Jovanovich, 1980.

Warner, Marina. *Alone of All Her Sex, the Myth and the Cult of the Virgin Mary*. New York: Vintage Books,1983.

Warner, Marina. "Child's Play" in *Janine Antoni*, edited by Janine Antoni. Kusnacht, Germany: Ink Tree Editions, 2000, p. 80-89 .

Watney, Simon. "In Purgatory: The Work of Felix Gonzales-Torres". *Parkett*. No. 39, 1994. p. 38-44.

Watney, Simon. *Talking Art!* London: Institute of Contemporary Art, 1993.

Woodward, Richard. "Joel Peter Witkin: An eye for the forbidden." *Vanity Fair*, April 1993, pp. 190-196, 216, 217.

Wills, Garry. *Papal Sin: Structures of Deceit*. New York: Doubleday, 2000

Wills, Garry. "With God on His Side". *New York Times Magazine*. March 30, 2003.

Wilson, Judith. "Ana Mendieta plants her garden". *Village Voice*. August 13, 1980.

Witkin, Joel Peter. "Danse Macabre". *Aperture*. 149, fall 1997.

Witkin, Joel Peter. "Revolt Against the Mystical." reprinted in Celant, Germano. *Joe-Peter Witkin*. Zurich: Scalo, 1995, pp. 49-63.

ACKNOWLEDGEMENTS

Since its first publication in 2004, *Postmodern Heretics* has taken me on a fascinating ride across usually impassible divide between art and religion. Many thanks to the readers for whom it has struck a chord, to the universities, galleries, conference organizers and other organizations who invited me to share my ideas with diverse audiences and especially to the artists whose work is proof that the poetry of religion is a powerful inspiration for contemporary art. Many thanks, as well, to Cynthia Navaretta, whose Midmarch Arts Press published the first edition of this book. I wish her well wherever she may be. When *Postmodern Heretics* fell out of print and my numerous efforts to contact Midmarch Arts Press failed, I turned to Silver Hollow Press, which has generously supported this new edition. I am also greatly indebted to Aldo Sampieri, whose expertise has yielded this beautiful redesign. And above all, thanks are due to Larry Litt, my inhouse critic and champion. Larry got me through the original composition of the book. His encouragement also enabled me to make it available again. I hope *Postmodern Heretics* continues to offer food for thought in these increasingly contentious times.

ELEANOR HEARTNEY is an author and Contributing Editor to Art in America and Artpress. Among her books are Art and Today, Postmodernism, and Postmodern Heretics: The Catholic Imagination in Contemporary Art. She is a co-author of After the Revolution: Women who Transformed Contemporary Art and The Reckoning: Women Artists in the New Millennium. Heartney is a past President of AICA-USA, the American section of the International Art Critics Association. Her awards include the College Art Association's Frank Jewett Mather Award and the French government's Chevalier dans l'Ordre des Arts et des Lettres. She is also a good Catholic girl who graduated from Saint Joseph Academy in Des Moines, Iowa in 1972.